Just The facts101

Textbook Key Facts

Turkey Country Study Guide

by **Cram101**
Textbook NOT Included

Table of Contents

Index: Answers

Just The Facts101

Exam Prep for

Turkey Country Study Guide

Just The Facts101 Exam Prep is your link from
the textbook and lecture to your exams.

**Just The Facts101 Exam Preps are unauthorized and comprehensive reviews
of your textbooks.**

All material provided by CTI Publications (c) 2019

Textbook publishers and textbook authors do not participate in or contribute to these reviews.

Just The Facts101 Exam Prep

eAIN 458303

Foundations of Business

A business, also known as an enterprise, agency or a firm, is an entity involved in the provision of goods and/or services to consumers. Businesses are prevalent in capitalist economies, where most of them are privately owned and provide goods and services to customers in exchange for other goods, services, or money.

:: Evaluation ::

A _____ is an evaluation of a publication, service, or company such as a movie , video game , musical composition , book ; a piece of hardware like a car, home appliance, or computer; or an event or performance, such as a live music concert, play, musical theater show, dance show, or art exhibition. In addition to a critical evaluation, the _____ 's author may assign the work a rating to indicate its relative merit. More loosely, an author may _____ current events, trends, or items in the news. A compilation of _____ s may itself be called a _____ . The New York _____ of Books, for instance, is a collection of essays on literature, culture, and current affairs. National _____ , founded by William F. Buckley, Jr., is an influential conservative magazine, and Monthly _____ is a long-running socialist periodical.

Exam Probability: **Low**

1. *Answer choices:*

(see index for correct answer)

- a. Cryptographic Module Testing Laboratory
- b. Server Efficiency Rating Tool
- c. Review
- d. XTS-400

Guidance: level 1

:: ::

An _____ is the production of goods or related services within an economy. The major source of revenue of a group or company is the indicator of its relevant _____ . When a large group has multiple sources of revenue generation, it is considered to be working in different industries. Manufacturing _____ became a key sector of production and labour in European and North American countries during the Industrial Revolution, upsetting previous mercantile and feudal economies. This came through many successive rapid advances in technology, such as the production of steel and coal.

Exam Probability: **Medium**

2. *Answer choices:*

(see index for correct answer)

- a. Character
- b. Industry
- c. hierarchical perspective
- d. imperative

Guidance: level 1

:: Electronic feedback ::

_____ occurs when outputs of a system are routed back as inputs as part of a chain of cause-and-effect that forms a circuit or loop. The system can then be said to feed back into itself. The notion of cause-and-effect has to be handled carefully when applied to _____ systems.

Exam Probability: **Medium**

3. *Answer choices:*

(see index for correct answer)

- a. feedback loop
- b. Positive feedback

Guidance: level 1

:: Strategic alliances ::

A _____ is an agreement between two or more parties to pursue a set of agreed upon objectives needed while remaining independent organizations. A _____ will usually fall short of a legal partnership entity, agency, or corporate affiliate relationship. Typically, two companies form a _____ when each possesses one or more business assets or have expertise that will help the other by enhancing their businesses. _____ s can develop in outsourcing relationships where the parties desire to achieve long-term win-win benefits and innovation based on mutually desired outcomes.

Exam Probability: **High**

4. *Answer choices:*

(see index for correct answer)

- a. Strategic alliance
- b. International joint venture

- c. Cross-licensing
- d. Management contract

Guidance: level 1

:: Competition regulators ::

The _____ is an independent agency of the United States government, established in 1914 by the _____ Act. Its principal mission is the promotion of consumer protection and the elimination and prevention of anticompetitive business practices, such as coercive monopoly. It is headquartered in the _____ Building in Washington, D.C.

Exam Probability: **Low**

5. *Answer choices:*

(see index for correct answer)

- a. Competition Bureau
- b. Federal Trade Commission
- c. Competition Commission of India
- d. Federal Cartel Office

Guidance: level 1

:: Business models ::

A _____ , _____ company or daughter company is a company that is owned or controlled by another company, which is called the parent company, parent, or holding company. The _____ can be a company, corporation, or limited liability company. In some cases it is a government or state-owned enterprise. In some cases, particularly in the music and book publishing industries, subsidiaries are referred to as imprints.

Exam Probability: **High**

6. *Answer choices:*

(see index for correct answer)

- a. Meta learning
- b. Volatility, uncertainty, complexity and ambiguity
- c. Consumer cooperative
- d. Strategy map

Guidance: level 1

:: Management ::

_____ is a process by which entities review the quality of all factors involved in production. ISO 9000 defines _____ as "A part of quality management focused on fulfilling quality requirements".

Exam Probability: **High**

7. *Answer choices:*

- a. Dominant design
- b. Action item
- c. Advisory board
- d. Security management

Guidance: level 1

:: Globalization-related theories ::

_____ is the process in which a nation is being improved in the sector of the economic, political, and social well-being of its people. The term has been used frequently by economists, politicians, and others in the 20th and 21st centuries. The concept, however, has been in existence in the West for centuries. "Modernization, "westernization", and especially "industrialization" are other terms often used while discussing _____ . _____ has a direct relationship with the environment and environmental issues. _____ is very often confused with industrial development, even in some academic sources.

Exam Probability: **Low**

8. *Answer choices:*

- a. Capitalism
- b. postmodernism

- c. Economic Development

Guidance: level 1

:: Management ::

A _____ is a method or technique that has been generally accepted as superior to any alternatives because it produces results that are superior to those achieved by other means or because it has become a standard way of doing things, e.g., a standard way of complying with legal or ethical requirements.

Exam Probability: **Medium**

9. *Answer choices:*
(see index for correct answer)

- a. Extended enterprise
- b. Best practice
- c. Context analysis
- d. Document automation

Guidance: level 1

:: Commerce ::

_____ relates to "the exchange of goods and services, especially on a large scale". It includes legal, economic, political, social, cultural and technological systems that operate in a country or in international trade.

Exam Probability: **Low**

10. *Answer choices:*

(see index for correct answer)

- a. Video rental shop
- b. Commerce
- c. RFM
- d. Factory

Guidance: level 1

:: Marketing techniques ::

_____ is the activity of dividing a broad consumer or business market, normally consisting of existing and potential customers, into sub-groups of consumers based on some type of shared characteristics. In dividing or segmenting markets, researchers typically look for common characteristics such as shared needs, common interests, similar lifestyles or even similar demographic profiles. The overall aim of segmentation is to identify high yield segments – that is, those segments that are likely to be the most profitable or that have growth potential – so that these can be selected for special attention .

11. *Answer choices:*

(see index for correct answer)

- a. Market segmentation
- b. REAN
- c. Freebie marketing
- d. Precision marketing

Guidance: level 1

:: Stock market ::

A shareholder is an individual or institution that legally owns one or more shares of stock in a public or private corporation. _____ may be referred to as members of a corporation. Legally, a person is not a shareholder in a corporation until their name and other details are entered in the corporation's register of _____ or members.

Exam Probability: **High**

12. *Answer choices:*

(see index for correct answer)

- a. Shareholders
- b. NorCom

- c. Rogue trader
- d. Alternative display facility

Guidance: level 1

:: Industry ::

_____ describes various measures of the efficiency of production. Often , a _____ measure is expressed as the ratio of an aggregate output to a single input or an aggregate input used in a production process, i.e. output per unit of input. Most common example is the labour _____ measure, e.g., such as GDP per worker. There are many different definitions of _____ and the choice among them depends on the purpose of the _____ measurement and/or data availability. The key source of difference between various _____ measures is also usually related to how the outputs and the inputs are aggregated into scalars to obtain such a ratio-type measure of

_____ .

Exam Probability: **High**

13. *Answer choices:*

(see index for correct answer)

- a. Productivity
- b. Wedge based mechanical exfoliation
- c. Economic importance of bacteria
- d. Sensory design

Guidance: level 1

:: Currency ::

A _____ , in the most specific sense is money in any form when in use or circulation as a medium of exchange, especially circulating banknotes and coins. A more general definition is that a _____ is a system of money in common use, especially for people in a nation. Under this definition, US dollars , pounds sterling , Australian dollars , European euros , Russian rubles and Indian Rupees are examples of currencies. These various currencies are recognized as stores of value and are traded between nations in foreign exchange markets, which determine the relative values of the different currencies. Currencies in this sense are defined by governments, and each type has limited boundaries of acceptance.

Exam Probability: **Low**

14. *Answer choices:*

(see index for correct answer)

- a. Representative money
- b. Debasement
- c. Currency money
- d. Currency

Guidance: level 1

:: Management ::

A _____ describes the rationale of how an organization creates, delivers, and captures value, in economic, social, cultural or other contexts. The process of _____ construction and modification is also called _____ innovation and forms a part of business strategy.

Exam Probability: **High**

15. *Answer choices:*

- a. Managerial hubris
- b. Business model
- c. Leadership Series
- d. Strategic lenses

Guidance: level 1

:: Marketing ::

The _____ is a foundation model for businesses. The _____ has been defined as the "set of marketing tools that the firm uses to pursue its marketing objectives in the target market". Thus the _____ refers to four broad levels of marketing decision, namely: product, price, place, and promotion. Marketing practice has been occurring for millennia, but marketing theory emerged in the early twentieth century. The contemporary _____ , or the 4 Ps, which has become the dominant framework for marketing management decisions, was first published in 1960. In services marketing, an extended _____ is used, typically comprising 7 Ps, made up of the original 4 Ps extended by process, people, and physical evidence. Occasionally service marketers will refer to 8 Ps, comprising these 7 Ps plus performance.

Exam Probability: **Low**

16. *Answer choices:*

(see index for correct answer)

- a. Market environment
- b. Pitching engine
- c. Marketing mix
- d. Law of primacy in persuasion

Guidance: level 1

:: Customs duties ::

A _____ is a tax on imports or exports between sovereign states. It is a form of regulation of foreign trade and a policy that taxes foreign products to encourage or safeguard domestic industry. _____ s are the simplest and oldest instrument of trade policy. Traditionally, states have used them as a source of income. Now, they are among the most widely used instruments of protection, along with import and export quotas.

Exam Probability: **Medium**

17. *Answer choices:*

(see index for correct answer)

- a. Customs racketeering
- b. Court of Exchequer
- c. Canadian import duties
- d. Tariff

Guidance: level 1

:: Classification systems ::

_____ is the practice of comparing business processes and performance metrics to industry bests and best practices from other companies. Dimensions typically measured are quality, time and cost.

Exam Probability: **Low**

18. *Answer choices:*

(see index for correct answer)

- a. ETIM
- b. Classification of percussion instruments
- c. Ecological land classification
- d. British undergraduate degree classification

Guidance: level 1

:: Production economics ::

_____ is the joint use of a resource or space. It is also the process of dividing and distributing. In its narrow sense, it refers to joint or alternating use of inherently finite goods, such as a common pasture or a shared residence. Still more loosely, "_____" can actually mean giving something as an outright gift: for example, to "share" one's food really means to give some of it as a gift. _____ is a basic component of human interaction, and is responsible for strengthening social ties and ensuring a person's well-being.

Exam Probability: **Low**

19. *Answer choices:*

(see index for correct answer)

- a. HMI quality
- b. Sharing

- c. Marginal product
- d. Synergy

Guidance: level 1

:: Foreign direct investment ::

A _____ is an investment in the form of a controlling ownership in a business in one country by an entity based in another country. It is thus distinguished from a foreign portfolio investment by a notion of direct control.

Exam Probability: **High**

20. *Answer choices:*

(see index for correct answer)

- a. Oligopolistic reaction
- b. Foreign direct investment
- c. International Centre for Settlement of Investment Disputes
- d. Expropriation

Guidance: level 1

:: Market research ::

_____ is an organized effort to gather information about target markets or customers. It is a very important component of business strategy. The term is commonly interchanged with marketing research; however, expert practitioners may wish to draw a distinction, in that marketing research is concerned specifically about marketing processes, while _____ is concerned specifically with markets.

Exam Probability: **Medium**

21. *Answer choices:*

(see index for correct answer)

- a. CRISIL
- b. Frugging
- c. Shanghai Metals Market
- d. Nonprobability sampling

Guidance: level 1

:: Industrial Revolution ::

The _____ , now also known as the First _____ , was the transition to new manufacturing processes in Europe and the US, in the period from about 1760 to sometime between 1820 and 1840. This transition included going from hand production methods to machines, new chemical manufacturing and iron production processes, the increasing use of steam power and water power, the development of machine tools and the rise of the mechanized factory system. The _____ also led to an unprecedented rise in the rate of population growth.

22. *Answer choices:*

(see index for correct answer)

- a. Masson Mill
- b. Industrial Revolution
- c. Coalbrookdale
- d. Textile manufacture during the Industrial Revolution

Guidance: level 1

:: Marketing ::

A _____ is something that is necessary for an organism to live a healthy life. _____ s are distinguished from wants in that, in the case of a _____ , a deficiency causes a clear adverse outcome: a dysfunction or death. In other words, a _____ is something required for a safe, stable and healthy life while a want is a desire, wish or aspiration. When _____ s or wants are backed by purchasing power, they have the potential to become economic demands.

23. *Answer choices:*

(see index for correct answer)

- a. Matomy Media

- b. Marketing channel
- c. Customer lifetime value
- d. Need

Guidance: level 1

:: Casting (manufacturing) ::

A _____ is a regularity in the world, man-made design, or abstract ideas. As such, the elements of a _____ repeat in a predictable manner. A geometric _____ is a kind of _____ formed of geometric shapes and typically repeated like a wallpaper design.

Exam Probability: **Medium**

24. *Answer choices:*

(see index for correct answer)

- a. Full-mold casting
- b. Institute of Cast Metals Engineers
- c. Core plug
- d. Juutila Foundry

Guidance: level 1

:: International trade ::

The law or principle of _____ holds that under free trade, an agent
will produce more of and consume less of a good for which they have a
_____ . _____ is the economic reality describing the work gains from
trade for individuals, firms, or nations, which arise from differences in their
factor endowments or technological progress. In an economic model, agents have
a _____ over others in producing a particular good if they can produce
that good at a lower relative opportunity cost or autarky price, i.e. at a
lower relative marginal cost prior to trade. One shouldn`t compare the monetary
costs of production or even the resource costs of production. Instead, one
must compare the opportunity costs of producing goods across countries.

Exam Probability: **Medium**

25. *Answer choices:*

(see index for correct answer)

- a. Comparative advantage
- b. Trade creation
- c. New Zealand Meat Producers Board
- d. Regional integration

Guidance: level 1

:: Credit cards ::

A _____ is a payment card issued to users to enable the cardholder to pay a merchant for goods and services based on the cardholder's promise to the card issuer to pay them for the amounts plus the other agreed charges. The card issuer creates a revolving account and grants a line of credit to the cardholder, from which the cardholder can borrow money for payment to a merchant or as a cash advance.

Exam Probability: **Low**

26. *Answer choices:*

(see index for correct answer)

- a. MPP Global Solutions
- b. North American Bancard
- c. EnRoute
- d. Credit card

Guidance: level 1

:: ::

In regulatory jurisdictions that provide for it , _____ is a group of laws and organizations designed to ensure the rights of consumers as well as fair trade, competition and accurate information in the marketplace. The laws are designed to prevent the businesses that engage in fraud or specified unfair practices from gaining an advantage over competitors. They may also provides additional protection for those most vulnerable in society. _____ laws are a form of government regulation that aim to protect the rights of consumers. For example, a government may require businesses to disclose detailed information about products—particularly in areas where safety or public health is an issue, such as food.

Exam Probability: **Medium**

27. *Answer choices:*

(see index for correct answer)

- a. Consumer Protection
- b. hierarchical
- c. cultural
- d. levels of analysis

Guidance: level 1

:: Statistical terminology ::

_____ is the magnitude or dimensions of a thing. _____ can be measured as length, width, height, diameter, perimeter, area, volume, or mass.

Exam Probability: **Low**

28. *Answer choices:*

(see index for correct answer)

- a. Error bar
- b. Core damage frequency
- c. Inherent zero
- d. Size

Guidance: level 1

:: Business ::

A _____ is a mathematical object used to count, measure, and label. The original examples are the natural _____ s 1, 2, 3, 4, and so forth. A written symbol like "5" that represents a _____ is called a numeral. A numeral system is an organized way to write and manipulate this type of symbol, for example the Hindu–Arabic numeral system allows combinations of numerical digits like "5" and "0" to represent larger _____ s like 50. A numeral in linguistics can refer to a symbol like 5, the words or phrase that names a _____ , like "five hundred", or other words that mean a specific _____ , like "dozen". In addition to their use in counting and measuring, numerals are often used for labels , for ordering , and for codes . In common usage, _____ may refer to a symbol, a word or phrase, or the mathematical object.

Exam Probability: **Low**

29. *Answer choices:*

(see index for correct answer)

- a. Psychic distance
- b. Office broker
- c. Ian McLeod
- d. Number

Guidance: level 1

:: Planning ::

_____ is a high level plan to achieve one or more goals under conditions of uncertainty. In the sense of the "art of the general," which included several subsets of skills including tactics, siegecraft, logistics etc., the term came into use in the 6th century C.E. in East Roman terminology, and was translated into Western vernacular languages only in the 18th century. From then until the 20th century, the word "_____" came to denote "a comprehensive way to try to pursue political ends, including the threat or actual use of force, in a dialectic of wills" in a military conflict, in which both adversaries interact.

Exam Probability: **Medium**

30. *Answer choices:*
(see index for correct answer)

- a. Strategy
- b. Commercial area
- c. Parish plan

- d. Resource-Task Network

Guidance: level 1

:: Problem solving ::

In other words, _____ is a situation where a group of people meet to generate new ideas and solutions around a specific domain of interest by removing inhibitions. People are able to think more freely and they suggest as many spontaneous new ideas as possible. All the ideas are noted down and those ideas are not criticized and after _____ session the ideas are evaluated. The term was popularized by Alex Faickney Osborn in the 1953 book Applied Imagination.

Exam Probability: **Low**

31. *Answer choices:*
(see index for correct answer)

- a. Use of force
- b. Syntegrity
- c. Brainstorming
- d. Calculation

Guidance: level 1

:: Business process ::

A _____ or business method is a collection of related, structured activities or tasks by people or equipment which in a specific sequence produce a service or product for a particular customer or customers. _____ es occur at all organizational levels and may or may not be visible to the customers. A _____ may often be visualized as a flowchart of a sequence of activities with interleaving decision points or as a process matrix of a sequence of activities with relevance rules based on data in the process. The benefits of using _____ es include improved customer satisfaction and improved agility for reacting to rapid market change. Process-oriented organizations break down the barriers of structural departments and try to avoid functional silos.

Exam Probability: **Low**

32. *Answer choices:*

(see index for correct answer)

- a. Intention mining
- b. Signavio
- c. IBM Blueworks Live
- d. Business process

Guidance: level 1

:: Free trade agreements ::

A _____ is a wide-ranging taxes, tariff and trade treaty that often includes investment guarantees. It exists when two or more countries agree on terms that helps them trade with each other. The most common _____ s are of the preferential and free trade types are concluded in order to reduce tariffs, quotas and other trade restrictions on items traded between the signatories.

Exam Probability: **Medium**

33. *Answer choices:*

(see index for correct answer)

- a. New West Partnership
- b. Comprehensive Economic Partnership Agreement
- c. Asia-Pacific Trade Agreement
- d. African Free Trade Zone

Guidance: level 1

:: Asset ::

In financial accounting, an _____ is any resource owned by the business. Anything tangible or intangible that can be owned or controlled to produce value and that is held by a company to produce positive economic value is an _____ . Simply stated, _____ s represent value of ownership that can be converted into cash . The balance sheet of a firm records the monetary value of the _____ s owned by that firm. It covers money and other valuables belonging to an individual or to a business.

34. *Answer choices:*

(see index for correct answer)

- a. Current asset
- b. Asset

Guidance: level 1

:: Management ::

_____ is the identification, evaluation, and prioritization of risks followed by coordinated and economical application of resources to minimize, monitor, and control the probability or impact of unfortunate events or to maximize the realization of opportunities.

35. *Answer choices:*

(see index for correct answer)

- a. PDCA
- b. Job rotation
- c. Marketing science
- d. IT performance management

:: Debt ::

_____ , in finance and economics, is payment from a borrower or deposit-taking financial institution to a lender or depositor of an amount above repayment of the principal sum , at a particular rate. It is distinct from a fee which the borrower may pay the lender or some third party. It is also distinct from dividend which is paid by a company to its shareholders from its profit or reserve, but not at a particular rate decided beforehand, rather on a pro rata basis as a share in the reward gained by risk taking entrepreneurs when the revenue earned exceeds the total costs.

Exam Probability: **Medium**

36. *Answer choices:*

(see index for correct answer)

- a. Debt wall
- b. Cohort default rate
- c. Debtors Anonymous
- d. Interest

:: Management ::

_____ is the process of thinking about the activities required to achieve a desired goal. It is the first and foremost activity to achieve desired results. It involves the creation and maintenance of a plan, such as psychological aspects that require conceptual skills. There are even a couple of tests to measure someone's capability of _____ well. As such, _____ is a fundamental property of intelligent behavior. An important further meaning, often just called " _____ " is the legal context of permitted building developments.

Exam Probability: **Low**

37. *Answer choices:*

(see index for correct answer)

- a. Process capability
- b. Logistics support analysis
- c. Production flow analysis
- d. Line of business

Guidance: level 1

:: Money ::

In economics, _____ is money in the physical form of currency, such as banknotes and coins. In bookkeeping and finance, _____ is current assets comprising currency or currency equivalents that can be accessed immediately or near-immediately . _____ is seen either as a reserve for payments, in case of a structural or incidental negative _____ flow or as a way to avoid a downturn on financial markets.

38. *Answer choices:*

(see index for correct answer)

- a. History of money
- b. Standard of deferred payment
- c. Money multiplier
- d. Cash

Guidance: level 1

:: Fraud ::

In law, _____ is intentional deception to secure unfair or unlawful gain, or to deprive a victim of a legal right. _____ can violate civil law , a criminal law , or it may cause no loss of money, property or legal right but still be an element of another civil or criminal wrong. The purpose of _____ may be monetary gain or other benefits, for example by obtaining a passport, travel document, or driver`s license, or mortgage _____ , where the perpetrator may attempt to qualify for a mortgage by way of false statements.

Exam Probability: **High**

39. *Answer choices:*

(see index for correct answer)

- a. Credit card fraud
- b. Corporate scandal
- c. Gone in 60 Seconds
- d. Sham marriage

Guidance: level 1

:: ::

_____ is the collection of mechanisms, processes and relations by which corporations are controlled and operated. Governance structures and principles identify the distribution of rights and responsibilities among different participants in the corporation and include the rules and procedures for making decisions in corporate affairs. _____ is necessary because of the possibility of conflicts of interests between stakeholders, primarily between shareholders and upper management or among shareholders.

Exam Probability: **Medium**

40. *Answer choices:*

(see index for correct answer)

- a. process perspective
- b. similarity-attraction theory
- c. Character
- d. Corporate governance

Guidance: level 1

:: Human resource management ::

_____ are the people who make up the workforce of an organization, business sector, or economy. "Human capital" is sometimes used synonymously with " _____ ", although human capital typically refers to a narrower effect . Likewise, other terms sometimes used include manpower, talent, labor, personnel, or simply people.

Exam Probability: **High**

41. *Answer choices:*

(see index for correct answer)

- a. Trust fall
- b. Person specification
- c. Human resources
- d. Adecco Group North America

Guidance: level 1

:: Management ::

In organizational studies, _____ is the efficient and effective development of an organization's resources when they are needed. Such resources may include financial resources, inventory, human skills, production resources, or information technology and natural resources.

42. *Answer choices:*

(see index for correct answer)

- a. Communities of innovation
- b. Resource management
- c. Business plan
- d. Customer Benefit Package

Guidance: level 1

:: Insolvency ::

_____ is a legal process through which people or other entities who cannot repay debts to creditors may seek relief from some or all of their debts. In most jurisdictions, _____ is imposed by a court order, often initiated by the debtor.

Exam Probability: **High**

43. *Answer choices:*

(see index for correct answer)

- a. United Kingdom insolvency law
- b. Bankruptcy
- c. Debt consolidation

- d. Insolvency

Guidance: level 1

:: Association of Southeast Asian Nations ::

The Association of Southeast Asian Nations is a regional intergovernmental organization comprising ten countries in Southeast Asia, which promotes intergovernmental cooperation and facilitates economic, political, security, military, educational, and sociocultural integration among its members and other countries in Asia. It also regularly engages other countries in the Asia-Pacific region and beyond. A major partner of Shanghai Cooperation Organisation, _____ maintains a global network of alliances and dialogue partners and is considered by many as a global powerhouse, the central union for cooperation in Asia-Pacific, and a prominent and influential organization. It is involved in numerous international affairs, and hosts diplomatic missions throughout the world.

Exam Probability: **Medium**

44. *Answer choices:*
(see index for correct answer)

- a. Hanoi Plan of Action
- b. ASEAN
- c. ASEAN Rise
- d. Flag of the Association of Southeast Asian Nations

Guidance: level 1

:: Rhetoric ::

_____ is the pattern of narrative development that aims to make vivid a place, object, character, or group. _____ is one of four rhetorical modes , along with exposition, argumentation, and narration. In practice it would be difficult to write literature that drew on just one of the four basic modes.

Exam Probability: **Medium**

45. *Answer choices:*

(see index for correct answer)

- a. Art of memory
- b. Communication Theory as a Field
- c. Suasoria
- d. Description

Guidance: level 1

:: Business models ::

_____ es are privately owned corporations, partnerships, or sole proprietorships that have fewer employees and/or less annual revenue than a regular-sized business or corporation. Businesses are defined as "small" in terms of being able to apply for government support and qualify for preferential tax policy varies depending on the country and industry.

_____ es range from fifteen employees under the Australian Fair Work Act 2009, fifty employees according to the definition used by the European Union, and fewer than five hundred employees to qualify for many U.S. _____ Administration programs. While _____ es can also be classified according to other methods, such as annual revenues, shipments, sales, assets, or by annual gross or net revenue or net profits, the number of employees is one of the most widely used measures.

Exam Probability: **Medium**

46. *Answer choices:*

(see index for correct answer)

- a. Small business
- b. Artel
- c. IASME
- d. Fractional ownership

Guidance: level 1

:: Stock market ::

A _____ , equity market or share market is the aggregation of buyers and sellers of stocks , which represent ownership claims on businesses; these may include securities listed on a public stock exchange, as well as stock that is only traded privately. Examples of the latter include shares of private companies which are sold to investors through equity crowdfunding platforms. Stock exchanges list shares of common equity as well as other security types, e.g. corporate bonds and convertible bonds.

Exam Probability: **High**

47. *Answer choices:*

(see index for correct answer)

- a. Direct participation program
- b. Witching hour
- c. Stock market
- d. CEE Stock Exchange Group

Guidance: level 1

:: Business terms ::

A _____ is a short statement of why an organization exists, what its overall goal is, identifying the goal of its operations: what kind of product or service it provides, its primary customers or market, and its geographical region of operation. It may include a short statement of such fundamental matters as the organization's values or philosophies, a business's main competitive advantages, or a desired future state—the "vision".

48. *Answer choices:*

(see index for correct answer)

- a. year-to-date
- b. front office
- c. noncommercial
- d. Mission statement

Guidance: level 1

:: Derivatives (finance) ::

_____ is any bodily activity that enhances or maintains physical
fitness and overall health and wellness. It is performed for various reasons,
to aid growth and improve strength, preventing aging, developing muscles and
the cardiovascular system, honing athletic skills, weight loss or maintenance,
improving health and also for enjoyment. Many individuals choose to _____
outdoors where they can congregate in groups, socialize, and enhance
well-being.

Exam Probability: **Medium**

49. *Answer choices:*

(see index for correct answer)

- a. Delivery month

- b. Interest rate derivative
- c. Exercise
- d. Foreign exchange derivative

Guidance: level 1

:: ::

A _____ is any person who contracts to acquire an asset in return for some form of consideration.

Exam Probability: **Medium**

50. *Answer choices:*

(see index for correct answer)

- a. open system
- b. empathy
- c. information systems assessment
- d. deep-level diversity

Guidance: level 1

:: Financial markets ::

A _____ is a financial market in which long-term debt or equity-backed securities are bought and sold. _____ s channel the wealth of savers to those who can put it to long-term productive use, such as companies or governments making long-term investments. Financial regulators like the Bank of England and the U.S. Securities and Exchange Commission oversee _____ s to protect investors against fraud, among other duties.

Exam Probability: **Medium**

51. *Answer choices:*

(see index for correct answer)

- a. Clearing
- b. Capital market
- c. Composite
- d. Broker-dealer

Guidance: level 1

:: ::

_____ is a means of protection from financial loss. It is a form of risk management, primarily used to hedge against the risk of a contingent or uncertain loss

Exam Probability: **Low**

52. *Answer choices:*

(see index for correct answer)

- a. open system
- b. Insurance
- c. deep-level diversity
- d. similarity-attraction theory

Guidance: level 1

:: Business models ::

A _____ is "an autonomous association of persons united voluntarily to meet their common economic, social, and cultural needs and aspirations through a jointly-owned and democratically-controlled enterprise". _____ s may include.

Exam Probability: **High**

53. *Answer choices:*

(see index for correct answer)

- a. Cooperative
- b. Small business
- c. Subsidiary
- d. Very small business

:: Generally Accepted Accounting Principles ::

An _____ or profit and loss account is one of the financial statements of a company and shows the company's revenues and expenses during a particular period.

Exam Probability: **Low**

54. *Answer choices:*

(see index for correct answer)

- a. Income statement
- b. Deprival value
- c. Trial balance
- d. Statement of recommended practice

:: Project management ::

In political science, an _____ is a means by which a petition signed by a certain minimum number of registered voters can force a government to choose to either enact a law or hold a public vote in parliament in what is called indirect _____ , or under direct _____ , the proposition is immediately put to a plebiscite or referendum, in what is called a Popular initiated Referendum or citizen-initiated referendum).

55. *Answer choices:*

(see index for correct answer)

- a. Responsibility assignment matrix
- b. Pre-construction services
- c. Initiative
- d. Task management

Guidance: level 1

:: Debt ::

_____ is the trust which allows one party to provide money or resources to another party wherein the second party does not reimburse the first party immediately , but promises either to repay or return those resources at a later date. In other words, _____ is a method of making reciprocity formal, legally enforceable, and extensible to a large group of unrelated people.

Exam Probability: **Medium**

56. *Answer choices:*

(see index for correct answer)

- a. Debt adjustment
- b. Perpetual subordinated debt
- c. Credit
- d. Compulsive buying disorder

Guidance: level 1

:: Real estate ::

_____ s serve several societal needs – primarily as shelter from weather, security, living space, privacy, to store belongings, and to comfortably live and work. A _____ as a shelter represents a physical division of the human habitat and the outside .

Exam Probability: **Low**

57. *Answer choices:*

(see index for correct answer)

- a. Owner-occupier
- b. Building
- c. 99-year lease

- d. Studio apartment

Guidance: level 1

:: ::

An _____ is a contingent motivator. Traditional _____ s are extrinsic motivators which reward actions to yield a desired outcome. The effectiveness of traditional _____ s has changed as the needs of Western society have evolved. While the traditional _____ model is effective when there is a defined procedure and goal for a task, Western society started to require a higher volume of critical thinkers, so the traditional model became less effective. Institutions are now following a trend in implementing strategies that rely on intrinsic motivations rather than the extrinsic motivations that the traditional _____ s foster.

Exam Probability: **Low**

58. *Answer choices:*

(see index for correct answer)

- a. process perspective
- b. hierarchical
- c. Incentive
- d. deep-level diversity

Guidance: level 1

:: Environmental economics ::

_____ is the process of people maintaining change in a balanced environment, in which the exploitation of resources, the direction of investments, the orientation of technological development and institutional change are all in harmony and enhance both current and future potential to meet human needs and aspirations. For many in the field, _____ is defined through the following interconnected domains or pillars: environment, economic and social, which according to Fritjof Capra is based on the principles of Systems Thinking. Sub-domains of sustainable development have been considered also: cultural, technological and political. While sustainable development may be the organizing principle for _____ for some, for others, the two terms are paradoxical . Sustainable development is the development that meets the needs of the present without compromising the ability of future generations to meet their own needs. Brundtland Report for the World Commission on Environment and Development introduced the term of sustainable development.

Exam Probability: **Medium**

59. *Answer choices:*

(see index for correct answer)

- a. Sustainability
- b. Hubbert peak theory
- c. Land Economics
- d. Peak minerals

Guidance: level 1

Management

Management is the administration of an organization, whether it is a business, a not-for-profit organization, or government body. Management includes the activities of setting the strategy of an organization and coordinating the efforts of its employees (or of volunteers) to accomplish its objectives through the application of available resources, such as financial, natural, technological, and human resources.

:: Evaluation ::

A _____ is an evaluation of a publication, service, or company such as a movie , video game , musical composition , book ; a piece of hardware like a car, home appliance, or computer; or an event or performance, such as a live music concert, play, musical theater show, dance show, or art exhibition. In addition to a critical evaluation, the _____ 's author may assign the work a rating to indicate its relative merit. More loosely, an author may _____ current events, trends, or items in the news. A compilation of _____ s may itself be called a _____ . The New York _____ of Books, for instance, is a collection of essays on literature, culture, and current affairs. National _____ , founded by William F. Buckley, Jr., is an influential conservative magazine, and Monthly _____ is a long-running socialist periodical.

Exam Probability: **High**

1. *Answer choices:*

(see index for correct answer)

- a. Integrity
- b. Teaching and Learning International Survey
- c. Review
- d. Scale of one to ten

Guidance: level 1

:: Statistical terminology ::

_____ is the ability to avoid wasting materials, energy, efforts, money, and time in doing something or in producing a desired result. In a more general sense, it is the ability to do things well, successfully, and without waste. In more mathematical or scientific terms, it is a measure of the extent to which input is well used for an intended task or function . It often specifically comprises the capability of a specific application of effort to produce a specific outcome with a minimum amount or quantity of waste, expense, or unnecessary effort. _____ refers to very different inputs and outputs in different fields and industries.

Exam Probability: **High**

2. *Answer choices:*

(see index for correct answer)

- a. Aggregate data
- b. Cause of death
- c. Efficiency
- d. Fisher consistency

Guidance: level 1

:: Quality management ::

A _____ or quality control circle is a group of workers who do the same or similar work, who meet regularly to identify, analyze and solve work-related problems. Normally small in size, the group is usually led by a supervisor or manager and presents its solutions to management; where possible, workers implement the solutions themselves in order to improve the performance of the organization and motivate employees. _____ s were at their most popular during the 1980s, but continue to exist in the form of Kaizen groups and similar worker participation schemes.

Exam Probability: **Medium**

3. *Answer choices:*

(see index for correct answer)

- a. Quality management system
- b. Informal Methods
- c. Regulatory translation
- d. Dana Ulery

Guidance: level 1

:: Types of marketing ::

In microeconomics and management, _____ is an arrangement in which the supply chain of a company is owned by that company. Usually each member of the supply chain produces a different product or service, and the products combine to satisfy a common need. It is contrasted with horizontal integration, wherein a company produces several items which are related to one another. _____ has also described management styles that bring large portions of the supply chain not only under a common ownership, but also into one corporation .

Exam Probability: **Medium**

4. *Answer choices:*

(see index for correct answer)

- a. Vertical integration
- b. Close Range Marketing
- c. Pre-installed software
- d. Affinity marketing

Guidance: level 1

:: Office administration ::

An _____ is generally a room or other area where an organization's employees perform administrative work in order to support and realize objects and goals of the organization. The word " _____ " may also denote a position within an organization with specific duties attached to it ; the latter is in fact an earlier usage. _____ as place originally referring to the location of one's duty. When used as an adjective, the term " _____ " may refer to business-related tasks. In law, a company or organization has _____ s in any place where it has an official presence, even if that presence consists of a storage silo rather than an establishment with desk-and-chair. An _____ is also an architectural and design phenomenon: ranging from a small _____ such as a bench in the corner of a small business of extremely small size , through entire floors of buildings, up to and including massive buildings dedicated entirely to one company. In modern terms an _____ is usually the location where white-collar workers carry out their functions. As per James Stephenson, " _____ is that part of business enterprise which is devoted to the direction and co-ordination of its various activities."

Exam Probability: **Low**

5. *Answer choices:*

(see index for correct answer)

- a. Office administration
- b. Fish! Philosophy
- c. Inter departmental communication
- d. Activity management

Guidance: level 1

:: ::

_____ or haggling is a type of negotiation in which the buyer and seller of a good or service debate the price and exact nature of a transaction. If the _____ produces agreement on terms, the transaction takes place. _____ is an alternative pricing strategy to fixed prices. Optimally, if it costs the retailer nothing to engage and allow _____ , s/he can divine the buyer's willingness to spend. It allows for capturing more consumer surplus as it allows price discrimination, a process whereby a seller can charge a higher price to one buyer who is more eager . Haggling has largely disappeared in parts of the world where the cost to haggle exceeds the gain to retailers for most common retail items. However, for expensive goods sold to uninformed buyers such as automobiles, _____ can remain commonplace.

Exam Probability: **High**

6. *Answer choices:*

(see index for correct answer)

- a. hierarchical
- b. empathy
- c. levels of analysis
- d. Sarbanes-Oxley act of 2002

Guidance: level 1

:: Social networks ::

_____ broadly refers to those factors of effectively functioning social groups that include such things as interpersonal relationships, a shared sense of identity, a shared understanding, shared norms, shared values, trust, cooperation, and reciprocity. However, the many views of this complex subject make a single definition difficult.

Exam Probability: **High**

7. *Answer choices:*

(see index for correct answer)

- a. Six Degrees patent
- b. Circular
- c. Fremont Arts Council
- d. Social capital

Guidance: level 1

:: ::

The _____ or just chief executive , is the most senior corporate, executive, or administrative officer in charge of managing an organization especially an independent legal entity such as a company or nonprofit institution. CEOs lead a range of organizations, including public and private corporations, non-profit organizations and even some government organizations . The CEO of a corporation or company typically reports to the board of directors and is charged with maximizing the value of the entity, which may include maximizing the share price, market share, revenues or another element. In the non-profit and government sector, CEOs typically aim at achieving outcomes related to the organization's mission, such as reducing poverty, increasing literacy, etc.

Exam Probability: **High**

8. *Answer choices:*

(see index for correct answer)

- a. corporate values
- b. open system
- c. Sarbanes-Oxley act of 2002
- d. process perspective

Guidance: level 1

:: ::

An _____ is a person temporarily or permanently residing in a country other than their native country. In common usage, the term often refers to professionals, skilled workers, or artists taking positions outside their home country, either independently or sent abroad by their employers, who can be companies, universities, governments, or non-governmental organisations. Effectively migrant workers, they usually earn more than they would at home, and less than local employees. However, the term ` _____ ` is also used for retirees and others who have chosen to live outside their native country. Historically, it has also referred to exiles.

Exam Probability: **Low**

9. *Answer choices:*

(see index for correct answer)

- a. functional perspective
- b. Expatriate
- c. interpersonal communication
- d. corporate values

Guidance: level 1

:: Outsourcing ::

_____ is the relocation of a business process from one country to another—typically an operational process, such as manufacturing, or supporting processes, such as accounting. Typically this refers to a company business, although state governments may also employ _____ . More recently, technical and administrative services have been offshored.

10. *Answer choices:*

(see index for correct answer)

- a. Government of Nova Scotia
- b. Cyient
- c. Offshoring
- d. Print and mail outsourcing

Guidance: level 1

:: Human resource management ::

_____ involves improving the effectiveness of organizations and the individuals and teams within them. Training may be viewed as related to immediate changes in organizational effectiveness via organized instruction, while development is related to the progress of longer-term organizational and employee goals. While _____ technically have differing definitions, the two are oftentimes used interchangeably and/or together. _____ has historically been a topic within applied psychology but has within the last two decades become closely associated with human resources management, talent management, human resources development, instructional design, human factors, and knowledge management.

Exam Probability: **Medium**

11. *Answer choices:*

(see index for correct answer)

- a. Employee value proposition
- b. Co-determination
- c. Income bracket
- d. Training and development

:: ::

A _____ is a professional who provides expert advice in a particular area such as security , management, education, accountancy, law, human resources, marketing , finance, engineering, science or any of many other specialized fields.

Exam Probability: **Medium**

12. *Answer choices:*

(see index for correct answer)

- a. hierarchical perspective
- b. surface-level diversity
- c. Consultant
- d. levels of analysis

:: Management ::

In organizational studies, _____ is the efficient and effective
development of an organization's resources when they are needed. Such resources
may include financial resources, inventory, human skills, production resources,
or information technology and natural resources.

Exam Probability: **Medium**

13. *Answer choices:*

(see index for correct answer)

- a. Omnex
- b. Resource management
- c. Logistics support analysis
- d. Top development

Guidance: level 1

:: ::

The _____ or labour force is the labour pool in employment. It is generally used to describe those working for a single company or industry, but can also apply to a geographic region like a city, state, or country. Within a company, its value can be labelled as its " _____ in Place". The _____ of a country includes both the employed and the unemployed. The labour force participation rate, LFPR , is the ratio between the labour force and the overall size of their cohort . The term generally excludes the employers or management, and can imply those involved in manual labour. It may also mean all those who are available for work.

Exam Probability: **Medium**

14. *Answer choices:*

(see index for correct answer)

- a. open system
- b. hierarchical perspective
- c. functional perspective
- d. Workforce

Guidance: level 1

:: Project management ::

_____ is a process of setting goals, planning and/or controlling the organizing and leading the execution of any type of activity, such as.

Exam Probability: **Low**

15. *Answer choices:*

- a. Management process
- b. Outcomes theory
- c. A Guide to the Project Management Body of Knowledge
- d. Gantt chart

Guidance: level 1

:: Management accounting ::

_____ s are costs that change as the quantity of the good or service that a business produces changes. _____ s are the sum of marginal costs over all units produced. They can also be considered normal costs. Fixed costs and _____ s make up the two components of total cost. Direct costs are costs that can easily be associated with a particular cost object. However, not all _____ s are direct costs. For example, variable manufacturing overhead costs are _____ s that are indirect costs, not direct costs. _____ s are sometimes called unit-level costs as they vary with the number of units produced.

Exam Probability: **High**

16. *Answer choices:*

- a. Variable cost
- b. Owner earnings

- c. activity based costing
- d. Job costing

Guidance: level 1

:: Employment discrimination ::

A _____ is a metaphor used to represent an invisible barrier that keeps a given demographic from rising beyond a certain level in a hierarchy.

Exam Probability: **High**

17. *Answer choices:*
(see index for correct answer)

- a. Employment discrimination
- b. Marriage bars
- c. Glass cliff
- d. Glass ceiling

Guidance: level 1

:: Evaluation ::

_____ is the practice of being honest and showing a consistent and uncompromising adherence to strong moral and ethical principles and values. In ethics, _____ is regarded as the honesty and truthfulness or accuracy of one's actions. _____ can stand in opposition to hypocrisy, in that judging with the standards of _____ involves regarding internal consistency as a virtue, and suggests that parties holding within themselves apparently conflicting values should account for the discrepancy or alter their beliefs. The word _____ evolved from the Latin adjective integer, meaning whole or complete. In this context, _____ is the inner sense of "wholeness" deriving from qualities such as honesty and consistency of character. As such, one may judge that others "have _____" to the extent that they act according to the values, beliefs and principles they claim to hold.

Exam Probability: **Medium**

18. *Answer choices:*

(see index for correct answer)

- a. Career portfolio
- b. Teaching and Learning International Survey
- c. SPECpower
- d. Evaluation approaches

Guidance: level 1

:: ::

_____ is the practice of protecting the natural environment by individuals, organizations and governments. Its objectives are to conserve natural resources and the existing natural environment and, where possible, to repair damage and reverse trends.

19. *Answer choices:*

(see index for correct answer)

- a. hierarchical
- b. Environmental protection
- c. hierarchical perspective
- d. empathy

Guidance: level 1

:: Export and import control ::

" _____ " means the Government Service which is responsible for the administration of _____ law and the collection of duties and taxes and which also has the responsibility for the application of other laws and regulations relating to the importation, exportation, movement or storage of goods.

20. *Answer choices:*

- a. Customs
- b. Canadian Export and Import Controls Bureau
- c. Import parity price
- d. CoCom

Guidance: level 1

:: Decision theory ::

Within economics the concept of _____ is used to model worth or value, but its usage has evolved significantly over time. The term was introduced initially as a measure of pleasure or satisfaction within the theory of utilitarianism by moral philosophers such as Jeremy Bentham and John Stuart Mill. But the term has been adapted and reapplied within neoclassical economics, which dominates modern economic theory, as a _____ function that represents a consumer's preference ordering over a choice set. As such, it is devoid of its original interpretation as a measurement of the pleasure or satisfaction obtained by the consumer from that choice.

Exam Probability: **High**

21. *Answer choices:*

- a. Litmus test
- b. Lock-in

- c. Utility
- d. Group decision-making

Guidance: level 1

:: Human resource management ::

_____ means increasing the scope of a job through extending the range of its job duties and responsibilities generally within the same level and periphery. _____ involves combining various activities at the same level in the organization and adding them to the existing job. It is also called the horizontal expansion of job activities. This contradicts the principles of specialisation and the division of labour whereby work is divided into small units, each of which is performed repetitively by an individual worker and the responsibilities are always clear. Some motivational theories suggest that the boredom and alienation caused by the division of labour can actually cause efficiency to fall. Thus, _____ seeks to motivate workers through reversing the process of specialisation. A typical approach might be to replace assembly lines with modular work; instead of an employee repeating the same step on each product, they perform several tasks on a single item. In order for employees to be provided with _____ they will need to be retrained in new fields to understand how each field works.

Exam Probability: **High**

22. *Answer choices:*

(see index for correct answer)

- a. Job enlargement
- b. war for talent

- c. Herrmann Brain Dominance Instrument
- d. Restructuring

Guidance: level 1

:: ::

_____ is the consumption and saving opportunity gained by an entity within a specified timeframe, which is generally expressed in monetary terms. For households and individuals, " _____ is the sum of all the wages, salaries, profits, interest payments, rents, and other forms of earnings received in a given period of time."

Exam Probability: **High**

23. *Answer choices:*

(see index for correct answer)

- a. Income
- b. surface-level diversity
- c. empathy
- d. interpersonal communication

Guidance: level 1

:: Asset ::

In financial accounting, an _____ is any resource owned by the business. Anything tangible or intangible that can be owned or controlled to produce value and that is held by a company to produce positive economic value is an _____ . Simply stated, _____ s represent value of ownership that can be converted into cash . The balance sheet of a firm records the monetary value of the _____ s owned by that firm. It covers money and other valuables belonging to an individual or to a business.

Exam Probability: **High**

24. *Answer choices:*

(see index for correct answer)

- a. Current asset
- b. Fixed asset

Guidance: level 1

:: ::

_____ refers to the overall process of attracting, shortlisting, selecting and appointing suitable candidates for jobs within an organization. _____ can also refer to processes involved in choosing individuals for unpaid roles. Managers, human resource generalists and _____ specialists may be tasked with carrying out _____ , but in some cases public-sector employment agencies, commercial _____ agencies, or specialist search consultancies are used to undertake parts of the process. Internet-based technologies which support all aspects of _____ have become widespread.

25. *Answer choices:*

(see index for correct answer)

- a. co-culture
- b. deep-level diversity
- c. Recruitment
- d. information systems assessment

Guidance: level 1

:: ::

A _____ or sample _____ is a single measure of some attribute of a sample . It is calculated by applying a function to the values of the items of the sample, which are known together as a set of data.

Exam Probability: **Low**

26. *Answer choices:*

(see index for correct answer)

- a. information systems assessment
- b. Statistic
- c. interpersonal communication
- d. empathy

:: Evaluation ::

_____ is a way of preventing mistakes and defects in manufactured products and avoiding problems when delivering products or services to customers; which ISO 9000 defines as "part of quality management focused on providing confidence that quality requirements will be fulfilled". This defect prevention in _____ differs subtly from defect detection and rejection in quality control and has been referred to as a shift left since it focuses on quality earlier in the process .

Exam Probability: **Low**

27. *Answer choices:*

(see index for correct answer)

- a. XTS-400
- b. Educational evaluation
- c. Technology assessment
- d. Health technology assessment

:: ::

_____ is the exchange of capital, goods, and services across international borders or territories.

Exam Probability: **High**

28. *Answer choices:*

- a. process perspective
- b. functional perspective
- c. empathy
- d. International trade

Guidance: level 1

:: Marketing ::

_____ or stock is the goods and materials that a business holds for the ultimate goal of resale .

Exam Probability: **High**

29. *Answer choices:*

- a. The Cellar

- b. Inventory
- c. Beat-sheet
- d. Accreditation in Public Relations

Guidance: level 1

:: Problem solving ::

A _____ is a unit or formation established to work on a single defined task or activity. Originally introduced by the United States Navy, the term has now caught on for general usage and is a standard part of NATO terminology. Many non-military organizations now create " _____ s" or task groups for temporary activities that might have once been performed by ad hoc committees.

Exam Probability: **Low**

30. *Answer choices:*

(see index for correct answer)

- a. Rhetorical reason
- b. Problem shaping
- c. Problem finding
- d. Parallel thinking

Guidance: level 1

:: Teams ::

A _____ usually refers to a group of individuals who work together from different geographic locations and rely on communication technology such as email, FAX, and video or voice conferencing services in order to collaborate. The term can also refer to groups or teams that work together asynchronously or across organizational levels. Powell, Piccoli and Ives define _____ s as "groups of geographically, organizationally and/or time dispersed workers brought together by information and telecommunication technologies to accomplish one or more organizational tasks." According to Ale Ebrahim et. al. , _____ s can also be defined as "small temporary groups of geographically, organizationally and/or time dispersed knowledge workers who coordinate their work predominantly with electronic information and communication technologies in order to accomplish one or more organization tasks."

Exam Probability: **Medium**

31. *Answer choices:*

(see index for correct answer)

- a. team composition
- b. Virtual team

Guidance: level 1

:: ::

_____ is a means of protection from financial loss. It is a form of risk management, primarily used to hedge against the risk of a contingent or uncertain loss

Exam Probability: **Low**

32. *Answer choices:*

(see index for correct answer)

- a. co-culture
- b. deep-level diversity
- c. Insurance
- d. cultural

Guidance: level 1

:: Power (social and political) ::

In a notable study of power conducted by social psychologists John R. P. French and Bertram Raven in 1959, power is divided into five separate and distinct forms. In 1965 Raven revised this model to include a sixth form by separating the informational power base as distinct from the _____ base.

Exam Probability: **High**

33. *Answer choices:*

(see index for correct answer)

- a. Hard power
- b. Referent power
- c. need for power

Guidance: level 1

:: Statistical terminology ::

_____ es can be learned implicitly within cultural contexts. People may develop _____ es toward or against an individual, an ethnic group, a sexual or gender identity, a nation, a religion, a social class, a political party, theoretical paradigms and ideologies within academic domains, or a species. _____ ed means one-sided, lacking a neutral viewpoint, or not having an open mind. _____ can come in many forms and is related to prejudice and intuition.

Exam Probability: **Low**

34. *Answer choices:*
(see index for correct answer)

- a. Iterated conditional modes
- b. Conditional expectation
- c. Gompertz function
- d. Bias

Guidance: level 1

:: Workplace ::

A _____ is a process through which feedback from an employee's subordinates, colleagues, and supervisor, as well as a self-evaluation by the employee themselves is gathered. Such feedback can also include, when relevant, feedback from external sources who interact with the employee, such as customers and suppliers or other interested stakeholders. _____ is so named because it solicits feedback regarding an employee's behavior from a variety of points of view . It therefore may be contrasted with "downward feedback" , or "upward feedback" delivered to supervisory or management employees by subordinates only.

Exam Probability: **Low**

35. *Answer choices:*

(see index for correct answer)

- a. Workplace relationships
- b. Workplace wellness
- c. labour turnover
- d. Queen bee syndrome

Guidance: level 1

:: ::

_____ comprises all of the processes of governing – whether undertaken by the government of a state, by a market or by a network – over a social system and whether through the laws, norms, power or language of an organized society. It relates to "the processes of interaction and decision-making among the actors involved in a collective problem that lead to the creation, reinforcement, or reproduction of social norms and institutions".In lay terms, it could be described as the political processes that exist in and between formal institutions.

Exam Probability: **Medium**

36. *Answer choices:*

(see index for correct answer)

- a. interpersonal communication
- b. Character
- c. co-culture
- d. Governance

Guidance: level 1

:: ::

In sales, commerce and economics, a _____ is the recipient of a good, service, product or an idea - obtained from a seller, vendor, or supplier via a financial transaction or exchange for money or some other valuable consideration.

Exam Probability: **Low**

37. *Answer choices:*

(see index for correct answer)

- a. Customer
- b. corporate values
- c. Character
- d. information systems assessment

Guidance: level 1

:: Time management ::

_____ is the process of planning and exercising conscious control of time spent on specific activities, especially to increase effectiveness, efficiency, and productivity. It involves a juggling act of various demands upon a person relating to work, social life, family, hobbies, personal interests and commitments with the finiteness of time. Using time effectively gives the person "choice" on spending/managing activities at their own time and expediency.

Exam Probability: **Medium**

38. *Answer choices:*

(see index for correct answer)

- a. Time perception

- b. Time management
- c. Maestro concept
- d. Time allocation

Guidance: level 1

:: ::

_____ is the amount of time someone works beyond normal working hours. The term is also used for the pay received for this time. Normal hours may be determined in several ways.

Exam Probability: **High**

39. *Answer choices:*

(see index for correct answer)

- a. imperative
- b. hierarchical perspective
- c. functional perspective
- d. Overtime

Guidance: level 1

:: ::

An _____ in international trade is a good or service produced in one country that is bought by someone in another country. The seller of such goods and services is an _____ er; the foreign buyer is an importer.

Exam Probability: **Medium**

40. *Answer choices:*

(see index for correct answer)

- a. surface-level diversity
- b. corporate values
- c. process perspective
- d. Export

Guidance: level 1

:: Cash flow ::

_____ s are narrowly interconnected with the concepts of value, interest rate and liquidity. A _____ that shall happen on a future day tN can be transformed into a _____ of the same value in t0.

Exam Probability: **Medium**

41. *Answer choices:*

(see index for correct answer)

- a. Discounted cash flow
- b. Cash flow
- c. Cash flow statement
- d. Valuation using discounted cash flows

Guidance: level 1

:: Industrial design ::

In physics and mathematics, the _____ of a mathematical space is informally defined as the minimum number of coordinates needed to specify any point within it. Thus a line has a _____ of one because only one coordinate is needed to specify a point on it for example, the point at 5 on a number line. A surface such as a plane or the surface of a cylinder or sphere has a _____ of two because two coordinates are needed to specify a point on it for example, both a latitude and longitude are required to locate a point on the surface of a sphere. The inside of a cube, a cylinder or a sphere is three- _____ al because three coordinates are needed to locate a point within these spaces.

Exam Probability: **Low**

42. *Answer choices:*

(see index for correct answer)

- a. Concept art
- b. I.D.
- c. International Council of Societies of Industrial Design
- d. Industrial design right

:: Management ::

The term _____ refers to measures designed to increase the degree of autonomy and self-determination in people and in communities in order to enable them to represent their interests in a responsible and self-determined way, acting on their own authority. It is the process of becoming stronger and more confident, especially in controlling one's life and claiming one's rights. _____ as action refers both to the process of self-_____ and to professional support of people, which enables them to overcome their sense of powerlessness and lack of influence, and to recognize and use their resources. To do work with power.

Exam Probability: **High**

43. *Answer choices:*

(see index for correct answer)

- a. Crisis management
- b. Empowerment
- c. Executive development
- d. Duality

:: Business ::

The seller, or the provider of the goods or services, completes a sale in response to an acquisition, appropriation, requisition or a direct interaction with the buyer at the point of sale. There is a passing of title of the item, and the settlement of a price, in which agreement is reached on a price for which transfer of ownership of the item will occur. The seller, not the purchaser typically executes the sale and it may be completed prior to the obligation of payment. In the case of indirect interaction, a person who sells goods or service on behalf of the owner is known as a _____ man or _____ woman or _____ person, but this often refers to someone selling goods in a store/shop, in which case other terms are also common, including _____ clerk, shop assistant, and retail clerk.

Exam Probability: **Low**

44. *Answer choices:*

(see index for correct answer)

- a. 24/7 service
- b. Sales
- c. Co-creation
- d. Corporate services

Guidance: level 1

:: ::

An _____ is a contingent motivator. Traditional _____ s are extrinsic motivators which reward actions to yield a desired outcome. The effectiveness of traditional _____ s has changed as the needs of Western society have evolved. While the traditional _____ model is effective when there is a defined procedure and goal for a task, Western society started to require a higher volume of critical thinkers, so the traditional model became less effective. Institutions are now following a trend in implementing strategies that rely on intrinsic motivations rather than the extrinsic motivations that the traditional _____ s foster.

Exam Probability: **High**

45. *Answer choices:*

(see index for correct answer)

- a. information systems assessment
- b. Incentive
- c. similarity-attraction theory
- d. surface-level diversity

Guidance: level 1

:: ::

A _____ is a fund into which a sum of money is added during an employee's employment years, and from which payments are drawn to support the person's retirement from work in the form of periodic payments. A _____ may be a "defined benefit plan" where a fixed sum is paid regularly to a person, or a "defined contribution plan" under which a fixed sum is invested and then becomes available at retirement age. _____ s should not be confused with severance pay; the former is usually paid in regular installments for life after retirement, while the latter is typically paid as a fixed amount after involuntary termination of employment prior to retirement.

Exam Probability: **Medium**

46. *Answer choices:*

(see index for correct answer)

- a. deep-level diversity
- b. functional perspective
- c. cultural
- d. hierarchical perspective

Guidance: level 1

:: Management ::

_____ is the identification, evaluation, and prioritization of risks followed by coordinated and economical application of resources to minimize, monitor, and control the probability or impact of unfortunate events or to maximize the realization of opportunities.

47. *Answer choices:*

(see index for correct answer)

- a. Overtime rate
- b. Staff management
- c. Board of governors
- d. Risk management

Guidance: level 1

:: ::

In logic and philosophy, an _____ is a series of statements , called the premises or premisses , intended to determine the degree of truth of another statement, the conclusion. The logical form of an _____ in a natural language can be represented in a symbolic formal language, and independently of natural language formally defined " _____ s" can be made in math and computer science.

Exam Probability: **Low**

48. *Answer choices:*

(see index for correct answer)

- a. Argument
- b. imperative

- c. hierarchical
- d. functional perspective

Guidance: level 1

:: ::

In mathematics, a _____ is a relationship between two numbers indicating how many times the first number contains the second. For example, if a bowl of fruit contains eight oranges and six lemons, then the _____ of oranges to lemons is eight to six . Similarly, the _____ of lemons to oranges is 6:8 and the _____ of oranges to the total amount of fruit is 8:14 .

Exam Probability: **Medium**

49. *Answer choices:*

(see index for correct answer)

- a. functional perspective
- b. deep-level diversity
- c. imperative
- d. Ratio

Guidance: level 1

:: ::

In a supply chain, a _____ , or a seller, is an enterprise that contributes goods or services. Generally, a supply chain _____ manufactures inventory/stock items and sells them to the next link in the chain. Today, these terms refer to a supplier of any good or service.

Exam Probability: **High**

50. *Answer choices:*

(see index for correct answer)

- a. interpersonal communication
- b. co-culture
- c. Vendor
- d. cultural

Guidance: level 1

:: Systems thinking ::

Systems theory is the interdisciplinary study of systems. A system is a cohesive conglomeration of interrelated and interdependent parts that is either natural or man-made. Every system is delineated by its spatial and temporal boundaries, surrounded and influenced by its environment, described by its structure and purpose or nature and expressed in its functioning. In terms of its effects, a system can be more than the sum of its parts if it expresses synergy or emergent behavior. Changing one part of the system usually affects other parts and the whole system, with predictable patterns of behavior. For systems that are self-learning and self-adapting, the positive growth and adaptation depend upon how well the system is adjusted with its environment. Some systems function mainly to support other systems by aiding in the maintenance of the other system to prevent failure. The goal of systems theory is systematically discovering a system's dynamics, constraints, conditions and elucidating principles that can be discerned and applied to systems at every level of nesting, and in every field for achieving optimized equifinality.

Exam Probability: **Medium**

51. *Answer choices:*

(see index for correct answer)

- a. The Arlington Institute
- b. The Energy and Resources Institute
- c. Futuribles International
- d. World Future Society

Guidance: level 1

:: Human resource management ::

_____ is the strategic approach to the effective management of people in an organization so that they help the business to gain a competitive advantage. It is designed to maximize employee performance in service of an employer's strategic objectives. HR is primarily concerned with the management of people within organizations, focusing on policies and on systems. HR departments are responsible for overseeing employee-benefits design, employee recruitment, training and development, performance appraisal, and Reward management . HR also concerns itself with organizational change and industrial relations, that is, the balancing of organizational practices with requirements arising from collective bargaining and from governmental laws.

Exam Probability: **Low**

52. *Answer choices:*

(see index for correct answer)

- a. Human resource management
- b. IDS HR in Practice
- c. Behavioral Competencies
- d. Occupational burnout

Guidance: level 1

:: Behaviorism ::

In behavioral psychology, _____ is a consequence applied that will strengthen an organism's future behavior whenever that behavior is preceded by a specific antecedent stimulus. This strengthening effect may be measured as a higher frequency of behavior , longer duration , greater magnitude , or shorter latency . There are two types of _____ , known as positive _____ and negative _____ ; positive is where by a reward is offered on expression of the wanted behaviour and negative is taking away an undesirable element in the persons environment whenever the desired behaviour is achieved.

Exam Probability: **High**

53. *Answer choices:*

(see index for correct answer)

- a. social facilitation
- b. chaining
- c. Systematic desensitization
- d. contingency management

Guidance: level 1

:: Leadership ::

_____ is a theory of leadership where a leader works with teams to identify needed change, creating a vision to guide the change through inspiration, and executing the change in tandem with committed members of a group; it is an integral part of the Full Range Leadership Model. _____ serves to enhance the motivation, morale, and job performance of followers through a variety of mechanisms; these include connecting the follower's sense of identity and self to a project and to the collective identity of the organization; being a role model for followers in order to inspire them and to raise their interest in the project; challenging followers to take greater ownership for their work, and understanding the strengths and weaknesses of followers, allowing the leader to align followers with tasks that enhance their performance.

Exam Probability: **High**

54. *Answer choices:*

(see index for correct answer)

- a. Transformational leadership
- b. Leadership analysis
- c. Sex differences in leadership
- d. The Saint, the Surfer, and the CEO

Guidance: level 1

:: ::

A _____ , or also known as foreman, overseer, facilitator, monitor, area coordinator, or sometimes gaffer, is the job title of a low level management position that is primarily based on authority over a worker or charge of a workplace. A _____ can also be one of the most senior in the staff at the place of work, such as a Professor who oversees a PhD dissertation. Supervision, on the other hand, can be performed by people without this formal title, for example by parents. The term _____ itself can be used to refer to any personnel who have this task as part of their job description.

Exam Probability: **High**

55. *Answer choices:*

(see index for correct answer)

- a. hierarchical perspective
- b. open system
- c. corporate values
- d. process perspective

Guidance: level 1

:: Marketing techniques ::

In industry, product lifecycle management is the process of managing the entire lifecycle of a product from inception, through engineering design and manufacture, to service and disposal of manufactured products. PLM integrates people, data, processes and business systems and provides a product information backbone for companies and their extended enterprise.

56. *Answer choices:*

(see index for correct answer)

- a. Seeding trial
- b. Social media in the fashion industry
- c. Lovemark
- d. Unique selling proposition

Guidance: level 1

:: Discrimination ::

In social psychology, a _____ is an over-generalized belief about a particular category of people. _____ s are generalized because one assumes that the _____ is true for each individual person in the category. While such generalizations may be useful when making quick decisions, they may be erroneous when applied to particular individuals. _____ s encourage prejudice and may arise for a number of reasons.

Exam Probability: **Low**

57. *Answer choices:*

(see index for correct answer)

- a. Economic discrimination
- b. Elitism

- c. Anti-Americanism

Guidance: level 1

:: Project management ::

_____ is the right to exercise power, which can be formalized by a state and exercised by way of judges, appointed executives of government, or the ecclesiastical or priestly appointed representatives of a God or other deities.

Exam Probability: **Low**

58. *Answer choices:*

(see index for correct answer)

- a. Fast-track construction
- b. Agile management
- c. Terms of reference
- d. Authority

Guidance: level 1

:: Analysis ::

_____ is the process of breaking a complex topic or substance into smaller parts in order to gain a better understanding of it. The technique has been applied in the study of mathematics and logic since before Aristotle , though _____ as a formal concept is a relatively recent development.

Exam Probability: **Low**

59. *Answer choices:*

(see index for correct answer)

- a. Analysis
- b. Configurational analysis
- c. SWOQe
- d. Rational analysis

Guidance: level 1

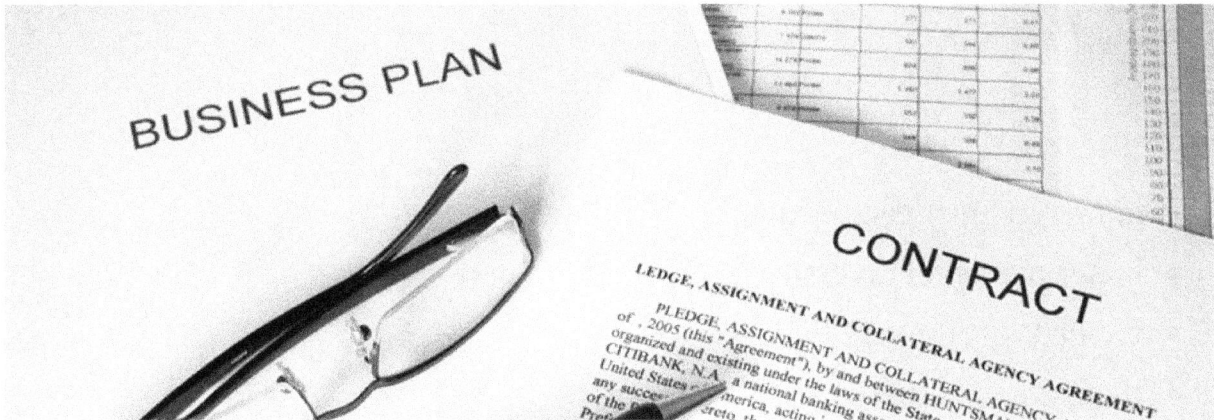

Business law

Corporate law (also known as business law) is the body of law governing the rights, relations, and conduct of persons, companies, organizations and businesses. It refers to the legal practice relating to, or the theory of corporations. Corporate law often describes the law relating to matters which derive directly from the life-cycle of a corporation. It thus encompasses the formation, funding, governance, and death of a corporation.

:: ::

In logic and philosophy, an _____ is a series of statements , called the premises or premisses , intended to determine the degree of truth of another statement, the conclusion. The logical form of an _____ in a natural language can be represented in a symbolic formal language, and independently of natural language formally defined " _____ s" can be made in math and computer science.

Exam Probability: **Medium**

1. *Answer choices:*

(see index for correct answer)

- a. hierarchical perspective
- b. surface-level diversity
- c. deep-level diversity
- d. personal values

Guidance: level 1

:: Equity (law) ::

An assignment is a legal term used in the context of the law of contract and of property. In both instances, assignment is the process whereby a person, the assignor, transfers rights or benefits to another, the _____ . An assignment may not transfer a duty, burden or detriment without the express agreement of the _____ . The right or benefit being assigned may be a gift or it may be paid for with a contractual consideration such as money.

Exam Probability: **Low**

2. *Answer choices:*

(see index for correct answer)

- a. Equitable conversion
- b. assignor

Guidance: level 1

:: Stock market ::

_____ is freedom from, or resilience against, potential harm caused by
others. Beneficiaries of _____ may be of persons and social groups,
objects and institutions, ecosystems or any other entity or phenomenon
vulnerable to unwanted change by its environment.

Exam Probability: **High**

3. *Answer choices:*

(see index for correct answer)

- a. Share
- b. Shareholders
- c. Paper valuation
- d. Security

Guidance: level 1

:: ::

_____ is an abstract concept of management of complex systems according
to a set of rules and trends. In systems theory, these types of rules exist in
various fields of biology and society, but the term has slightly different
meanings according to context. For example.

4. *Answer choices:*

(see index for correct answer)

- a. Regulation
- b. co-culture
- c. open system
- d. functional perspective

Guidance: level 1

:: ::

Advertising is a marketing communication that employs an openly sponsored, non-personal message to promote or sell a product, service or idea. Sponsors of advertising are typically businesses wishing to promote their products or services. Advertising is differentiated from public relations in that an advertiser pays for and has control over the message. It differs from personal selling in that the message is non-personal, i.e., not directed to a particular individual.Advertising is communicated through various mass media, including traditional media such as newspapers, magazines, television, radio, outdoor advertising or direct mail; and new media such as search results, blogs, social media, websites or text messages. The actual presentation of the message in a medium is referred to as an _____ , or "ad" or advert for short.

5. *Answer choices:*

(see index for correct answer)

- a. corporate values
- b. Sarbanes-Oxley act of 2002
- c. interpersonal communication
- d. surface-level diversity

Guidance: level 1

:: Debt ::

_____ is the trust which allows one party to provide money or resources to another party wherein the second party does not reimburse the first party immediately , but promises either to repay or return those resources at a later date. In other words, _____ is a method of making reciprocity formal, legally enforceable, and extensible to a large group of unrelated people.

Exam Probability: **High**

6. *Answer choices:*

(see index for correct answer)

- a. Debt-lag
- b. Credit
- c. Compulsive buying disorder
- d. Student debt

:: ::

An _____ , for United States federal income tax, is a closely held corporation that makes a valid election to be taxed under Subchapter S of Chapter 1 of the Internal Revenue Code. In general, _____ s do not pay any income taxes. Instead, the corporation's income or losses are divided among and passed through to its shareholders. The shareholders must then report the income or loss on their own individual income tax returns.

Exam Probability: **High**

7. *Answer choices:*

(see index for correct answer)

- a. deep-level diversity
- b. cultural
- c. information systems assessment
- d. S corporation

:: Law ::

_____ is a body of law which defines the role, powers, and structure of different entities within a state, namely, the executive, the parliament or legislature, and the judiciary; as well as the basic rights of citizens and, in federal countries such as the United States and Canada, the relationship between the central government and state, provincial, or territorial governments.

Exam Probability: **Low**

8. *Answer choices:*

(see index for correct answer)

- a. Constitutional law
- b. Comparative law

Guidance: level 1

:: ::

In law, a _____ is the formal finding of fact made by a jury on matters or questions submitted to the jury by a judge. In a bench trial, the judge's decision near the end of the trial is simply referred to as a finding. In England and Wales, a coroner's findings are called _____ s .

Exam Probability: **Low**

9. *Answer choices:*

(see index for correct answer)

- a. Verdict
- b. co-culture
- c. empathy
- d. deep-level diversity

Guidance: level 1

:: International trade ::

_____ involves the transfer of goods or services from one person or entity to another, often in exchange for money. A system or network that allows _____ is called a market.

Exam Probability: **Medium**

10. *Answer choices:*

(see index for correct answer)

- a. Trade
- b. Bullionism
- c. Competitiveness Policy Council
- d. Trade Act

Guidance: level 1

:: Marketing ::

A _____ is an overall experience of a customer that distinguishes an organization or product from its rivals in the eyes of the customer. _____ s are used in business, marketing, and advertising. Name _____ s are sometimes distinguished from generic or store _____ s.

Exam Probability: **Medium**

11. *Answer choices:*

(see index for correct answer)

- a. Double bottom line
- b. Corporate anniversary
- c. Experiential marketing
- d. Customer acquisition management

Guidance: level 1

:: ::

The _____ of 1973, , is a federal law, codified as 29 U.S.C. § 701 et seq. The principal sponsor of the bill was Rep. John Brademas [IN-3]. The _____ of 1973 replaces the Vocational _____ of 1973, to extend and revise the authorization of grants to States for vocational rehabilitation services, with special emphasis on services to those with the most severe disabilities, to expand special Federal responsibilities and research and training programs with respect to individuals with disabilities, to establish special responsibilities in the Secretary of Health, Education, and Welfare for coordination of all programs with respect to individuals with disabilities within the Department of Health, Education, and Welfare, and for other purposes.

Exam Probability: **Medium**

12. *Answer choices:*

(see index for correct answer)

- a. information systems assessment
- b. hierarchical perspective
- c. Character
- d. personal values

Guidance: level 1

:: ::

A _____ is a person who trades in commodities produced by other people. Historically, a _____ is anyone who is involved in business or trade. _____ s have operated for as long as industry, commerce, and trade have existed. During the 16th-century, in Europe, two different terms for _____ s emerged: One term, meerseniers, described local traders such as bakers, grocers, etc.; while a new term, koopman (Dutch: koopman, described _____ s who operated on a global stage, importing and exporting goods over vast distances, and offering added-value services such as credit and finance.

Exam Probability: **Low**

13. *Answer choices:*

(see index for correct answer)

- a. empathy
- b. levels of analysis
- c. Merchant
- d. open system

Guidance: level 1

:: Judgment (law) ::

In law, a _____ is a judgment entered by a court for one party and against another party summarily, i.e., without a full trial. Such a judgment may be issued on the merits of an entire case, or on discrete issues in that case.

14. *Answer choices:*

(see index for correct answer)

- a. Entry of judgment
- b. Summary judgment

Guidance: level 1

:: Business models ::

A _____ , _____ company or daughter company is a company that is owned or controlled by another company, which is called the parent company, parent, or holding company. The _____ can be a company, corporation, or limited liability company. In some cases it is a government or state-owned enterprise. In some cases, particularly in the music and book publishing industries, subsidiaries are referred to as imprints.

Exam Probability: **Low**

15. *Answer choices:*

(see index for correct answer)

- a. Business networking
- b. Parent company
- c. Subsidiary
- d. Paid To Click

:: ::

_____ or accountancy is the measurement, processing, and communication of financial information about economic entities such as businesses and corporations. The modern field was established by the Italian mathematician Luca Pacioli in 1494. _____ , which has been called the "language of business", measures the results of an organization's economic activities and conveys this information to a variety of users, including investors, creditors, management, and regulators. Practitioners of _____ are known as accountants. The terms " _____ " and "financial reporting" are often used as synonyms.

Exam Probability: **Medium**

16. *Answer choices:*

(see index for correct answer)

- a. functional perspective
- b. Character
- c. personal values
- d. Accounting

:: Forgery ::

_____ is a white-collar crime that generally refers to the false making or material alteration of a legal instrument with the specific intent to defraud anyone . Tampering with a certain legal instrument may be forbidden by law in some jurisdictions but such an offense is not related to _____ unless the tampered legal instrument was actually used in the course of the crime to defraud another person or entity. Copies, studio replicas, and reproductions are not considered forgeries, though they may later become forgeries through knowing and willful misrepresentations.

Exam Probability: **Medium**

17. *Answer choices:*

(see index for correct answer)

- a. Forgery of Foreign Bills Act 1803
- b. Unapproved aircraft part
- c. Archaeological forgery
- d. Void pantograph

Guidance: level 1

:: ::

_____ Motor Company is an American multinational automaker that has its main headquarter in Dearborn, Michigan, a suburb of Detroit. It was founded by Henry _____ and incorporated on June 16, 1903. The company sells automobiles and commercial vehicles under the _____ brand and most luxury cars under the Lincoln brand. _____ also owns Brazilian SUV manufacturer Troller, an 8% stake in Aston Martin of the United Kingdom and a 32% stake in Jiangling Motors. It also has joint-ventures in China , Taiwan , Thailand , Turkey , and Russia . The company is listed on the New York Stock Exchange and is controlled by the _____ family; they have minority ownership but the majority of the voting power.

Exam Probability: **High**

18. *Answer choices:*

(see index for correct answer)

- a. open system
- b. co-culture
- c. cultural
- d. surface-level diversity

Guidance: level 1

:: Contract law ::

Offer and acceptance analysis is a traditional approach in contract law. The offer and acceptance formula, developed in the 19th century, identifies a moment of formation when the parties are of one mind. This classical approach to contract formation has been modified by developments in the law of estoppel, misleading conduct, misrepresentation and unjust enrichment.

Exam Probability: **Low**

19. *Answer choices:*

(see index for correct answer)

- a. History of contract law
- b. Third-party beneficiary
- c. Escalator clause
- d. End-user license agreement

Guidance: level 1

:: Manufacturing ::

A _____ is a building for storing goods. _____ s are used by manufacturers, importers, exporters, wholesalers, transport businesses, customs, etc. They are usually large plain buildings in industrial parks on the outskirts of cities, towns or villages.

Exam Probability: **Low**

20. *Answer choices:*

(see index for correct answer)

- a. Eneas
- b. Build to order
- c. Universal gateway
- d. Carton flow

Guidance: level 1

:: ::

_____ is the collection of techniques, skills, methods, and processes used in the production of goods or services or in the accomplishment of objectives, such as scientific investigation. _____ can be the knowledge of techniques, processes, and the like, or it can be embedded in machines to allow for operation without detailed knowledge of their workings. Systems applying _____ by taking an input, changing it according to the system's use, and then producing an outcome are referred to as _____ systems or technological systems.

Exam Probability: **Low**

21. *Answer choices:*

(see index for correct answer)

- a. hierarchical
- b. open system

- c. process perspective
- d. empathy

Guidance: level 1

:: ::

A _____ is a request to do something, most commonly addressed to a government official or public entity. _____ s to a deity are a form of prayer called supplication.

Exam Probability: **High**

22. *Answer choices:*

(see index for correct answer)

- a. Petition
- b. Sarbanes-Oxley act of 2002
- c. Character
- d. cultural

Guidance: level 1

:: ::

A federation is a political entity characterized by a union of partially self-governing provinces, states, or other regions under a central _____ . In a federation, the self-governing status of the component states, as well as the division of power between them and the central government, is typically constitutionally entrenched and may not be altered by a unilateral decision of either party, the states or the federal political body. Alternatively, federation is a form of government in which sovereign power is formally divided between a central authority and a number of constituent regions so that each region retains some degree of control over its internal affairs. It is often argued that federal states where the central government has the constitutional authority to suspend a constituent state's government by invoking gross mismanagement or civil unrest, or to adopt national legislation that overrides or infringe on the constituent states' powers by invoking the central government's constitutional authority to ensure "peace and good government" or to implement obligations contracted under an international treaty, are not truly federal states.

Exam Probability: **High**

23. *Answer choices:*

(see index for correct answer)

- a. Federal government
- b. personal values
- c. Sarbanes-Oxley act of 2002
- d. deep-level diversity

Guidance: level 1

:: ::

_____ is a type of government support for the citizens of that society. _____ may be provided to people of any income level, as with social security , but it is usually intended to ensure that the poor can meet their basic human needs such as food and shelter. _____ attempts to provide poor people with a minimal level of well-being, usually either a free- or a subsidized-supply of certain goods and social services, such as healthcare, education, and vocational training.

Exam Probability: **Low**

24. *Answer choices:*

(see index for correct answer)

- a. Welfare
- b. deep-level diversity
- c. surface-level diversity
- d. personal values

Guidance: level 1

:: Film production ::

_____ is a legal term more comprehensive and of higher import than either warranty or "security". It most commonly designates a private transaction by means of which one person, to obtain some trust, confidence or credit for another, engages to be answerable for him. It may also designate a treaty through which claims, rights or possessions are secured. It is to be differentiated from the colloquial "personal _____ " in that a _____ is a legal concept which produces an economic effect. A personal _____ by contrast is often used to refer to a promise made by an individual which is supported by, or assured through, the word of the individual. In the same way, a _____ produces a legal effect wherein one party affirms the promise of another by promising to themselves pay if default occurs.

Exam Probability: **Medium**

25. *Answer choices:*

(see index for correct answer)

- a. Central Asian and Southern Caucasus Film Festivals Confederation
- b. Guarantee
- c. Martini Shot
- d. Cinematographic shooting

Guidance: level 1

:: Progressive Era in the United States ::

The Clayton Antitrust Act of 1914 , was a part of United States antitrust law with the goal of adding further substance to the U.S. antitrust law regime; the _____ sought to prevent anticompetitive practices in their incipiency. That regime started with the Sherman Antitrust Act of 1890, the first Federal law outlawing practices considered harmful to consumers . The _____ specified particular prohibited conduct, the three-level enforcement scheme, the exemptions, and the remedial measures.

Exam Probability: **Medium**

26. *Answer choices:*

(see index for correct answer)

- a. pragmatism
- b. Clayton Antitrust Act
- c. Clayton Act

Guidance: level 1

:: White-collar criminals ::

_____ refers to financially motivated, nonviolent crime committed by businesses and government professionals. It was first defined by the sociologist Edwin Sutherland in 1939 as "a crime committed by a person of respectability and high social status in the course of their occupation". Typical _____ s could include wage theft, fraud, bribery, Ponzi schemes, insider trading, labor racketeering, embezzlement, cybercrime, copyright infringement, money laundering, identity theft, and forgery. Lawyers can specialize in _____ .

27. *Answer choices:*

(see index for correct answer)

- a. Tongsun Park
- b. White-collar crime

Guidance: level 1

:: Monopoly (economics) ::

A _____ is a form of intellectual property that gives its owner the legal right to exclude others from making, using, selling, and importing an invention for a limited period of years, in exchange for publishing an enabling public disclosure of the invention. In most countries _____ rights fall under civil law and the _____ holder needs to sue someone infringing the _____ in order to enforce his or her rights. In some industries _____ s are an essential form of competitive advantage; in others they are irrelevant.

Exam Probability: **Low**

28. *Answer choices:*

(see index for correct answer)

- a. Economies of scope
- b. Patent

- c. Ramsey problem
- d. Natural monopoly

Guidance: level 1

:: Legal terms ::

_____ , or non-absolute contributory negligence outside the United States, is a partial legal defense that reduces the amount of damages that a plaintiff can recover in a negligence-based claim, based upon the degree to which the plaintiff's own negligence contributed to cause the injury. When the defense is asserted, the factfinder, usually a jury, must decide the degree to which the plaintiff's negligence and the combined negligence of all other relevant actors all contributed to cause the plaintiff's damages. It is a modification of the doctrine of contributory negligence that disallows any recovery by a plaintiff whose negligence contributed even minimally to causing the damages.

Exam Probability: **Low**

29. *Answer choices:*

(see index for correct answer)

- a. Advisory jury
- b. European Authorized Representative
- c. Government interest
- d. Comparative negligence

Guidance: level 1

:: ::

The _____ of 1933, also known as the 1933 Act, the _____ , the Truth in _____ , the Federal _____ , and the `33 Act, was enacted by the United States Congress on May 27, 1933, during the Great Depression, after the stock market crash of 1929. Legislated pursuant to the Interstate Commerce Clause of the Constitution, it requires every offer or sale of securities that uses the means and instrumentalities of interstate commerce to be registered with the SEC pursuant to the 1933 Act, unless an exemption from registration exists under the law. The term "means and instrumentalities of interstate commerce" is extremely broad and it is virtually impossible to avoid the operation of the statute by attempting to offer or sell a security without using an "instrumentality" of interstate commerce. Any use of a telephone, for example, or the mails would probably be enough to subject the transaction to the statute.

Exam Probability: **Low**

30. *Answer choices:*

(see index for correct answer)

- a. Character
- b. Securities Act
- c. functional perspective
- d. interpersonal communication

Guidance: level 1

:: Contract law ::

A _____ is a legally-binding agreement which recognises and governs the rights and duties of the parties to the agreement. A _____ is legally enforceable because it meets the requirements and approval of the law. An agreement typically involves the exchange of goods, services, money, or promises of any of those. In the event of breach of _____ , the law awards the injured party access to legal remedies such as damages and cancellation.

Exam Probability: **Medium**

31. *Answer choices:*

(see index for correct answer)

- a. Voidable contract
- b. Severable contract
- c. Heads of loss
- d. Pre-existing duty rule

Guidance: level 1

:: Contract law ::

_____ is a doctrine in contract law that describes terms that are so extremely unjust, or overwhelmingly one-sided in favor of the party who has the superior bargaining power, that they are contrary to good conscience. Typically, an unconscionable contract is held to be unenforceable because no reasonable or informed person would otherwise agree to it. The perpetrator of the conduct is not allowed to benefit, because the consideration offered is lacking, or is so obviously inadequate, that to enforce the contract would be unfair to the party seeking to escape the contract.

32. *Answer choices:*

(see index for correct answer)

- a. Oral contract
- b. Cover
- c. Unconscionability
- d. Time is of the essence

Guidance: level 1

:: ::

_____ is the act or practice of forbidding something by law; more particularly the term refers to the banning of the manufacture, storage , transportation, sale, possession, and consumption of alcoholic beverages. The word is also used to refer to a period of time during which such bans are enforced.

33. *Answer choices:*

(see index for correct answer)

- a. levels of analysis
- b. hierarchical perspective

- c. interpersonal communication
- d. Prohibition

Guidance: level 1

:: Contract law ::

An _____ , or simply option, is defined as "a promise which meets the requirements for the formation of a contract and limits the promisor`s power to revoke an offer."

Exam Probability: **High**

34. *Answer choices:*

(see index for correct answer)

- a. Baseball business rules
- b. Seal
- c. Option contract
- d. Cover

Guidance: level 1

:: Marketing ::

_____ comes from the Latin neg and otsia referring to businessmen who, unlike the patricians, had no leisure time in their industriousness; it held the meaning of business until the 17th century when it took on the diplomatic connotation as a dialogue between two or more people or parties intended to reach a beneficial outcome over one or more issues where a conflict exists with respect to at least one of these issues. Thus, _____ is a process of combining divergent positions into a joint agreement under a decision rule of unanimity.

Exam Probability: **High**

35. *Answer choices:*

(see index for correct answer)

- a. Exploratory research
- b. Negotiation
- c. elaboration likelihood
- d. Consumer culture theory

Guidance: level 1

:: Business law ::

The term is used to designate a range of diverse, if often kindred, concepts. These have historically been addressed in a number of discrete disciplines, notably mathematics, physics, chemistry, ethics, aesthetics, ontology, and theology.

36. *Answer choices:*

(see index for correct answer)

- a. Perfection
- b. Fraudulent trading
- c. Administration
- d. Bulk sale

Guidance: level 1

:: Contract law ::

_____ are damages whose amount the parties designate during the formation of a contract for the injured party to collect as compensation upon a specific breach .

Exam Probability: **Medium**

37. *Answer choices:*

(see index for correct answer)

- a. Service plan
- b. Indian contract law
- c. Extinguishment
- d. Liquidated damages

:: ::

Competition arises whenever at least two parties strive for a goal which cannot be shared: where one's gain is the other's loss .

Exam Probability: **Low**

38. *Answer choices:*

(see index for correct answer)

- a. hierarchical perspective
- b. Competitor
- c. empathy
- d. levels of analysis

:: Negotiable instrument law ::

In the United States, The Preservation of Consumers' Claims and Defenses [
_____ Rule], formally known as the "Trade Regulation Rule Concerning
Preservation of Consumers' Claims and Defenses," protects consumers when
merchants sell a consumer's credit contracts to other lenders. Specifically, it
preserves consumers' right to assert the same legal claims and defenses against
anyone who purchases the credit contract, as they would have against the seller
who originally provided the credit. [16 Code of Federal Regulations Part 433]

Exam Probability: **High**

39. *Answer choices:*

(see index for correct answer)

- a. Clearfield Trust Co. v. United States
- b. Regulation CC
- c. Holder in due course
- d. Real defense

Guidance: level 1

:: Contract law ::

_____ , also called an anticipatory breach, is a term in the law of
contracts that describes a declaration by the promising party to a contract
that he or she does not intend to live up to his or her obligations under the
contract.

Exam Probability: **Low**

40. *Answer choices:*

(see index for correct answer)

- a. Anticipatory repudiation
- b. Lease purchase contract
- c. Mistake
- d. Offeree

Guidance: level 1

:: Insurance terms ::

A _____ in the broadest sense is a natural person or other legal entity who receives money or other benefits from a benefactor. For example, the _____ of a life insurance policy is the person who receives the payment of the amount of insurance after the death of the insured.

Exam Probability: **Low**

41. *Answer choices:*

(see index for correct answer)

- a. Pro rata
- b. Beneficiary
- c. Contingent coverage
- d. Co-insurance

:: ::

A _____ can mean the holder of a license, or in U.S. tort law, a _____ is a person who is on the property of another, despite the fact that the property is not open to the general public, because the owner of the property has allowed the _____ to enter. The status of a visitor as a _____ defines the legal rights of the visitor if they are injured due to the negligence of the property possessor .

Exam Probability: **Low**

42. *Answer choices:*

(see index for correct answer)

- a. Sarbanes-Oxley act of 2002
- b. empathy
- c. similarity-attraction theory
- d. hierarchical perspective

:: Legal doctrines and principles ::

In law, a _____ is an event sufficiently related to an injury that the courts deem the event to be the cause of that injury. There are two types of causation in the law: cause-in-fact, and proximate cause. Cause-in-fact is determined by the "but for" test: But for the action, the result would not have happened. The action is a necessary condition, but may not be a sufficient condition, for the resulting injury. A few circumstances exist where the but for test is ineffective . Since but-for causation is very easy to show , a second test is used to determine if an action is close enough to a harm in a "chain of events" to be legally valid. This test is called _____ .
_____ is a key principle of Insurance and is concerned with how the loss or damage actually occurred. There are several competing theories of _____ . For an act to be deemed to cause a harm, both tests must be met; _____ is a legal limitation on cause-in-fact.

Exam Probability: **Low**

43. *Answer choices:*

(see index for correct answer)

- a. Parol evidence
- b. Duty to rescue
- c. Acquiescence
- d. Proximate cause

Guidance: level 1

:: Product liability ::

_____ is the area of law in which manufacturers, distributors, suppliers, retailers, and others who make products available to the public are held responsible for the injuries those products cause. Although the word "product" has broad connotations, _____ as an area of law is traditionally limited to products in the form of tangible personal property.

Exam Probability: **High**

44. *Answer choices:*

(see index for correct answer)

- a. Chinese drywall
- b. Consumer Protection Act 1987
- c. Domestic Fuels Protection Act
- d. Product Liability Directive

Guidance: level 1

:: Competition law ::

In competition law, a _____ is a market in which a particular product or service is sold. It is the intersection of a relevant product market and a relevant geographic market. The European Commission defines a _____ and its product and geographic components as follows.

Exam Probability: **Low**

45. *Answer choices:*

(see index for correct answer)

- a. European Union competition law
- b. Relevant market
- c. Canadian Football Act
- d. Antitrust law

Guidance: level 1

:: Utilitarianism ::

_____ is a family of consequentialist ethical theories that promotes actions that maximize happiness and well-being for the majority of a population. Although different varieties of _____ admit different characterizations, the basic idea behind all of them is to in some sense maximize utility, which is often defined in terms of well-being or related concepts. For instance, Jeremy Bentham, the founder of _____ , described utility as

Exam Probability: **Medium**

46. *Answer choices:*

(see index for correct answer)

- a. Rule utilitarianism
- b. Paradox of hedonism
- c. Utilitarianism

- d. Global Happiness Organization

Guidance: level 1

:: Criminal procedure ::

_____ is the adjudication process of the criminal law. While _____ differs dramatically by jurisdiction, the process generally begins with a formal criminal charge with the person on trial either being free on bail or incarcerated, and results in the conviction or acquittal of the defendant. _____ can be either in form of inquisitorial or adversarial _____ .

Exam Probability: **High**

47. *Answer choices:*

(see index for correct answer)

- a. directed verdict
- b. Criminal procedure

Guidance: level 1

:: Monopoly (economics) ::

_____ is a category of property that includes intangible creations of the human intellect. _____ encompasses two types of rights: industrial property rights and copyright. It was not until the 19th century that the term " _____ " began to be used, and not until the late 20th century that it became commonplace in the majority of the world.

Exam Probability: **High**

48. *Answer choices:*

(see index for correct answer)

- a. Monopoly
- b. Intellectual property
- c. Practice of law
- d. Coercive monopoly

Guidance: level 1

:: ::

A _____ is monetary compensation paid by an employer to an employee in exchange for work done. Payment may be calculated as a fixed amount for each task completed , or at an hourly or daily rate , or based on an easily measured quantity of work done.

Exam Probability: **Low**

49. *Answer choices:*

(see index for correct answer)

- a. cultural
- b. similarity-attraction theory
- c. open system
- d. Wage

Guidance: level 1

:: Business law ::

A _____ is a legal right granted by a debtor to a creditor over the debtor's property which enables the creditor to have recourse to the property if the debtor defaults in making payment or otherwise performing the secured obligations. One of the most common examples of a _____ is a mortgage: When person, by the action of an expressed conveyance, pledges by a promise to pay a certain sum of money, with certain conditions, on a said date or dates for a said period, that action on the page with wet ink applied on the part of the one wishing the exchange creates the original funds and negotiable Instrument. That action of pledging conveys a promise binding upon the mortgagee which creates a face value upon the Instrument of the amount of currency being asked for in exchange. It is therein in good faith offered to the Bank in exchange for local currency from the Bank to buy a house. The particular country's Bank Acts usually requires the Banks to deliver such fund bearing negotiable instruments to the Countries Main Bank such as is the case in Canada. This creates a _____ in the land the house sits on for the Bank and they file a caveat at land titles on the house as evidence of that _____ . If the mortgagee fails to pay defaulting in his promise to repay the exchange, the bank then applies to the court to for-close on your property to eventually sell the house and apply the proceeds to the outstanding exchange.

50. *Answer choices:*

(see index for correct answer)

- a. Unfair Commercial Practices Directive
- b. Tacit relocation
- c. Independent contractor
- d. Security interest

Guidance: level 1

:: Debt ::

_____ , in finance and economics, is payment from a borrower or deposit-taking financial institution to a lender or depositor of an amount above repayment of the principal sum , at a particular rate. It is distinct from a fee which the borrower may pay the lender or some third party. It is also distinct from dividend which is paid by a company to its shareholders from its profit or reserve, but not at a particular rate decided beforehand, rather on a pro rata basis as a share in the reward gained by risk taking entrepreneurs when the revenue earned exceeds the total costs.

Exam Probability: **Medium**

51. *Answer choices:*

(see index for correct answer)

- a. Perpetual subordinated debt
- b. Household debt
- c. External debt
- d. Interest

Guidance: level 1

:: Information technology audit ::

_____ is the act of using a computer to take or alter electronic data, or to gain unlawful use of a computer or system. In the United States, _____ is specifically proscribed by the _____ and Abuse Act, which criminalizes computer-related acts under federal jurisdiction. Types of _____ include.

Exam Probability: **Low**

52. *Answer choices:*

(see index for correct answer)

- a. National Information Infrastructure Protection Act
- b. Mobile device forensics
- c. Statement on Auditing Standards No. 99: Consideration of Fraud
- d. Information security audit

Guidance: level 1

_____ is a marketing communication that employs an openly sponsored, non-personal message to promote or sell a product, service or idea. Sponsors of _____ are typically businesses wishing to promote their products or services. _____ is differentiated from public relations in that an advertiser pays for and has control over the message. It differs from personal selling in that the message is non-personal, i.e., not directed to a particular individual. _____ is communicated through various mass media, including traditional media such as newspapers, magazines, television, radio, outdoor _____ or direct mail; and new media such as search results, blogs, social media, websites or text messages. The actual presentation of the message in a medium is referred to as an advertisement, or "ad" or advert for short.

Exam Probability: **Low**

53. *Answer choices:*

(see index for correct answer)

- a. interpersonal communication
- b. process perspective
- c. similarity-attraction theory
- d. information systems assessment

Guidance: level 1

A _____ is the party who initiates a lawsuit before a court. By doing so, the _____ seeks a legal remedy; if this search is successful, the court will issue judgment in favor of the _____ and make the appropriate court order . " _____ " is the term used in civil cases in most English-speaking jurisdictions, the notable exception being England and Wales, where a _____ has, since the introduction of the Civil Procedure Rules in 1999, been known as a "claimant", but that term also has other meanings. In criminal cases, the prosecutor brings the case against the defendant, but the key complaining party is often called the "complainant".

Exam Probability: **Medium**

54. *Answer choices:*

(see index for correct answer)

- a. Plaintiff
- b. cultural
- c. Sarbanes-Oxley act of 2002
- d. functional perspective

Guidance: level 1

:: Fraud ::

_____ is the deliberate use of someone else's identity, usually as a method to gain a financial advantage or obtain credit and other benefits in the other person's name, and perhaps to the other person's disadvantage or loss. The person whose identity has been assumed may suffer adverse consequences, especially if they are held responsible for the perpetrator's actions.

_____ occurs when someone uses another's personally identifying information, like their name, identifying number, or credit card number, without their permission, to commit fraud or other crimes. The term _____ was coined in 1964. Since that time, the definition of _____ has been statutorily prescribed throughout both the U.K. and the United States as the theft of personally identifying information, generally including a person's name, date of birth, social security number, driver's license number, bank account or credit card numbers, PIN numbers, electronic signatures, fingerprints, passwords, or any other information that can be used to access a person's financial resources.

Exam Probability: **High**

55. *Answer choices:*

(see index for correct answer)

- a. Adoption fraud
- b. Pious fraud
- c. Workers Resistance
- d. Identity theft

Guidance: level 1

:: Insolvency ::

_____ is the state of being unable to pay the money owed, by a person or company, on time; those in a state of _____ are said to be insolvent. There are two forms: cash-flow _____ and balance-sheet _____ .

Exam Probability: **High**

56. *Answer choices:*

(see index for correct answer)

- a. Insolvency
- b. Official Committee of Equity Security Holders
- c. Personal Insolvency Arrangement
- d. Insolvency law of Russia

Guidance: level 1

:: False advertising law ::

The Lanham Act is the primary federal trademark statute of law in the United States. The Act prohibits a number of activities, including trademark infringement, trademark dilution, and false advertising.

Exam Probability: **High**

57. *Answer choices:*

(see index for correct answer)

- a. POM Wonderful LLC v. Coca-Cola Co.
- b. Lanham Act

Guidance: level 1

:: Legal terms ::

_____ , a form of alternative dispute resolution , is a way to resolve disputes outside the courts. The dispute will be decided by one or more persons , which renders the " _____ award". An _____ award is legally binding on both sides and enforceable in the courts.

Exam Probability: **Low**

58. *Answer choices:*

(see index for correct answer)

- a. Appearance
- b. Position of trust
- c. Plain meaning rule
- d. Arbitration

Guidance: level 1

:: Business ethics ::

Banking secrecy, alternately known as _____ , banking discretion, or bank safety, is a conditional agreement between a bank and its clients that all foregoing activities remain secure, confidential, and private. While some banking institutions voluntarily impose banking secrecy institutionally, others operate in regions where the practice is legally mandated and protected . Almost all banking secrecy standards prohibit the disclosure of client information to third parties without consent or an accepted criminal complaint. Additional privacy is provided to select clients via numbered bank accounts or underground bank vaults. Most often associated with banking in Switzerland, banking secrecy is prevalent in Luxembourg, Monaco, Hong Kong, Singapore, Ireland, Lebanon and the Cayman Islands, among other off-shore banking institutions.

Exam Probability: **Medium**

59. *Answer choices:*

(see index for correct answer)

- a. The FCPA Blog
- b. Corporate social entrepreneurship
- c. FRISK Software International
- d. Integrity management

Guidance: level 1

Finance

Finance is a field that is concerned with the allocation (investment) of assets and liabilities over space and time, often under conditions of risk or uncertainty. Finance can also be defined as the science of money management. Participants in the market aim to price assets based on their risk level, fundamental value, and their expected rate of return. Finance can be split into three sub-categories: public finance, corporate finance and personal finance.

:: Banking ::

A _____ is a financial institution that accepts deposits from the public and creates credit. Lending activities can be performed either directly or indirectly through capital markets. Due to their importance in the financial stability of a country, _____ s are highly regulated in most countries. Most nations have institutionalized a system known as fractional reserve _____ ing under which _____ s hold liquid assets equal to only a portion of their current liabilities. In addition to other regulations intended to ensure liquidity, _____ s are generally subject to minimum capital requirements based on an international set of capital standards, known as the Basel Accords.

Exam Probability: **Low**

1. *Answer choices:*

(see index for correct answer)

- a. Short term deposit
- b. Tier 2 capital
- c. Bank secrecy
- d. Branch manager

Guidance: level 1

:: Market research ::

_____ , an acronym for Information through Disguised Experimentation is an annual market research fair conducted by the students of IIM-Lucknow. Students create games and use various other simulated environments to capture consumers' subconscious thoughts. This innovative method of market research removes the sensitization effect that might bias peoples answers to questions. This ensures that the most truthful answers are captured to research questions. The games are designed in such a way that the observers can elicit all the required information just by observing and noting down the behaviour and the responses of the participants.

Exam Probability: **High**

2. *Answer choices:*

(see index for correct answer)

- a. AbsolutData
- b. Australian Market and Social Research Society Limited
- c. INDEX
- d. IModerate

Guidance: level 1

:: Portfolio theories ::

In finance, the _____ is a model used to determine a theoretically appropriate required rate of return of an asset, to make decisions about adding assets to a well-diversified portfolio.

3. *Answer choices:*

(see index for correct answer)

- a. Capital asset pricing model
- b. Intertemporal portfolio choice
- c. Behavioral portfolio theory
- d. Tail risk parity

Guidance: level 1

:: Investment ::

_____ , and investment appraisal, is the planning process used to determine whether an organization's long term investments such as new machinery, replacement of machinery, new plants, new products, and research development projects are worth the funding of cash through the firm's capitalization structure . It is the process of allocating resources for major capital, or investment, expenditures. One of the primary goals of _____ investments is to increase the value of the firm to the shareholders.

Exam Probability: **Medium**

4. *Answer choices:*

(see index for correct answer)

- a. Insurance bond

- b. Advisors Sentiment
- c. Do-it-yourself investing
- d. Investing online

Guidance: level 1

:: ::

In finance, return is a profit on an investment. It comprises any change in value of the investment, and/or cash flows which the investor receives from the investment, such as interest payments or dividends. It may be measured either in absolute terms or as a percentage of the amount invested. The latter is also called the holding period return.

Exam Probability: **High**

5. *Answer choices:*

(see index for correct answer)

- a. hierarchical
- b. surface-level diversity
- c. similarity-attraction theory
- d. open system

Guidance: level 1

:: Derivatives (finance) ::

In finance, a _____ or simply a forward is a non-standardized contract between two parties to buy or to sell an asset at a specified future time at a price agreed upon today, making it a type of derivative instrument. The party agreeing to buy the underlying asset in the future assumes a long position, and the party agreeing to sell the asset in the future assumes a short position. The price agreed upon is called the delivery price, which is equal to the forward price at the time the contract is entered into.

Exam Probability: **Medium**

6. *Answer choices:*

(see index for correct answer)

- a. Options arbitrage
- b. Contango
- c. Triple witching hour
- d. Forward contract

Guidance: level 1

:: Financial markets ::

_____ s are monetary contracts between parties. They can be created, traded, modified and settled. They can be cash , evidence of an ownership interest in an entity , or a contractual right to receive or deliver cash .

7. *Answer choices:*

(see index for correct answer)

- a. Financial instrument
- b. Odd lot
- c. Thomson Reuters league tables
- d. Private equity fund

Guidance: level 1

:: Accounting source documents ::

A _____ or account statement is a summary of financial transactions which have occurred over a given period on a bank account held by a person or business with a financial institution.

Exam Probability: **High**

8. *Answer choices:*

(see index for correct answer)

- a. Bank statement
- b. Parcel audit
- c. Remittance advice
- d. Credit memorandum

:: United States Generally Accepted Accounting Principles ::

In a companies' financial reporting, _____ "includes all changes in equity during a period except those resulting from investments by owners and distributions to owners". Because that use excludes the effects of changing ownership interest, an economic measure of _____ is necessary for financial analysis from the shareholders' point of view

Exam Probability: **Low**

9. *Answer choices:*

(see index for correct answer)

- a. Impaired asset
- b. FIN 46
- c. Comprehensive income
- d. Single Audit

:: ::

_____ Corporation was an American energy, commodities, and services company based in Houston, Texas. It was founded in 1985 as a merger between Houston Natural Gas and InterNorth, both relatively small regional companies. Before its bankruptcy on December 3, 2001, _____ employed approximately 29,000 staff and was a major electricity, natural gas, communications and pulp and paper company, with claimed revenues of nearly $101 billion during 2000. Fortune named _____ "America's Most Innovative Company" for six consecutive years.

Exam Probability: **Low**

10. *Answer choices:*

(see index for correct answer)

- a. Enron
- b. Character
- c. Sarbanes-Oxley act of 2002
- d. similarity-attraction theory

Guidance: level 1

:: ::

_____ , often abbreviated as B/E in finance, is the point of balance making neither a profit nor a loss. The term originates in finance but the concept has been applied in other fields.

Exam Probability: **High**

11. *Answer choices:*

(see index for correct answer)

- a. empathy
- b. Break-even
- c. hierarchical
- d. Character

Guidance: level 1

:: Mathematical finance ::

In economics and finance, _____ , also known as present discounted value, is the value of an expected income stream determined as of the date of valuation. The _____ is always less than or equal to the future value because money has interest-earning potential, a characteristic referred to as the time value of money, except during times of negative interest rates, when the _____ will be more than the future value. Time value can be described with the simplified phrase, "A dollar today is worth more than a dollar tomorrow". Here, `worth more` means that its value is greater. A dollar today is worth more than a dollar tomorrow because the dollar can be invested and earn a day's worth of interest, making the total accumulate to a value more than a dollar by tomorrow. Interest can be compared to rent. Just as rent is paid to a landlord by a tenant without the ownership of the asset being transferred, interest is paid to a lender by a borrower who gains access to the money for a time before paying it back. By letting the borrower have access to the money, the lender has sacrificed the exchange value of this money, and is compensated for it in the form of interest. The initial amount of the borrowed funds is less than the total amount of money paid to the lender.

Exam Probability: **Medium**

12. *Answer choices:*

(see index for correct answer)

- a. AZFinText
- b. Stochastic calculus
- c. Present value
- d. Stochastic discount factor

Guidance: level 1

:: Business law ::

A _____ , also known as the sole trader, individual entrepreneurship or proprietorship, is a type of enterprise that is owned and run by one person and in which there is no legal distinction between the owner and the business entity. A sole trader does not necessarily work `alone`—it is possible for the sole trader to employ other people.

Exam Probability: **Low**

13. *Answer choices:*

(see index for correct answer)

- a. Sole proprietorship
- b. Legal tender
- c. Tax patent
- d. Holder

:: Generally Accepted Accounting Principles ::

In accounting, an economic item's _____ is the original nominal monetary value of that item. _____ accounting involves reporting assets and liabilities at their _____ s, which are not updated for changes in the items' values. Consequently, the amounts reported for these balance sheet items often differ from their current economic or market values.

Exam Probability: **Low**

14. *Answer choices:*

(see index for correct answer)

- a. Earnings before interest, taxes, depreciation, and amortization
- b. Historical cost
- c. Indian Accounting Standards
- d. Trial balance

:: Fixed income market ::

In finance, the _____ is a curve showing several yields or interest rates across different contract lengths for a similar debt contract. The curve shows the relation between the interest rate and the time to maturity, known as the "term", of the debt for a given borrower in a given currency. For example, the U.S. dollar interest rates paid on U.S. Treasury securities for various maturities are closely watched by many traders, and are commonly plotted on a graph such as the one on the right which is informally called "the _____ ". More formal mathematical descriptions of this relation are often called the term structure of interest rates.

Exam Probability: **Low**

15. *Answer choices:*

(see index for correct answer)

- a. Inter-dealer broker
- b. Basis point
- c. Yield curve
- d. Pool factor

Guidance: level 1

:: Inventory ::

_____ is the amount of inventory a company has in stock at the end of its fiscal year. It is closely related with _____ cost, which is the amount of money spent to get these goods in stock. It should be calculated at the lower of cost or market.

16. *Answer choices:*

(see index for correct answer)

- a. Consignment stock
- b. Reorder point
- c. Ending inventory
- d. Inventory optimization

Guidance: level 1

:: Generally Accepted Accounting Principles ::

A _____ , in accrual accounting, is any account where the asset or liability is not realized until a future date , e.g. annuities, charges, taxes, income, etc. The deferred item may be carried, dependent on type of _____ , as either an asset or liability. See also accrual.

Exam Probability: **High**

17. *Answer choices:*

(see index for correct answer)

- a. Net profit
- b. Goodwill
- c. Gross sales

- d. Deferral

Guidance: level 1

:: ::

_____ s and acquisitions are transactions in which the ownership of companies, other business organizations, or their operating units are transferred or consolidated with other entities. As an aspect of strategic management, M&A can allow enterprises to grow or downsize, and change the nature of their business or competitive position.

Exam Probability: **High**

18. *Answer choices:*

(see index for correct answer)

- a. hierarchical
- b. cultural
- c. Character
- d. personal values

Guidance: level 1

:: Corporate finance ::

_____ in corporate finance is the way a corporation finances its assets through some combination of equity, debt, or hybrid securities.

Exam Probability: **High**

19. *Answer choices:*

(see index for correct answer)

- a. Trapped equity theory
- b. Targeted repurchase
- c. Capital structure
- d. Avellum Partners

Guidance: level 1

:: Government bonds ::

A _____ or sovereign bond is a bond issued by a national government, generally with a promise to pay periodic interest payments called coupon payments and to repay the face value on the maturity date. The aim of a _____ is to support government spending. _____ s are usually denominated in the country's own currency, in which case the government cannot be forced to default, although it may choose to do so. If a government is close to default on its debt the media often refer to this as a sovereign debt crisis.

Exam Probability: **Low**

20. *Answer choices:*

(see index for correct answer)

- a. Brady Bonds
- b. Government bond
- c. South Carolina v. Baker
- d. War bond

Guidance: level 1

:: Inventory ::

In business and accounting/accountancy, _____ or continuous inventory describes systems of inventory where information on inventory quantity and availability is updated on a continuous basis as a function of doing business. Generally this is accomplished by connecting the inventory system with order entry and in retail the point of sale system. In this case, book inventory would be exactly the same as, or almost the same, as the real inventory.

Exam Probability: **Low**

21. *Answer choices:*

(see index for correct answer)

- a. Perpetual inventory
- b. Reorder point
- c. Stock-taking
- d. Order picking

:: ::

Business is the activity of making one's living or making money by producing or buying and selling products . Simply put, it is "any activity or enterprise entered into for profit. It does not mean it is a company, a corporation, partnership, or have any such formal organization, but it can range from a street peddler to General Motors."

Exam Probability: **Medium**

22. *Answer choices:*

(see index for correct answer)

- a. cultural
- b. similarity-attraction theory
- c. empathy
- d. imperative

:: ::

_____ is a costing method that identifies activities in an organization and assigns the cost of each activity to all products and services according to the actual consumption by each. This model assigns more indirect costs into direct costs compared to conventional costing.

Exam Probability: **Low**

23. *Answer choices:*

(see index for correct answer)

- a. open system
- b. levels of analysis
- c. hierarchical
- d. Activity-based costing

Guidance: level 1

:: Financial markets ::

A _____ is a market in which people trade financial securities and derivatives such as futures and options at low transaction costs. Securities include stocks and bonds, and precious metals.

Exam Probability: **Medium**

24. *Answer choices:*

(see index for correct answer)

- a. Limits to arbitrage
- b. Noise trader
- c. Reset
- d. Systematic trading

Guidance: level 1

:: Generally Accepted Accounting Principles ::

In accrual accounting, the revenue recognition principle states that expenses should be recorded during the period in which they are incurred, regardless of when the transfer of cash occurs. Conversely, cash basis accounting calls for the recognition of an expense when the cash is paid, regardless of when the expense was actually incurred.

Exam Probability: **Medium**

25. *Answer choices:*

(see index for correct answer)

- a. Treasury stock
- b. Vendor-specific objective evidence
- c. Matching principle
- d. Normal balance

Guidance: level 1

:: Business economics ::

_____ is one of the constituents of a leasing calculus or operation. It describes the future value of a good in terms of absolute value in monetary terms and it is sometimes abbreviated into a percentage of the initial price when the item was new.

Exam Probability: **Medium**

26. *Answer choices:*

(see index for correct answer)

- a. Residual value
- b. Units of transportation measurement
- c. Disclosed fees
- d. Average daily rate

Guidance: level 1

:: Insolvency ::

_____ is the process in accounting by which a company is brought to an end in the United Kingdom, Republic of Ireland and United States. The assets and property of the company are redistributed. _____ is also sometimes referred to as winding-up or dissolution, although dissolution technically refers to the last stage of _____ . The process of _____ also arises when customs, an authority or agency in a country responsible for collecting and safeguarding customs duties, determines the final computation or ascertainment of the duties or drawback accruing on an entry.

Exam Probability: **High**

27. *Answer choices:*

(see index for correct answer)

- a. George Samuel Ford
- b. Liquidation
- c. Liquidator
- d. Insolvency law of Russia

Guidance: level 1

:: Hazard analysis ::

Broadly speaking, a _____ is the combined effort of 1. identifying and analyzing potential events that may negatively impact individuals, assets, and/or the environment ; and 2. making judgments "on the tolerability of the risk on the basis of a risk analysis" while considering influencing factors .
Put in simpler terms, a _____ analyzes what can go wrong, how likely it is to happen, what the potential consequences are, and how tolerable the identified risk is. As part of this process, the resulting determination of risk may be expressed in a quantitative or qualitative fashion. The _____ is an inherent part of an overall risk management strategy, which attempts to, after a _____ , "introduce control measures to eliminate or reduce" any potential risk-related consequences.

Exam Probability: **Low**

28. *Answer choices:*

(see index for correct answer)

- a. Hazard identification
- b. Risk assessment
- c. Hazardous Materials Identification System

Guidance: level 1

:: Data analysis ::

In statistics, the _____ is a measure that is used to quantify the amount of variation or dispersion of a set of data values. A low _____ indicates that the data points tend to be close to the mean of the set, while a high _____ indicates that the data points are spread out over a wider range of values.

Exam Probability: **Low**

29. *Answer choices:*

(see index for correct answer)

- a. Health care analytics
- b. Ariel Beresniak
- c. Exponential smoothing
- d. Standard deviation

Guidance: level 1

:: Financial accounting ::

_____ is the value of all the non-financial and financial assets owned by an institutional unit or sector minus the value of all its outstanding liabilities. Since financial assets minus outstanding liabilities equal net financial assets, _____ can also be conveniently expressed as non-financial assets plus net financial assets. _____ can apply to companies, individuals, governments or economic sectors such as the sector of financial corporations or to entire countries.

30. *Answer choices:*

(see index for correct answer)

- a. Net worth
- b. Holding gains
- c. Book value
- d. Money measurement

Guidance: level 1

:: Financial crises ::

A _____ is any of a broad variety of situations in which some financial assets suddenly lose a large part of their nominal value. In the 19th and early 20th centuries, many financial crises were associated with banking panics, and many recessions coincided with these panics. Other situations that are often called financial crises include stock market crashes and the bursting of other financial bubbles, currency crises, and sovereign defaults. Financial crises directly result in a loss of paper wealth but do not necessarily result in significant changes in the real economy .

Exam Probability: **High**

31. *Answer choices:*

(see index for correct answer)

- a. Neal, James, Fordyce and Down
- b. Financial crisis
- c. Chinese Banking Liquidity Crisis of 2013
- d. Kennedy Slide of 1962

Guidance: level 1

:: Stock market ::

_____ or stock market launch is a type of public offering in which shares of a company are sold to institutional investors and usually also retail investors; an IPO is underwritten by one or more investment banks, who also arrange for the shares to be listed on one or more stock exchanges. Through this process, colloquially known as floating, or going public, a privately held company is transformed into a public company. _____ s can be used: to raise new equity capital for the company concerned; to monetize the investments of private shareholders such as company founders or private equity investors; and to enable easy trading of existing holdings or future capital raising by becoming publicly traded enterprises.

Exam Probability: **Low**

32. *Answer choices:*

(see index for correct answer)

- a. Wash sale
- b. Fill or kill
- c. Hybrid market
- d. Instinet

:: Management accounting ::

In _____ or managerial accounting, managers use the provisions of accounting information in order to better inform themselves before they decide matters within their organizations, which aids their management and performance of control functions.

Exam Probability: **High**

33. *Answer choices:*

(see index for correct answer)

- a. Extended cost
- b. Management accounting
- c. Management control system
- d. Fixed assets management

:: ::

_____ is the quantity of three-dimensional space enclosed by a closed surface, for example, the space that a substance or shape occupies or contains. _____ is often quantified numerically using the SI derived unit, the cubic metre. The _____ of a container is generally understood to be the capacity of the container; i. e., the amount of fluid that the container could hold, rather than the amount of space the container itself displaces. Three dimensional mathematical shapes are also assigned _____ s. _____ s of some simple shapes, such as regular, straight-edged, and circular shapes can be easily calculated using arithmetic formulas. _____ s of complicated shapes can be calculated with integral calculus if a formula exists for the shape's boundary. One-dimensional figures and two-dimensional shapes are assigned zero _____ in the three-dimensional space.

Exam Probability: **High**

34. *Answer choices:*

(see index for correct answer)

- a. co-culture
- b. Volume
- c. hierarchical
- d. empathy

Guidance: level 1

:: Stock market ::

The _____ of a corporation is all of the shares into which ownership of the corporation is divided. In American English, the shares are commonly known as " _____ s". A single share of the _____ represents fractional ownership of the corporation in proportion to the total number of shares. This typically entitles the _____ holder to that fraction of the company's earnings, proceeds from liquidation of assets , or voting power, often dividing these up in proportion to the amount of money each _____ holder has invested. Not all _____ is necessarily equal, as certain classes of _____ may be issued for example without voting rights, with enhanced voting rights, or with a certain priority to receive profits or liquidation proceeds before or after other classes of shareholders.

Exam Probability: **Medium**

35. *Answer choices:*

(see index for correct answer)

- a. Nifty Fifty
- b. Direct finance
- c. Stock
- d. Stub

Guidance: level 1

:: Accounting terminology ::

_____ is a legally enforceable claim for payment held by a business for goods supplied and/or services rendered that customers/clients have ordered but not paid for. These are generally in the form of invoices raised by a business and delivered to the customer for payment within an agreed time frame.

_____ is shown in a balance sheet as an asset. It is one of a series of accounting transactions dealing with the billing of a customer for goods and services that the customer has ordered. These may be distinguished from notes receivable, which are debts created through formal legal instruments called promissory notes.

Exam Probability: **High**

36. *Answer choices:*

(see index for correct answer)

- a. General ledger
- b. Chart of accounts
- c. Capital appreciation
- d. Enterprise liquidity

Guidance: level 1

:: Money ::

Cash and _____ s are the most liquid current assets found on a business's balance sheet. _____ s are short-term commitments "with temporarily idle cash and easily convertible into a known cash amount". An investment normally counts to be a _____ when it has a short maturity period of 90 days or less, and can be included in the cash and _____ s balance from the date of acquisition when it carries an insignificant risk of changes in the asset value; with more than 90 days maturity, the asset is not considered as cash and _____ s. Equity investments mostly are excluded from _____ s, unless they are essentially _____ s, for instance, if the preferred shares acquired within a short maturity period and with specified recovery date.

Exam Probability: **High**

37. *Answer choices:*

(see index for correct answer)

- a. Dam
- b. Lump sum
- c. Metallism
- d. Constant dollars

Guidance: level 1

:: ::

An _____ is a contingent motivator. Traditional _____ s are extrinsic motivators which reward actions to yield a desired outcome. The effectiveness of traditional _____ s has changed as the needs of Western society have evolved. While the traditional _____ model is effective when there is a defined procedure and goal for a task, Western society started to require a higher volume of critical thinkers, so the traditional model became less effective. Institutions are now following a trend in implementing strategies that rely on intrinsic motivations rather than the extrinsic motivations that the traditional _____ s foster.

Exam Probability: **Medium**

38. *Answer choices:*

(see index for correct answer)

- a. Character
- b. information systems assessment
- c. empathy
- d. process perspective

Guidance: level 1

:: Auditing ::

_____ , as defined by accounting and auditing, is a process for assuring of an organization's objectives in operational effectiveness and efficiency, reliable financial reporting, and compliance with laws, regulations and policies. A broad concept, _____ involves everything that controls risks to an organization.

39. *Answer choices:*

(see index for correct answer)

- a. Sales tax audit
- b. International Association of Airline Internal Auditors
- c. Quality audit
- d. Internal control

Guidance: level 1

:: Generally Accepted Accounting Principles ::

A _____ or reacquired stock is stock which is bought back by the issuing company, reducing the amount of outstanding stock on the open market .

40. *Answer choices:*

(see index for correct answer)

- a. Access to finance
- b. Closing entries
- c. Generally Accepted Accounting Practice
- d. Treasury stock

:: Occupations ::

An _____ is a practitioner of accounting or accountancy, which is the measurement, disclosure or provision of assurance about financial information that helps managers, investors, tax authorities and others make decisions about allocating resource.

Exam Probability: **Low**

41. *Answer choices:*

(see index for correct answer)

- a. Accountant
- b. Expeditor
- c. Mixing engineer
- d. Manciple

:: Debt ::

_____ is the trust which allows one party to provide money or resources to another party wherein the second party does not reimburse the first party immediately , but promises either to repay or return those resources at a later date. In other words, _____ is a method of making reciprocity formal, legally enforceable, and extensible to a large group of unrelated people.

Exam Probability: **High**

42. *Answer choices:*

(see index for correct answer)

- a. Credit
- b. Debit commission
- c. Creditor
- d. Perpetual subordinated debt

Guidance: level 1

:: ::

_____ focuses on ratios, equities and debts. It is useful for portfolio management, distribution of dividend, capital raising, hedging and looking after fluctuations in foreign currency and product cycles. Financial managers are the people who will do research and based on the research, decide what sort of capital to obtain in order to fund the company's assets as well as maximizing the value of the firm for all the stakeholders. It also refers to the efficient and effective management of money in such a manner as to accomplish the objectives of the organization. It is the specialized function directly associated with the top management. The significance of this function is not seen in the `Line` but also in the capacity of the `Staff` in overall of a company. It has been defined differently by different experts in the field.

Exam Probability: **Medium**

43. *Answer choices:*

(see index for correct answer)

- a. Financial management
- b. similarity-attraction theory
- c. corporate values
- d. surface-level diversity

Guidance: level 1

:: Retirement ::

An _____ is a series of payments made at equal intervals. Examples of annuities are regular deposits to a savings account, monthly home mortgage payments, monthly insurance payments and pension payments. Annuities can be classified by the frequency of payment dates. The payments may be made weekly, monthly, quarterly, yearly, or at any other regular interval of time.

Exam Probability: **High**

44. *Answer choices:*

(see index for correct answer)

- a. Social protection
- b. Mandatory retirement
- c. Elder Village
- d. Annuity

Guidance: level 1

:: ::

A _____ , or holiday, is a leave of absence from a regular occupation, or a specific trip or journey, usually for the purpose of recreation or tourism. People often take a _____ during specific holiday observances, or for specific festivals or celebrations. _____ s are often spent with friends or family.

Exam Probability: **Medium**

45. *Answer choices:*

(see index for correct answer)

- a. empathy
- b. imperative
- c. cultural
- d. open system

Guidance: level 1

:: Business ::

The seller, or the provider of the goods or services, completes a sale in response to an acquisition, appropriation, requisition or a direct interaction with the buyer at the point of sale. There is a passing of title of the item, and the settlement of a price, in which agreement is reached on a price for which transfer of ownership of the item will occur. The seller, not the purchaser typically executes the sale and it may be completed prior to the obligation of payment. In the case of indirect interaction, a person who sells goods or service on behalf of the owner is known as a _____ man or _____ woman or _____ person, but this often refers to someone selling goods in a store/shop, in which case other terms are also common, including _____ clerk, shop assistant, and retail clerk.

Exam Probability: **High**

46. *Answer choices:*

(see index for correct answer)

- a. SONGZIO
- b. Attribution
- c. Student@Home
- d. Sales

Guidance: level 1

:: Financial ratios ::

In finance, the _____ , also known as the acid-test ratio is a type of liquidity ratio which measures the ability of a company to use its near cash or quick assets to extinguish or retire its current liabilities immediately. Quick assets include those current assets that presumably can be quickly converted to cash at close to their book values. It is the ratio between quickly available or liquid assets and current liabilities.

Exam Probability: **Medium**

47. *Answer choices:*

(see index for correct answer)

- a. Quick ratio
- b. Net profit margin
- c. Omega ratio
- d. EV/GCI

Guidance: level 1

_____ is the study and management of exchange relationships. _____ is the business process of creating relationships with and satisfying customers. With its focus on the customer, _____ is one of the premier components of business management.

Exam Probability: **Medium**

48. *Answer choices:*

(see index for correct answer)

- a. functional perspective
- b. process perspective
- c. hierarchical
- d. Marketing

Guidance: level 1

:: Marketing ::

_____ is a financial mechanism in which a debtor obtains the right to delay payments to a creditor, for a defined period of time, in exchange for a charge or fee. Essentially, the party that owes money in the present purchases the right to delay the payment until some future date. The discount, or charge, is the difference between the original amount owed in the present and the amount that has to be paid in the future to settle the debt.

49. *Answer choices:*

(see index for correct answer)

- a. Digital strategy
- b. Osborne effect
- c. Online marketing platform
- d. Discounting

Guidance: level 1

:: Generally Accepted Accounting Principles ::

In accounting and finance, earnings before interest and taxes is a measure of a firm's profit that includes all incomes and expenses except interest expenses and income tax expenses.

Exam Probability: **High**

50. *Answer choices:*

(see index for correct answer)

- a. Liability
- b. Insurance asset management
- c. Earnings before interest, taxes, depreciation, and amortization
- d. Matching principle

:: Generally Accepted Accounting Principles ::

_____ , or non-current liabilities, are liabilities that are due beyond a year or the normal operation period of the company. The normal operation period is the amount of time it takes for a company to turn inventory into cash. On a classified balance sheet, liabilities are separated between current and _____ to help users assess the company's financial standing in short-term and long-term periods. _____ give users more information about the long-term prosperity of the company, while current liabilities inform the user of debt that the company owes in the current period. On a balance sheet, accounts are listed in order of liquidity, so _____ come after current liabilities. In addition, the specific long-term liability accounts are listed on the balance sheet in order of liquidity. Therefore, an account due within eighteen months would be listed before an account due within twenty-four months. Examples of _____ are bonds payable, long-term loans, capital leases, pension liabilities, post-retirement healthcare liabilities, deferred compensation, deferred revenues, deferred income taxes, and derivative liabilities.

Exam Probability: **Low**

51. *Answer choices:*

(see index for correct answer)

- a. Operating income
- b. Cash method of accounting
- c. net realisable value
- d. Long-term liabilities

:: Basel II ::

All businesses take risks based on two factors: the probability an adverse circumstance will come about and the cost of such adverse circumstance.Risk management is the study of how to control risks and balance the possibility of gains.

Exam Probability: **Medium**

52. *Answer choices:*

(see index for correct answer)

- a. Market risk
- b. Jaime Caruana
- c. Legal risk
- d. Basic indicator approach

:: Social security ::

_____ is "any government system that provides monetary assistance to people with an inadequate or no income." In the United States, this is usually called welfare or a social safety net, especially when talking about Canada and European countries.

Exam Probability: **Low**

53. *Answer choices:*

(see index for correct answer)

- a. Employees%27 State Insurance
- b. Social Security System
- c. SNILS
- d. Social security

Guidance: level 1

:: Management accounting ::

_____ s are costs that change as the quantity of the good or service that a business produces changes. _____ s are the sum of marginal costs over all units produced. They can also be considered normal costs. Fixed costs and _____ s make up the two components of total cost. Direct costs are costs that can easily be associated with a particular cost object. However, not all _____ s are direct costs. For example, variable manufacturing overhead costs are _____ s that are indirect costs, not direct costs. _____ s are sometimes called unit-level costs as they vary with the number of units produced.

54. *Answer choices:*

(see index for correct answer)

- a. Accounting management
- b. Variable cost
- c. Standard cost
- d. Certified Management Accountant

Guidance: level 1

:: ::

A _____ is the period used by governments for accounting and budget purposes, which varies between countries. It is also used for financial reporting by business and other organizations. Laws in many jurisdictions require company financial reports to be prepared and published on an annual basis, but generally do not require the reporting period to align with the calendar year . Taxation laws generally require accounting records to be maintained and taxes calculated on an annual basis, which usually corresponds to the _____ used for government purposes. The calculation of tax on an annual basis is especially relevant for direct taxation, such as income tax. Many annual government fees—such as Council rates, licence fees, etc.—are also levied on a _____ basis, while others are charged on an anniversary basis.

55. *Answer choices:*

(see index for correct answer)

- a. empathy
- b. Fiscal year
- c. Character
- d. functional perspective

Guidance: level 1

:: Inventory ::

Costs are associated with particular goods using one of the several formulas, including specific identification, first-in first-out , or average cost. Costs include all costs of purchase, costs of conversion and other costs that are incurred in bringing the inventories to their present location and condition. Costs of goods made by the businesses include material, labor, and allocated overhead. The costs of those goods which are not yet sold are deferred as costs of inventory until the inventory is sold or written down in value.

Exam Probability: **High**

56. *Answer choices:*

(see index for correct answer)

- a. Spare part
- b. Phantom inventory
- c. Ending inventory

- d. Cost of goods sold

Guidance: level 1

:: Financial ratios ::

_____ or asset turns is a financial ratio that measures the efficiency of a company's use of its assets in generating sales revenue or sales income to the company.

Exam Probability: **Medium**

57. *Answer choices:*

(see index for correct answer)

- a. Total revenue share
- b. Asset turnover
- c. Statutory liquidity ratio
- d. interest margin

Guidance: level 1

:: Costs ::

In microeconomic theory, the _____ , or alternative cost, of making a particular choice is the value of the most valuable choice out of those that were not taken. In other words, opportunity that will require sacrifices.

Exam Probability: **Low**

58. *Answer choices:*

(see index for correct answer)

- a. Khozraschyot
- b. Direct materials cost
- c. Manufacturing cost
- d. Opportunity cost

Guidance: level 1

:: Bonds (finance) ::

In finance, a _____ or convertible note or convertible debt is a type of bond that the holder can convert into a specified number of shares of common stock in the issuing company or cash of equal value. It is a hybrid security with debt- and equity-like features. It originated in the mid-19th century, and was used by early speculators such as Jacob Little and Daniel Drew to counter market cornering.

Exam Probability: **Medium**

59. *Answer choices:*

(see index for correct answer)

- a. Accretion
- b. Senior debt
- c. I-spread
- d. Convertible bond

Guidance: level 1

Human resource management

Human resource (HR) management is the strategic approach to the effective management of organization workers so that they help the business gain a competitive advantage. It is designed to maximize employee performance in service of an employer's strategic objectives. HR is primarily concerned with the management of people within organizations, focusing on policies and on systems. HR departments are responsible for overseeing employee-benefits design, employee recruitment, training and development, performance appraisal, and rewarding (e.g., managing pay and benefit systems). HR also concerns itself with organizational change and industrial relations, that is, the balancing of organizational practices with requirements arising from collective bargaining and from governmental laws.

:: Employment ::

_____ is a relationship between two parties, usually based on a contract where work is paid for, where one party, which may be a corporation, for profit, not-for-profit organization, co-operative or other entity is the employer and the other is the employee. Employees work in return for payment, which may be in the form of an hourly wage, by piecework or an annual salary, depending on the type of work an employee does or which sector she or he is working in. Employees in some fields or sectors may receive gratuities, bonus payment or stock options. In some types of _____ , employees may receive benefits in addition to payment. Benefits can include health insurance, housing, disability insurance or use of a gym. _____ is typically governed by _____ laws, regulations or legal contracts.

Exam Probability: **High**

1. *Answer choices:*

(see index for correct answer)

- a. Job security
- b. Location independence
- c. Effective altruism
- d. Employment

Guidance: level 1

:: Industrial agreements ::

A _____ , in labor relations, is a group of employees with a clear and identifiable community of interests who are represented by a single labor union in collective bargaining and other dealings with management. Examples would be non-management professors, law enforcement professionals, blue-collar workers, clerical and administrative employees, etc. Geographic location as well as the number of facilities included in _____ s can be at issue during representation cases.

Exam Probability: **Medium**

2. *Answer choices:*
(see index for correct answer)

- a. Compromise agreement
- b. Federal Labor Relations Act
- c. Workplace Authority
- d. Bargaining unit

Guidance: level 1

:: ::

_____ is a form of development in which a person called a coach supports a learner or client in achieving a specific personal or professional goal by providing training and guidance. The learner is sometimes called a coachee. Occasionally, _____ may mean an informal relationship between two people, of whom one has more experience and expertise than the other and offers advice and guidance as the latter learns; but _____ differs from mentoring in focusing on specific tasks or objectives, as opposed to more general goals or overall development.

Exam Probability: **Medium**

3. *Answer choices:*

(see index for correct answer)

- a. hierarchical perspective
- b. deep-level diversity
- c. Coaching
- d. empathy

Guidance: level 1

:: ::

On December 31, 2016, Xerox separated its business process service operations into a new publicly traded company, Conduent. Xerox focuses on its document technology and document outsourcing business, and continues to trade on the NYSE. On January 31, 2018, Xerox announced that it would sell a controlling stake to Fujifilm, which has maintained a joint venture in the Asia-Pacific region known as Fuji Xerox.

Exam Probability: **Low**

4. *Answer choices:*

(see index for correct answer)

- a. imperative
- b. Xerox Corporation
- c. deep-level diversity
- d. co-culture

Guidance: level 1

:: Human resource management ::

_____ is a continual process used to align the needs and priorities of the organization with those of its workforce to ensure it can meet its legislative, regulatory, service and production requirements and organizational objectives. _____ enables evidence based workforce development strategies.

Exam Probability: **Medium**

5. *Answer choices:*

(see index for correct answer)

- a. At-will employment
- b. Workforce sciences

- c. Talent management system
- d. Workforce planning

Guidance: level 1

:: Labour relations ::

_____ is the practice of hiring more workers than are needed to perform a given job, or to adopt work procedures which appear pointless, complex and time-consuming merely to employ additional workers. The term "make-work" is sometimes used as a synonym for _____ .

Exam Probability: **High**

6. *Answer choices:*

(see index for correct answer)

- a. Comprehensive campaign
- b. Merit shop
- c. Featherbedding
- d. Union representative

Guidance: level 1

:: Sexual harassment in the United States ::

In law, a _____ , reasonable man, or the man on the Clapham omnibus is a hypothetical person of legal fiction crafted by the courts and communicated through case law and jury instructions.

Exam Probability: **Low**

7. *Answer choices:*

(see index for correct answer)

- a. Charol Shakeshaft
- b. Reasonable person
- c. Fitzgerald v. Barnstable School Committee
- d. Puerto Rican Day Parade attacks

Guidance: level 1

:: ::

An _____ is a person temporarily or permanently residing in a country other than their native country. In common usage, the term often refers to professionals, skilled workers, or artists taking positions outside their home country, either independently or sent abroad by their employers, who can be companies, universities, governments, or non-governmental organisations. Effectively migrant workers, they usually earn more than they would at home, and less than local employees. However, the term ` _____ ` is also used for retirees and others who have chosen to live outside their native country. Historically, it has also referred to exiles.

8. *Answer choices:*

(see index for correct answer)

- a. personal values
- b. Sarbanes-Oxley act of 2002
- c. Expatriate
- d. deep-level diversity

Guidance: level 1

:: Validity (statistics) ::

_____ is a type of evidence that can be gathered to defend the use of a test for predicting other outcomes. It is a parameter used in sociology, psychology, and other psychometric or behavioral sciences. _____ is demonstrated when a test correlates well with a measure that has previously been validated. The two measures may be for the same construct, but more often used for different, but presumably related, constructs.

Exam Probability: **Medium**

9. *Answer choices:*

(see index for correct answer)

- a. Concurrent validity
- b. Criterion validity

- c. Convergent validity
- d. Ecological validity

Guidance: level 1

:: Employment compensation ::

_____ s and benefits in kind include various types of non-wage compensation provided to employees in addition to their normal wages or salaries. Instances where an employee exchanges wages for some other form of benefit is generally referred to as a "salary packaging" or "salary exchange" arrangement. In most countries, most kinds of _____ s are taxable to at least some degree. Examples of these benefits include: housing furnished or not, with or without free utilities; group insurance ; disability income protection; retirement benefits; daycare; tuition reimbursement; sick leave; vacation ; social security; profit sharing; employer student loan contributions; conveyancing; domestic help ; and other specialized benefits.

Exam Probability: **High**

10. *Answer choices:*
(see index for correct answer)

- a. Holidays with Pay Convention, 1936
- b. Total Reward
- c. Wages for housework
- d. Stock appreciation right

Guidance: level 1

:: Human resource management ::

_____ are transactions in which the ownership of companies, other business organizations, or their operating units are transferred or consolidated with other entities. As an aspect of strategic management, M&A can allow enterprises to grow or downsize, and change the nature of their business or competitive position.

Exam Probability: **High**

11. *Answer choices:*

(see index for correct answer)

- a. Work activity management
- b. Onboarding
- c. Mentorship
- d. Personal development planning

Guidance: level 1

:: Outsourcing ::

_____ is the practice of sourcing from the global market for goods and services across geopolitical boundaries. _____ often aims to exploit global efficiencies in the delivery of a product or service. These efficiencies include low cost skilled labor, low cost raw material and other economic factors like tax breaks and low trade tariffs. A large number of Information Technology projects and Services, including IS Applications and Mobile Apps and database services are outsourced globally to countries like Pakistan and India for more economical pricing.

Exam Probability: **Low**

12. *Answer choices:*

(see index for correct answer)

- a. Shared services center
- b. Global sourcing
- c. NetRom Software BV
- d. Engineering process outsourcing

Guidance: level 1

:: ::

_____ , also known as drug abuse, is a patterned use of a drug in which the user consumes the substance in amounts or with methods which are harmful to themselves or others, and is a form of substance-related disorder. Widely differing definitions of drug abuse are used in public health, medical and criminal justice contexts. In some cases criminal or anti-social behaviour occurs when the person is under the influence of a drug, and long term personality changes in individuals may occur as well. In addition to possible physical, social, and psychological harm, use of some drugs may also lead to criminal penalties, although these vary widely depending on the local jurisdiction.

Exam Probability: **Low**

13. *Answer choices:*

(see index for correct answer)

- a. corporate values
- b. hierarchical
- c. Substance abuse
- d. hierarchical perspective

Guidance: level 1

:: ::

_____ is an important topic of Human Resource Management. It helps develop the career of the individual and the prosperous growth of the organization. On the job training is a form of training provided at the workplace. During the training, employees are familiarized with the working environment they will become part of. Employees also get a hands-on experience using machinery, equipment, tools, materials, etc. Part of is to face the challenges that occur during the performance of the job. An experienced employee or a manager are executing the role of the mentor who through written, or verbal instructions and demonstrations are passing on his/her knowledge and company-specific skills to the new employee. Executing the training on at the job location, rather than the classroom, creates a stress-free environment for the employees. _____ is the most popular method of training not only in the United States but in most of the developed countries, such as the United Kingdom, China, Russia, etc. Its effectiveness is based on the use of existing workplace tools, machines, documents and equipment, and the knowledge of specialists who are working in this field. _____ is easy to arrange and manage and it simplifies the process of adapting to the new workplace. OJT is highly used for practical tasks. It is inexpensive, and it doesn't require special equipment that is normally used for a specific job. Upon satisfaction of completion of the training, the employer is expected to retain participants as regular employees.

Exam Probability: **Low**

14. *Answer choices:*

(see index for correct answer)

- a. information systems assessment
- b. Character
- c. cultural
- d. open system

Guidance: level 1

:: Legal terms ::

_____ , a form of alternative dispute resolution , is a way to resolve disputes outside the courts. The dispute will be decided by one or more persons , which renders the "_____ award". An _____ award is legally binding on both sides and enforceable in the courts.

Exam Probability: **Low**

15. *Answer choices:*

(see index for correct answer)

- a. Legal transplant
- b. Hardship clause
- c. Appropriation
- d. Champerty and maintenance

Guidance: level 1

:: Options (finance) ::

_____ is a contractual agreement between a corporation and recipients of phantom shares that bestow upon the grantee the right to a cash payment at a designated time or in association with a designated event in the future, which payment is to be in an amount tied to the market value of an equivalent number of shares of the corporation's stock. Thus, the amount of the payout will increase as the stock price rises, and decrease if the stock falls, but without the recipient actually receiving any stock. Like other forms of stock-based compensation plans, _____ broadly serves to align the interests of recipients and shareholders, incent contribution to share value, and encourage the retention or continued participation of contributors. Recipients are typically employees, but may also be directors, third-party vendors, or others.

Exam Probability: **Low**

16. *Answer choices:*

(see index for correct answer)

- a. Phantom stock
- b. Interest rate guarantee
- c. Warrant
- d. Option symbol

Guidance: level 1

:: Leadership ::

_____ is a theory of leadership where a leader works with teams to identify needed change, creating a vision to guide the change through inspiration, and executing the change in tandem with committed members of a group; it is an integral part of the Full Range Leadership Model. _____ serves to enhance the motivation, morale, and job performance of followers through a variety of mechanisms; these include connecting the follower's sense of identity and self to a project and to the collective identity of the organization; being a role model for followers in order to inspire them and to raise their interest in the project; challenging followers to take greater ownership for their work, and understanding the strengths and weaknesses of followers, allowing the leader to align followers with tasks that enhance their performance.

Exam Probability: **Low**

17. *Answer choices:*

(see index for correct answer)

- a. Consideration and Initiating Structure
- b. The Saint, the Surfer, and the CEO
- c. Spirit of Enniskillen Trust
- d. Sex differences in leadership

Guidance: level 1

:: Human resource management ::

_____ are the people who make up the workforce of an organization, business sector, or economy. "Human capital" is sometimes used synonymously with " _____ ", although human capital typically refers to a narrower effect . Likewise, other terms sometimes used include manpower, talent, labor, personnel, or simply people.

Exam Probability: **Low**

18. *Answer choices:*

(see index for correct answer)

- a. Human resources
- b. Individual development plan
- c. ROWE
- d. Parallel running

Guidance: level 1

:: Training ::

_____ is a phase of training needs analysis directed at identifying which individuals within an organization should receive training.

Exam Probability: **Low**

19. *Answer choices:*

(see index for correct answer)

- a. Question Writer
- b. Enforcement
- c. American Council on Exercise
- d. Leonardo da Vinci programme

Guidance: level 1

:: Psychometrics ::

_____ is a dynamic, structured, interactive process where a neutral third party assists disputing parties in resolving conflict through the use of specialized communication and negotiation techniques. All participants in _____ are encouraged to actively participate in the process. _____ is a "party-centered" process in that it is focused primarily upon the needs, rights, and interests of the parties. The mediator uses a wide variety of techniques to guide the process in a constructive direction and to help the parties find their optimal solution. A mediator is facilitative in that she/he manages the interaction between parties and facilitates open communication. _____ is also evaluative in that the mediator analyzes issues and relevant norms , while refraining from providing prescriptive advice to the parties .

Exam Probability: **Low**

20. *Answer choices:*

(see index for correct answer)

- a. Online assessment
- b. Situational judgement test

- c. Non-response bias
- d. Mediation

:: Employment compensation ::

In government contracting, a _____ is defined as the hourly wage, usual benefits and overtime, paid to the majority of workers, laborers, and mechanics within a particular area. This is usually the union wage.

Exam Probability: **Medium**

21. *Answer choices:*
(see index for correct answer)

- a. Wage regulation
- b. Compa-ratio
- c. Golden parachute
- d. Dearness allowance

:: Labor rights ::

A _____ is a wrong or hardship suffered, real or supposed, which forms legitimate grounds of complaint. In the past, the word meant the infliction or cause of hardship.

Exam Probability: **High**

22. *Answer choices:*

(see index for correct answer)

- a. Kim Bobo
- b. Labor rights
- c. Grievance
- d. Right to work

Guidance: level 1

:: Human resource management ::

_____ assesses whether a person performs a job well. _____, studied academically as part of industrial and organizational psychology, also forms a part of human resources management. Performance is an important criterion for organizational outcomes and success. John P. Campbell describes _____ as an individual-level variable, or something a single person does. This differentiates it from more encompassing constructs such as organizational performance or national performance, which are higher-level variables.

Exam Probability: **Low**

23. *Answer choices:*

(see index for correct answer)

- a. Organizational chart
- b. Human resource consulting
- c. Onboarding
- d. Job design

Guidance: level 1

:: Belief ::

_____ is the ability to acquire knowledge without proof, evidence, or conscious reasoning, or without understanding how the knowledge was acquired. Different writers give the word " _____ " a great variety of different meanings, ranging from direct access to unconscious knowledge, unconscious cognition, inner sensing, inner insight to unconscious pattern-recognition and the ability to understand something instinctively, without the need for conscious reasoning.

Exam Probability: **Medium**

24. *Answer choices:*

(see index for correct answer)

- a. Ignorance
- b. Intuition
- c. Hold come what may

- d. Philosophy

Guidance: level 1

:: Project management ::

_____ is a name for various theories of human motivation built on Douglas McGregor's Theory X and Theory Y. Theories X, Y and various versions of Z have been used in human resource management, organizational behavior, organizational communication and organizational development.

Exam Probability: **Medium**

25. *Answer choices:*

(see index for correct answer)

- a. Trenegy Incorporated
- b. Theory Z
- c. Cost estimate
- d. Mandated lead arranger

Guidance: level 1

:: Management ::

A _____ is when two or more people come together to discuss one or more topics, often in a formal or business setting, but _____ s also occur in a variety of other environments. Many various types of _____ s exist.

Exam Probability: **Medium**

26. *Answer choices:*

(see index for correct answer)

- a. Performance management
- b. Production flow analysis
- c. Meeting
- d. Goal

Guidance: level 1

:: ::

_____ is the administration of an organization, whether it is a business, a not-for-profit organization, or government body. _____ includes the activities of setting the strategy of an organization and coordinating the efforts of its employees to accomplish its objectives through the application of available resources, such as financial, natural, technological, and human resources. The term " _____ " may also refer to those people who manage an organization.

Exam Probability: **Medium**

27. *Answer choices:*

(see index for correct answer)

- a. co-culture
- b. Management
- c. interpersonal communication
- d. process perspective

Guidance: level 1

:: Majority–minority relations ::

_____ , also known as reservation in India and Nepal, positive discrimination / action in the United Kingdom, and employment equity in Canada and South Africa, is the policy of promoting the education and employment of members of groups that are known to have previously suffered from discrimination. Historically and internationally, support for _____ has sought to achieve goals such as bridging inequalities in employment and pay, increasing access to education, promoting diversity, and redressing apparent past wrongs, harms, or hindrances.

Exam Probability: **Low**

28. *Answer choices:*

(see index for correct answer)

- a. cultural Relativism
- b. cultural dissonance

- c. Affirmative action

Guidance: level 1

:: Human resource management ::

_____ is a family of procedures to identify the content of a job in terms of activities involved and attributes or job requirements needed to perform the activities. _____ provides information of organizations which helps to determine which employees are best fit for specific jobs. Through _____ , the analyst needs to understand what the important tasks of the job are, how they are carried out, and the necessary human qualities needed to complete the job successfully.

Exam Probability: **High**

29. *Answer choices:*
(see index for correct answer)

- a. Job analysis
- b. Multiculturalism
- c. Health human resources
- d. Human resource management

Guidance: level 1

:: ::

_____ is the process of gathering and measuring information on targeted variables in an established system, which then enables one to answer relevant questions and evaluate outcomes. _____ is a component of research in all fields of study including physical and social sciences, humanities, and business. While methods vary by discipline, the emphasis on ensuring accurate and honest collection remains the same. The goal for all _____ is to capture quality evidence that allows analysis to lead to the formulation of convincing and credible answers to the questions that have been posed.

Exam Probability: **Low**

30. *Answer choices:*

(see index for correct answer)

- a. interpersonal communication
- b. levels of analysis
- c. corporate values
- d. Data collection

Guidance: level 1

:: ::

Domestic violence is violence or other abuse by one person against another in a domestic setting, such as in marriage or cohabitation. It may be termed intimate partner violence when committed by a spouse or partner in an intimate relationship against the other spouse or partner, and can take place in heterosexual or same-sex relationships, or between former spouses or partners. Domestic violence can also involve violence against children, parents, or the elderly. It takes a number of forms, including physical, verbal, emotional, economic, religious, reproductive, and sexual abuse, which can range from subtle, coercive forms to marital rape and to violent physical abuse such as choking, beating, female genital mutilation, and acid throwing that results in disfigurement or death. Domestic murders include stoning, bride burning, honor killings, and dowry deaths.

Exam Probability: **Medium**

31. *Answer choices:*

(see index for correct answer)

- a. information systems assessment
- b. surface-level diversity
- c. functional perspective
- d. Family violence

Guidance: level 1

:: Human resource management ::

_____ involves improving the effectiveness of organizations and the individuals and teams within them. Training may be viewed as related to immediate changes in organizational effectiveness via organized instruction, while development is related to the progress of longer-term organizational and employee goals. While _____ technically have differing definitions, the two are oftentimes used interchangeably and/or together. _____ has historically been a topic within applied psychology but has within the last two decades become closely associated with human resources management, talent management, human resources development, instructional design, human factors, and knowledge management.

Exam Probability: **Medium**

32. *Answer choices:*

(see index for correct answer)

- a. Bradford Factor
- b. Occupational burnout
- c. Competency-based job description
- d. Training and development

Guidance: level 1

:: Multiple choice ::

The _____ is a standardized psychometric test of adult personality and psychopathology. Psychologists and other mental health professionals use various versions of the MMPI to help develop treatment plans; assist with differential diagnosis; help answer legal questions ; screen job candidates during the personnel selection process; or as part of a therapeutic assessment procedure.

Exam Probability: **High**

33. *Answer choices:*

(see index for correct answer)

- a. Multiple choice
- b. Minnesota Multiphasic Personality Inventory
- c. Eddy Test
- d. Millon Clinical Multiaxial Inventory

Guidance: level 1

:: Human resource management ::

Frederick Herzberg, an American psychologist, originally developed the concept of ` _____ ` in 1968, in an article that he published on pioneering studies at A T&T. The concept stemmed from Herzberg's motivator-hygiene theory, which is based on the premise that job attitude is a construct of two independent factors, namely job satisfaction and job dissatisfaction. Job satisfaction encompasses intrinsic factors that arise from the work itself, including achievement and advancement; whilst job dissatisfaction stems from factors external to the actual work, including company policy and the quality of supervision.

Exam Probability: **Low**

34. *Answer choices:*

(see index for correct answer)

- a. Behavioral Competencies
- b. Job knowledge
- c. Job enrichment
- d. Domestic inquiry

Guidance: level 1

:: Survey methodology ::

_____ is often used to assess thoughts, opinions, and feelings. Surveys can be specific and limited, or they can have more global, widespread goals. Psychologists and sociologists often use surveys to analyze behavior, while it is also used to meet the more pragmatic needs of the media, such as, in evaluating political candidates, public health officials, professional organizations, and advertising and marketing directors. A survey consists of a predetermined set of questions that is given to a sample. With a representative sample, that is, one that is representative of the larger population of interest, one can describe the attitudes of the population from which the sample was drawn. Further, one can compare the attitudes of different populations as well as look for changes in attitudes over time. A good sample selection is key as it allows one to generalize the findings from the sample to the population, which is the whole purpose of _____ .

Exam Probability: **Low**

35. *Answer choices:*

(see index for correct answer)

- a. National Health Interview Survey
- b. Census
- c. Self-report
- d. Survey research

Guidance: level 1

:: Business law ::

A pre-entry _____ is a form of union security agreement under which the employer agrees to hire union members only, and employees must remain members of the union at all times in order to remain employed. This is different from a post-entry _____ , which is an agreement requiring all employees to join the union if they are not already members. In a union shop, the union must accept as a member any person hired by the employer.

Exam Probability: **Medium**

36. *Answer choices:*

(see index for correct answer)

- a. Complex structured finance transactions
- b. Limited liability limited partnership
- c. Time-and-a-half
- d. Business license

Guidance: level 1

:: Business ethics ::

_____ is a type of harassment technique that relates to a sexual nature and the unwelcome or inappropriate promise of rewards in exchange for sexual favors. _____ includes a range of actions from mild transgressions to sexual abuse or assault. Harassment can occur in many different social settings such as the workplace, the home, school, churches, etc. Harassers or victims may be of any gender.

37. *Answer choices:*

(see index for correct answer)

- a. Sexual harassment
- b. Moral hazard
- c. Hypernorms
- d. Anatomy of Greed

Guidance: level 1

:: United States employment discrimination case law ::

_____ , 411 U.S. 792 , is a US employment law case by the United States Supreme Court regarding the burdens and nature of proof in proving a Title VII case and the order in which plaintiffs and defendants present proof. It was the seminal case in the McDonnell Douglas burden-shifting framework.

Exam Probability: **Low**

38. *Answer choices:*

(see index for correct answer)

- a. Dothard v. Rawlinson
- b. Bundy v. Jackson
- c. McDonnell Douglas Corp. v. Green

- d. Shyamala Rajender v. University of Minnesota

Guidance: level 1

:: Human resource management ::

_____ refers to the ability of an organization to retain its employees. _____ can be represented by a simple statistic . However, many consider _____ as relating to the efforts by which employers attempt to retain the employees in their workforce. In this sense, retention becomes the strategies rather than the outcome.

Exam Probability: **Medium**

39. *Answer choices:*

(see index for correct answer)

- a. Employee retention
- b. Skill mix
- c. Employee relationship management
- d. Cross-cultural capital

Guidance: level 1

:: Employment ::

_____ s are experiential learning opportunities, similar to internships but generally shorter, provided by partnerships between educational institutions and employers to give students short practical experiences in their field of study. In medicine it may refer to a visiting physician who is not part of the regular staff. In law, it usually refers to rigorous legal work opportunities undertaken by law students for law school credit and pay, similar to that of a junior attorney. It is derived from Latin externus and from English -ship.

Exam Probability: **High**

40. *Answer choices:*

(see index for correct answer)

- a. Gofer
- b. Externship
- c. Paradox of toil
- d. Saudization

Guidance: level 1

:: Organizational theory ::

_____ is the process of creating, retaining, and transferring knowledge within an organization. An organization improves over time as it gains experience. From this experience, it is able to create knowledge. This knowledge is broad, covering any topic that could better an organization. Examples may include ways to increase production efficiency or to develop beneficial investor relations. Knowledge is created at four different units: individual, group, organizational, and inter organizational.

Exam Probability: **Medium**

41. *Answer choices:*

(see index for correct answer)

- a. Staff augmentation
- b. Stages of growth model
- c. Swift trust
- d. Organizational field

Guidance: level 1

:: Recruitment ::

A _____ is a quantitative research method commonly employed in survey research. The aim of this approach is to ensure that each interview is presented with exactly the same questions in the same order. This ensures that answers can be reliably aggregated and that comparisons can be made with confidence between sample subgroups or between different survey periods.

42. *Answer choices:*

(see index for correct answer)

- a. NotchUp
- b. E-recruitment
- c. Global Career Development Facilitator
- d. Structured interview

Guidance: level 1

:: Employment compensation ::

Compensation and benefits is a sub-discipline of human resources, focused on employee compensation and benefits policy-making. While compensation and benefits are tangible, there are intangible rewards such as recognition, work-life and development. Combined, these are referred to as _____ s . The term "compensation and benefits" refers to the discipline as well as the rewards themselves.

Exam Probability: **Low**

43. *Answer choices:*

(see index for correct answer)

- a. Pay scale
- b. ADP, LLC

- c. Total Reward
- d. Explanation of benefits

Guidance: level 1

:: Unemployment by country ::

Unemployment benefits are payments made by back authorized bodies to unemployed people. In the United States, benefits are funded by a compulsory governmental insurance system, not taxes on individual citizens. Depending on the jurisdiction and the status of the person, those sums may be small, covering only basic needs, or may compensate the lost time proportionally to the previous earned salary.

Exam Probability: **Low**

44. *Answer choices:*

(see index for correct answer)

- a. Unemployment in Spain
- b. Unemployment insurance
- c. Unemployment in Brazil

Guidance: level 1

:: Human resource management ::

_____ is an institutional process that maximizes performance levels and competency for an organization. The process includes all the activities needed to maintain a productive workforce, such as field service management, human resource management, performance and training management, data collection, recruiting, budgeting, forecasting, scheduling and analytics.

Exam Probability: **High**

45. *Answer choices:*

(see index for correct answer)

- a. Upward communication
- b. Resource-based view
- c. Workforce management
- d. Restructuring

Guidance: level 1

:: Grounds for termination of employment ::

_____ is a habitual pattern of absence from a duty or obligation without good reason. Generally, _____ is unplanned absences. _____ has been viewed as an indicator of poor individual performance, as well as a breach of an implicit contract between employee and employer. It is seen as a management problem, and framed in economic or quasi-economic terms. More recent scholarship seeks to understand _____ as an indicator of psychological, medical, or social adjustment to work.

46. *Answer choices:*

(see index for correct answer)

- a. Department of Defense Whistleblower Program
- b. Sleeping while on duty
- c. Presidential Policy Directive 19
- d. No call, no show

Guidance: level 1

:: Parental leave ::

_____ , or family leave, is an employee benefit available in almost all countries. The term " _____ " may include maternity, paternity, and adoption leave; or may be used distinctively from "maternity leave" and "paternity leave" to describe separate family leave available to either parent to care for small children. In some countries and jurisdictions, "family leave" also includes leave provided to care for ill family members. Often, the minimum benefits and eligibility requirements are stipulated by law.

Exam Probability: **Medium**

47. *Answer choices:*

(see index for correct answer)

- a. Pregnancy discrimination

- b. Sara Hlupekile Longwe
- c. Maternity and Parental Leave, etc Regulations 1999
- d. Parental leave

Guidance: level 1

:: Corporate governance ::

An _____ is generally a person responsible for running an organization, although the exact nature of the role varies depending on the organization. In many militaries, an _____ , or "XO," is the second-in-command, reporting to the commanding officer. The XO is typically responsible for the management of day-to-day activities, freeing the commander to concentrate on strategy and planning the unit's next move.

Exam Probability: **Low**

48. *Answer choices:*
(see index for correct answer)

- a. King II
- b. Headquarters
- c. King Committee
- d. Executive officer

Guidance: level 1

_____ is a belief that hard work and diligence have a moral benefit and an inherent ability, virtue or value to strengthen character and individual abilities. It is a set of values centered on importance of work and manifested by determination or desire to work hard. Social ingrainment of this value is considered to enhance character through hard work that is respective to an individual's field of work.

Exam Probability: **High**

49. *Answer choices:*

(see index for correct answer)

- a. hierarchical
- b. open system
- c. Work ethic
- d. imperative

Guidance: level 1

:: Working time ::

The shift plan, rota or roster is the central component of a shift schedule in shift work. The schedule includes considerations of shift overlap, shift change times and alignment with the clock, vacation, training, shift differentials, holidays, etc. The shift plan determines the sequence of work and free days within a shift system.

50. *Answer choices:*

(see index for correct answer)

- a. Gallagher v. Crown Kosher Super Market of Massachusetts, Inc.
- b. Graveyard shift
- c. Waiting for the Weekend
- d. Watch system

Guidance: level 1

:: Analysis ::

_____ is the process of breaking a complex topic or substance into smaller parts in order to gain a better understanding of it. The technique has been applied in the study of mathematics and logic since before Aristotle , though _____ as a formal concept is a relatively recent development.

Exam Probability: **Medium**

51. *Answer choices:*

(see index for correct answer)

- a. Irreducibility
- b. Analysis
- c. EATPUT

- d. Water cascade analysis

Guidance: level 1

:: Sociological theories ::

A _____ is a systematic process for determining and addressing needs, or "gaps" between current conditions and desired conditions or "wants". The discrepancy between the current condition and wanted condition must be measured to appropriately identify the need. The need can be a desire to improve current performance or to correct a deficiency.

Exam Probability: **Medium**

52. *Answer choices:*

(see index for correct answer)

- a. Needs assessment
- b. social constructionism
- c. Compliance gaining
- d. comfort zone

Guidance: level 1

:: Management ::

_____ is a set of activities that ensure goals are met in an effective and efficient manner. _____ can focus on the performance of an organization, a department, an employee, or the processes in place to manage particular tasks. _____ standards are generally organized and disseminated by senior leadership at an organization, and by task owners.

Exam Probability: **High**

53. *Answer choices:*

(see index for correct answer)

- a. Interim management
- b. Business workflow analysis
- c. Performance management
- d. Quick response manufacturing

Guidance: level 1

:: ::

The _____ of 1938 29 U.S.C. § 203 is a United States labor law that creates the right to a minimum wage, and "time-and-a-half" overtime pay when people work over forty hours a week. It also prohibits most employment of minors in "oppressive child labor". It applies to employees engaged in interstate commerce or employed by an enterprise engaged in commerce or in the production of goods for commerce, unless the employer can claim an exemption from coverage.

54. *Answer choices:*

(see index for correct answer)

- a. hierarchical perspective
- b. Sarbanes-Oxley act of 2002
- c. Fair Labor Standards Act
- d. surface-level diversity

Guidance: level 1

:: Persuasion techniques ::

_____ is a psychological technique in which an individual attempts to influence another person by becoming more likeable to their target. This term was coined by social psychologist Edward E. Jones, who further defined _____ as "a class of strategic behaviors illicitly designed to influence a particular other person concerning the attractiveness of one`s personal qualities." _____ research has identified some specific tactics of employing _____ .

55. *Answer choices:*

(see index for correct answer)

- a. Kolakeia

- b. Crocodile tears
- c. Foot-in-the-door technique
- d. Fairy tale

Guidance: level 1

:: Socialism ::

In sociology, _____ is the process of internalizing the norms and ideologies of society. _____ encompasses both learning and teaching and is thus "the means by which social and cultural continuity are attained".

Exam Probability: **Low**

56. *Answer choices:*

(see index for correct answer)

- a. Social class
- b. Utopian socialism
- c. Harvest Hills Cooperative Community
- d. Socialization

Guidance: level 1

:: Business ethics ::

A _____ is a person who exposes any kind of information or activity that is deemed illegal, unethical, or not correct within an organization that is either private or public. The information of alleged wrongdoing can be classified in many ways: violation of company policy/rules, law, regulation, or threat to public interest/national security, as well as fraud, and corruption. Those who become _____ s can choose to bring information or allegations to surface either internally or externally. Internally, a _____ can bring his/her accusations to the attention of other people within the accused organization such as an immediate supervisor. Externally, a _____ can bring allegations to light by contacting a third party outside of an accused organization such as the media, government, law enforcement, or those who are concerned. _____ s, however, take the risk of facing stiff reprisal and retaliation from those who are accused or alleged of wrongdoing.

Exam Probability: **Medium**

57. *Answer choices:*

(see index for correct answer)

- a. Price discrimination
- b. Whistleblower
- c. Destructionism
- d. Creative destruction

Guidance: level 1

:: ::

_____ , also known as alcohol use disorder , is a broad term for any drinking of alcohol that results in mental or physical health problems. The disorder was previously divided into two types: alcohol abuse and alcohol dependence. In a medical context, _____ is said to exist when two or more of the following conditions are present: a person drinks large amounts of alcohol over a long time period, has difficulty cutting down, acquiring and drinking alcohol takes up a great deal of time, alcohol is strongly desired, usage results in not fulfilling responsibilities, usage results in social problems, usage results in health problems, usage results in risky situations, withdrawal occurs when stopping, and alcohol tolerance has occurred with use. Risky situations include drinking and driving or having unsafe sex, among other things. Alcohol use can affect all parts of the body, but it particularly affects the brain, heart, liver, pancreas and immune system. This can result in mental illness, Wernicke–Korsakoff syndrome, irregular heartbeat, an impaired immune response, liver cirrhosis and increased cancer risk, among other diseases. Drinking during pregnancy can cause damage to the baby resulting in fetal alcohol spectrum disorders. Women are generally more sensitive than men to the harmful physical and mental effects of alcohol.

Exam Probability: **Medium**

58. *Answer choices:*

(see index for correct answer)

- a. functional perspective
- b. personal values
- c. empathy
- d. Alcoholism

Guidance: level 1

:: Employment compensation ::

A _____ is a type of employee benefit plan offered in the United States pursuant to Section 125 of the Internal Revenue Code. Its name comes from the earliest such plans that allowed employees to choose between different types of benefits, similar to the ability of a customer to choose among available items in a cafeteria. Qualified _____ s are excluded from gross income. To qualify, a _____ must allow employees to choose from two or more benefits consisting of cash or qualified benefit plans. The Internal Revenue Code explicitly excludes deferred compensation plans from qualifying as a _____ subject to a gross income exemption. Section 125 also provides two exceptions.

Exam Probability: **High**

59. *Answer choices:*

(see index for correct answer)

- a. Cafeteria plan
- b. Medical Care and Sickness Benefits Convention, 1969
- c. Commission
- d. Long service leave

Guidance: level 1

Information systems

Information systems (IS) are formal, sociotechnical, organizational systems designed to collect, process, store, and distribute information. In a sociotechnical perspective Information Systems are composed by four components: technology, process, people and organizational structure.

:: Data transmission ::

In telecommunications and computing, _____ is the number of bits that are conveyed or processed per unit of time.

Exam Probability: **Low**

1. *Answer choices:*

(see index for correct answer)

- a. Asynchronous serial communication
- b. SENT
- c. Ultra-wideband
- d. Bit rate

Guidance: level 1

:: Computing output devices ::

An _____ is any piece of computer hardware equipment which converts information into human-readable form.

Exam Probability: **Low**

2. *Answer choices:*

(see index for correct answer)

- a. Output device
- b. Flicker fixer
- c. Smart Display
- d. Palette

Guidance: level 1

:: Confidence tricks ::

_____ is the fraudulent attempt to obtain sensitive information such as usernames, passwords and credit card details by disguising oneself as a trustworthy entity in an electronic communication. Typically carried out by email spoofing or instant messaging, it often directs users to enter personal information at a fake website which matches the look and feel of the legitimate site.

Exam Probability: **Medium**

3. *Answer choices:*

(see index for correct answer)

- a. Phishing
- b. Television Preview
- c. Hustling
- d. Technical support scam

Guidance: level 1

:: Global Positioning System ::

A _____ is a mechanism for determining the location of an object in space. Technologies for this task exist ranging from worldwide coverage with meter accuracy to workspace coverage with sub-millimetre accuracy.

4. *Answer choices:*

(see index for correct answer)

- a. Positioning system
- b. Gpsd
- c. Wide Area Augmentation System
- d. Precise Point Positioning

Guidance: level 1

:: ::

_____ , Inc. is an American online social media and social networking service company based in Menlo Park, California. It was founded by Mark Zuckerberg, along with fellow Harvard College students and roommates Eduardo Saverin, Andrew McCollum, Dustin Moskovitz and Chris Hughes. It is considered one of the Big Four technology companies along with Amazon, Apple, and Google.

Exam Probability: **High**

5. *Answer choices:*

(see index for correct answer)

- a. levels of analysis
- b. Facebook

- c. similarity-attraction theory
- d. empathy

Guidance: level 1

:: ::

A _____ is an abstract model that organizes elements of data and standardizes how they relate to one another and to properties of the real world entities. For instance, a _____ may specify that the data element representing a car be composed of a number of other elements which, in turn, represent the color and size of the car and define its owner.

Exam Probability: **High**

6. *Answer choices:*

(see index for correct answer)

- a. Character
- b. levels of analysis
- c. corporate values
- d. Data model

Guidance: level 1

:: Computer access control protocols ::

An _____ is a type of computer communications protocol or cryptographic protocol specifically designed for transfer of authentication data between two entities. It allows the receiving entity to authenticate the connecting entity as well as authenticate itself to the connecting entity by declaring the type of information needed for authentication as well as syntax. It is the most important layer of protection needed for secure communication within computer networks.

Exam Probability: **High**

7. *Answer choices:*

(see index for correct answer)

- a. Ticket Granting Ticket
- b. Yahalom
- c. Authentication protocol
- d. LAN Manager

Guidance: level 1

:: Big data ::

_____ is the discovery, interpretation, and communication of meaningful patterns in data; and the process of applying those patterns towards effective decision making. In other words, _____ can be understood as the connective tissue between data and effective decision making, within an organization. Especially valuable in areas rich with recorded information, _____ relies on the simultaneous application of statistics, computer programming and operations research to quantify performance.

Exam Probability: **Low**

8. *Answer choices:*

(see index for correct answer)

- a. SAP HANA
- b. Social IT
- c. Hack/reduce
- d. RelateIQ

Guidance: level 1

:: ::

A _____ is a control panel usually located directly ahead of a vehicle's driver, displaying instrumentation and controls for the vehicle's operation.

Exam Probability: **Low**

9. *Answer choices:*

(see index for correct answer)

- a. Dashboard
- b. surface-level diversity
- c. Character
- d. corporate values

:: Google services ::

A blog is a discussion or informational website published on the World Wide Web consisting of discrete, often informal diary-style text entries . Posts are typically displayed in reverse chronological order, so that the most recent post appears first, at the top of the web page. Until 2009, blogs were usually the work of a single individual, occasionally of a small group, and often covered a single subject or topic. In the 2010s, "multi-author blogs" emerged, featuring the writing of multiple authors and sometimes professionally edited. MABs from newspapers, other media outlets, universities, think tanks, advocacy groups, and similar institutions account for an increasing quantity of blog traffic. The rise of Twitter and other "microblogging" systems helps integrate MABs and single-author blogs into the news media. Blog can also be used as a verb, meaning to maintain or add content to a blog.

Exam Probability: **High**

10. *Answer choices:*

(see index for correct answer)

- a. Blogger
- b. Freebase
- c. Gizmo5
- d. AdSense

:: History of human–computer interaction ::

A _____ , plural mice, is a small rodent characteristically having a pointed snout, small rounded ears, a body-length scaly tail and a high breeding rate. The best known _____ species is the common house _____ . It is also a popular pet. In some places, certain kinds of field mice are locally common. They are known to invade homes for food and shelter.

Exam Probability: **High**

11. *Answer choices:*

(see index for correct answer)

- a. Trackball
- b. Mouse
- c. In the Beginning... Was the Command Line
- d. File Retrieval and Editing System

Guidance: level 1

:: Information technology management ::

In information technology to _____ means to move from one place to another, information to detailed data by focusing in on something. In a GUI-environment, "drilling-down" may involve clicking on some representation in order to reveal more detail.

12. *Answer choices:*

(see index for correct answer)

- a. Information repository
- b. Definitive Media Library
- c. Piazza telematica
- d. Drill down

Guidance: level 1

:: Service-oriented (business computing) ::

_____ is a style of software design where services are provided to the other components by application components, through a communication protocol over a network. The basic principles of _____ are independent of vendors, products and technologies.A service is a discrete unit of functionality that can be accessed remotely and acted upon and updated independently, such as retrieving a credit card statement online.

Exam Probability: **Medium**

13. *Answer choices:*

(see index for correct answer)

- a. Service-oriented architecture
- b. Service-oriented modeling

- c. Machine to machine
- d. Cudamail

Guidance: level 1

:: Database theory ::

A _____ is a digital database based on the relational model of data, as proposed by E. F. Codd in 1970. A software system used to maintain _____ s is a _____ management system . Virtually all _____ systems use SQL for querying and maintaining the database.

Exam Probability: **High**

14. *Answer choices:*
(see index for correct answer)

- a. Range searching
- b. Dependency theory
- c. Database catalog
- d. Chase

Guidance: level 1

:: Industrial automation ::

_____ is the technology by which a process or procedure is performed with minimal human assistance. _____ or automatic control is the use of various control systems for operating equipment such as machinery, processes in factories, boilers and heat treating ovens, switching on telephone networks, steering and stabilization of ships, aircraft and other applications and vehicles with minimal or reduced human intervention.

Exam Probability: **High**

15. *Answer choices:*

(see index for correct answer)

- a. EtherCAT
- b. RAPIEnet
- c. I/Gear
- d. Advanced Plant Management System

Guidance: level 1

:: Transaction processing ::

Transaction processing is information processing in computer science that is divided into individual, indivisible operations called transactions. Each transaction must succeed or fail as a complete unit; it can never be only partially complete.

Exam Probability: **Low**

16. *Answer choices:*

(see index for correct answer)

- a. Purchase-to-pay
- b. Atomic commit
- c. Transaction processing
- d. SafePeak

Guidance: level 1

:: Data ::

In computer main memory, auxiliary storage and computer buses, _____ is the existence of data that is additional to the actual data and permits correction of errors in stored or transmitted data. The additional data can simply be a complete copy of the actual data, or only select pieces of data that allow detection of errors and reconstruction of lost or damaged data up to a certain level.

Exam Probability: **Medium**

17. *Answer choices:*

(see index for correct answer)

- a. Infonomics
- b. Metro Chicago Information Center
- c. Biological data
- d. Humanities Indicators

:: ::

A _____ is a published declaration of the intentions, motives, or views of the issuer, be it an individual, group, political party or government. A _____ usually accepts a previously published opinion or public consensus or promotes a new idea with prescriptive notions for carrying out changes the author believes should be made. It often is political or artistic in nature, but may present an individual's life stance. _____ s relating to religious belief are generally referred to as creeds.

Exam Probability: **Medium**

18. *Answer choices:*

(see index for correct answer)

- a. similarity-attraction theory
- b. open system
- c. imperative
- d. co-culture

:: Computer data ::

In computer science, _____ is the ability to access an arbitrary element of a sequence in equal time or any datum from a population of addressable elements roughly as easily and efficiently as any other, no matter how many elements may be in the set. It is typically contrasted to sequential access.

19. *Answer choices:*

(see index for correct answer)

- a. Machine-generated data
- b. Lilian date
- c. Random access
- d. Data in Use

Guidance: level 1

:: Automatic identification and data capture ::

_____ is the trademark for a type of matrix barcode first designed in 1994 for the automotive industry in Japan. A barcode is a machine-readable optical label that contains information about the item to which it is attached. In practice, _____ s often contain data for a locator, identifier, or tracker that points to a website or application. A _____ uses four standardized encoding modes to store data efficiently; extensions may also be used.

20. *Answer choices:*

(see index for correct answer)

- a. IBeacon
- b. QR code
- c. Intermec
- d. Smart label

Guidance: level 1

:: Search engine optimization ::

_____ is an algorithm used by Google Search to rank web pages in their search engine results. _____ was named after Larry Page, one of the founders of Google. _____ is a way of measuring the importance of website pages. According to Google.

Exam Probability: **High**

21. *Answer choices:*

(see index for correct answer)

- a. PageRank
- b. Competitor backlinking
- c. Ultimate Research Assistant

- d. Dartboard optimization matrix

Guidance: level 1

:: Virtual economies ::

_____ Inc. is an American social game developer running social video game services founded in April 2007 and headquartered in San Francisco, California, United States. The company primarily focuses on mobile and social networking platforms. _____ states its mission as "connecting the world through games."

Exam Probability: **High**

22. *Answer choices:*

(see index for correct answer)

- a. Zynga
- b. Viximo
- c. TirNua
- d. Mytopia

Guidance: level 1

:: Data management ::

_____ is a form of intellectual property that grants the creator of an original creative work an exclusive legal right to determine whether and under what conditions this original work may be copied and used by others, usually for a limited term of years. The exclusive rights are not absolute but limited by limitations and exceptions to _____ law, including fair use. A major limitation on _____ on ideas is that _____ protects only the original expression of ideas, and not the underlying ideas themselves.

Exam Probability: **Low**

23. *Answer choices:*

(see index for correct answer)

- a. Copyright
- b. Data field
- c. Head/tail Breaks
- d. Data extraction

Guidance: level 1

:: E-commerce ::

Customer to customer markets provide an innovative way to allow customers to interact with each other. Traditional markets require business to customer relationships, in which a customer goes to the business in order to purchase a product or service. In customer to customer markets, the business facilitates an environment where customers can sell goods or services to each other. Other types of markets include business to business and business to customer .

24. *Answer choices:*

(see index for correct answer)

- a. Consumer-to-consumer
- b. Standard Interchange Language
- c. Billing and Settlement Plan
- d. Automated Clearing House

Guidance: level 1

:: Reputation management ::

_____ refers to the influencing and controlling of an individual's or group's reputation. Originally a public relations term, the growth of the internet and social media, along with _____ companies, have made search results a core part of an individual's or group's reputation. Online _____ , sometimes abbreviated as ORM, focuses on the management of product and service search website results. Ethical grey areas include mug shot removal sites, astroturfing customer review sites, censoring negative complaints, and using search engine optimization tactics to influence results.

Exam Probability: **High**

25. *Answer choices:*

(see index for correct answer)

- a. Meta-moderation system
- b. Slashdot
- c. Reputation management
- d. Moderation system

Guidance: level 1

:: Finance ::

_____ is a financial estimate intended to help buyers and owners determine the direct and indirect costs of a product or system. It is a management accounting concept that can be used in full cost accounting or even ecological economics where it includes social costs.

Exam Probability: **Low**

26. *Answer choices:*

(see index for correct answer)

- a. Cram down
- b. PVIFA
- c. Non-operating income
- d. Private sector involvement

Guidance: level 1

Within the Internet, _____ s are formed by the rules and procedures of the _____ System . Any name registered in the DNS is a _____ . _____ s are used in various networking contexts and for application-specific naming and addressing purposes. In general, a _____ represents an Internet Protocol resource, such as a personal computer used to access the Internet, a server computer hosting a web site, or the web site itself or any other service communicated via the Internet. In 2017, 330.6 million _____ s had been registered.

Exam Probability: **Medium**

27. *Answer choices:*

(see index for correct answer)

- a. hierarchical
- b. cultural
- c. hierarchical perspective
- d. Domain name

Guidance: level 1

:: Fraud ::

In law, _____ is intentional deception to secure unfair or unlawful gain, or to deprive a victim of a legal right. _____ can violate civil law , a criminal law , or it may cause no loss of money, property or legal right but still be an element of another civil or criminal wrong. The purpose of _____ may be monetary gain or other benefits, for example by obtaining a passport, travel document, or driver`s license, or mortgage _____ , where the perpetrator may attempt to qualify for a mortgage by way of false statements.

Exam Probability: **Medium**

28. *Answer choices:*

(see index for correct answer)

- a. Subex
- b. Fraud Alert
- c. Claims Conference
- d. Fraud

Guidance: level 1

:: World Wide Web Consortium standards ::

_____ is a markup language that defines a set of rules for encoding documents in a format that is both human-readable and machine-readable. The W3C`s XML 1.0 Specification and several other related specifications—all of them free open standards—define XML.

Exam Probability: **Low**

29. *Answer choices:*

(see index for correct answer)

- a. Hypertext markup language
- b. Hyper Text Markup Language

Guidance: level 1

:: Distribution, retailing, and wholesaling ::

_____ measures the performance of a system. Certain goals are defined and the _____ gives the percentage to which those goals should be achieved. Fill rate is different from _____ .

Exam Probability: **Medium**

30. *Answer choices:*

(see index for correct answer)

- a. Open Payment Initiative
- b. Pallet rack mover
- c. Service level
- d. 350 West Mart Center

Guidance: level 1

:: Payment systems ::

_____ is a mobile phone-based money transfer, financing and microfinancing service, launched in 2007 by Vodafone for Safaricom and Vodacom, the largest mobile network operators in Kenya and Tanzania. It has since expanded to Afghanistan, South Africa, India and in 2014 to Romania and in 2015 to Albania. _____ allows users to deposit, withdraw, transfer money and pay for goods and services easily with a mobile device.

Exam Probability: **Low**

31. *Answer choices:*

(see index for correct answer)

- a. WorldNet TPS
- b. QC Record Format
- c. Electronic Recording Machine, Accounting
- d. Saudi Payments Network

Guidance: level 1

:: ::

Sustainability is the process of people maintaining change in a balanced environment, in which the exploitation of resources, the direction of investments, the orientation of technological development and institutional change are all in harmony and enhance both current and future potential to meet human needs and aspirations. For many in the field, sustainability is defined through the following interconnected domains or pillars: environment, economic and social, which according to Fritjof Capra is based on the principles of Systems Thinking. Sub-domains of _____ development have been considered also: cultural, technological and political. While _____ development may be the organizing principle for sustainability for some, for others, the two terms are paradoxical . _____ development is the development that meets the needs of the present without compromising the ability of future generations to meet their own needs. Brundtland Report for the World Commission on Environment and Development introduced the term of _____ development.

Exam Probability: **High**

32. *Answer choices:*

(see index for correct answer)

- a. Sustainable
- b. co-culture
- c. empathy
- d. surface-level diversity

Guidance: level 1

:: Intrusion detection systems ::

An _____ is a device or software application that monitors a network or systems for malicious activity or policy violations. Any malicious activity or violation is typically reported either to an administrator or collected centrally using a security information and event management system. A SIEM system combines outputs from multiple sources, and uses alarm filtering techniques to distinguish malicious activity from false alarms.

Exam Probability: **High**

33. *Answer choices:*

(see index for correct answer)

- a. IDMEF
- b. Host-based intrusion detection system
- c. Protocol-based intrusion detection system
- d. Intrusion detection system

Guidance: level 1

:: Procurement practices ::

_____ or commercially available off-the-shelf products are packaged solutions which are then adapted to satisfy the needs of the purchasing organization, rather than the commissioning of custom-made, or bespoke, solutions. A related term, Mil-COTS, refers to COTS products for use by the U.S. military.

Exam Probability: **Medium**

34. *Answer choices:*

(see index for correct answer)

- a. Commercial off-the-shelf
- b. Construction by configuration

Guidance: level 1

:: Google services ::

_____ is a word processor included as part of a free, web-based software office suite offered by Google within its Google Drive service. This service also includes Google Sheets and Google Slides, a spreadsheet and presentation program respectively. _____ is available as a web application, mobile app for Android, iOS, Windows, BlackBerry, and as a desktop application on Google's ChromeOS. The app is compatible with Microsoft Office file formats. The application allows users to create and edit files online while collaborating with other users in real-time. Edits are tracked by user with a revision history presenting changes. An editor's position is highlighted with an editor-specific color and cursor. A permissions system regulates what users can do. Updates have introduced features using machine learning, including "Explore", offering search results based on the contents of a document, and "Action items", allowing users to assign tasks to other users.

Exam Probability: **Medium**

35. *Answer choices:*

(see index for correct answer)

- a. Google Videos

- b. Google Docs
- c. Google Safe Browsing
- d. Google Public DNS

Guidance: level 1

:: ::

_____ is a set of values of subjects with respect to qualitative or quantitative variables.

Exam Probability: **Low**

36. *Answer choices:*
(see index for correct answer)

- a. deep-level diversity
- b. information systems assessment
- c. cultural
- d. levels of analysis

Guidance: level 1

:: Computer access control ::

_____ is the act of confirming the truth of an attribute of a single piece of data claimed true by an entity. In contrast with identification, which refers to the act of stating or otherwise indicating a claim purportedly attesting to a person or thing's identity, _____ is the process of actually confirming that identity. It might involve confirming the identity of a person by validating their identity documents, verifying the authenticity of a website with a digital certificate, determining the age of an artifact by carbon dating, or ensuring that a product is what its packaging and labeling claim to be. In other words, _____ often involves verifying the validity of at least one form of identification.

Exam Probability: **Low**

37. *Answer choices:*

(see index for correct answer)

- a. Digital identity
- b. WS-Trust
- c. Authentication
- d. FinFisher

Guidance: level 1

:: ::

A database is an organized collection of data, generally stored and accessed electronically from a computer system. Where databases are more complex they are often developed using formal design and modeling techniques.

38. *Answer choices:*

(see index for correct answer)

- a. functional perspective
- b. co-culture
- c. Database management system
- d. imperative

Guidance: level 1

:: Data interchange standards ::

_____ is the concept of businesses electronically communicating information that was traditionally communicated on paper, such as purchase orders and invoices. Technical standards for EDI exist to facilitate parties transacting such instruments without having to make special arrangements.

Exam Probability: **Low**

39. *Answer choices:*

(see index for correct answer)

- a. ASC X12
- b. Uniform Communication Standard
- c. Interaction protocol

- d. Domain Application Protocol

Guidance: level 1

:: ::

_____ is a kind of action that occur as two or more objects have an effect upon one another. The idea of a two-way effect is essential in the concept of _____ , as opposed to a one-way causal effect. A closely related term is interconnectivity, which deals with the _____ s of _____ s within systems: combinations of many simple _____ s can lead to surprising emergent phenomena. _____ has different tailored meanings in various sciences. Changes can also involve _____ .

Exam Probability: **Low**

40. *Answer choices:*

(see index for correct answer)

- a. co-culture
- b. information systems assessment
- c. similarity-attraction theory
- d. open system

Guidance: level 1

:: Fault tolerance ::

_____ is the property that enables a system to continue operating properly in the event of the failure of some of its components. If its operating quality decreases at all, the decrease is proportional to the severity of the failure, as compared to a naively designed system, in which even a small failure can cause total breakdown. _____ is particularly sought after in high-availability or life-critical systems. The ability of maintaining functionality when portions of a system break down is referred to as graceful degradation.

Exam Probability: **High**

41. *Answer choices:*

(see index for correct answer)

- a. Byzantine fault tolerance
- b. Repetition code
- c. Elegant degradation
- d. Control reconfiguration

Guidance: level 1

:: Information retrieval ::

_____ is the practice of making content from multiple enterprise-type sources, such as databases and intranets, searchable to a defined audience .

Exam Probability: **Medium**

42. *Answer choices:*

(see index for correct answer)

- a. Enterprise search
- b. Uncertain inference
- c. Rocchio algorithm
- d. Information Retrieval Facility

Guidance: level 1

:: Data management ::

_____ s or data _____ s are computer languages used to make queries in databases and information systems.

Exam Probability: **Low**

43. *Answer choices:*

(see index for correct answer)

- a. Query language
- b. Enterprise bus matrix
- c. PerformancePoint
- d. Distributed transaction

Guidance: level 1

:: Google services ::

_____ is a web mapping service developed by Google. It offers satellite imagery, aerial photography, street maps, 360° panoramic views of streets, real-time traffic conditions, and route planning for traveling by foot, car, bicycle and air , or public transportation.

Exam Probability: **Medium**

44. *Answer choices:*

(see index for correct answer)

- a. Google Voice Search
- b. Google Schemer
- c. Google Maps
- d. Google Insights for Search

Guidance: level 1

:: Production and manufacturing ::

_____ is the manufacturing approach of using computers to control entire production process. This integration allows individual processes to exchange information with each other and initiate actions. Although manufacturing can be faster and less error-prone by the integration of computers, the main advantage is the ability to create automated manufacturing processes. Typically CIM relies of closed-loop control processes, based on real-time input from sensors. It is also known as flexible design and manufacturing.

Exam Probability: **Low**

45. *Answer choices:*

(see index for correct answer)

- a. Computer-integrated manufacturing
- b. ISO/IEC 17025
- c. Enterprise control
- d. Expediting

Guidance: level 1

:: Data quality ::

_____ or data cleaning is the process of detecting and correcting corrupt or inaccurate records from a record set, table, or database and refers to identifying incomplete, incorrect, inaccurate or irrelevant parts of the data and then replacing, modifying, or deleting the dirty or coarse data. _____ may be performed interactively with data wrangling tools, or as batch processing through scripting.

46. *Answer choices:*

(see index for correct answer)

- a. Data truncation
- b. One-for-one checking
- c. Input mask
- d. Dirty data

Guidance: level 1

:: Information science ::

In discourse-based grammatical theory, _____ is any tracking of referential information by speakers. Information may be new, just introduced into the conversation; given, already active in the speakers' consciousness; or old, no longer active. The various types of activation, and how these are defined, are model-dependent.

Exam Probability: **Medium**

47. *Answer choices:*

(see index for correct answer)

- a. Informatics
- b. Informing science

- c. Information flow
- d. Information logistics

Guidance: level 1

:: Data ::

_____ is viewed by many disciplines as a modern equivalent of visual communication. It involves the creation and study of the visual representation of data.

Exam Probability: **High**

48. *Answer choices:*
(see index for correct answer)

- a. GS1 DataBar Coupon
- b. One Source Networks
- c. Synthetic data
- d. primary data

Guidance: level 1

:: Economic globalization ::

_____ is an agreement in which one company hires another company to be responsible for a planned or existing activity that is or could be done internally,and sometimes involves transferring employees and assets from one firm to another.

Exam Probability: **High**

49. *Answer choices:*

(see index for correct answer)

- a. reshoring
- b. global financial

Guidance: level 1

:: Market research ::

_____ is the action of defining, gathering, analyzing, and distributing intelligence about products, customers, competitors, and any aspect of the environment needed to support executives and managers in strategic decision making for an organization.

Exam Probability: **High**

50. *Answer choices:*

(see index for correct answer)

- a. Competitive intelligence
- b. Vehicle Dependability Study
- c. Customer satisfaction research
- d. ISO 20252

Guidance: level 1

:: ::

_____ is a set of documents provided on paper, or online, or on digital or analog media, such as audio tape or CDs. Examples are user guides, white papers, on-line help, quick-reference guides. It is becoming less common to see paper _____ . _____ is distributed via websites, software products, and other on-line applications.

Exam Probability: **Medium**

51. *Answer choices:*

(see index for correct answer)

- a. personal values
- b. open system
- c. Documentation
- d. corporate values

Guidance: level 1

:: Statistical laws ::

In statistics and business, a _____ of some distributions of numbers is the portion of the distribution having a large number of occurrences far from the "head" or central part of the distribution. The distribution could involve popularities, random numbers of occurrences of events with various probabilities, etc. The term is often used loosely, with no definition or arbitrary definition, but precise definitions are possible.

Exam Probability: **High**

52. *Answer choices:*

(see index for correct answer)

- a. Long tail
- b. Safety in numbers
- c. Rank-size distribution
- d. Law of total expectation

Guidance: level 1

:: Monopoly (economics) ::

A _____ exists when a specific person or enterprise is the only supplier of a particular commodity. This contrasts with a monopsony which relates to a single entity's control of a market to purchase a good or service, and with oligopoly which consists of a few sellers dominating a market. Monopolies are thus characterized by a lack of economic competition to produce the good or service, a lack of viable substitute goods, and the possibility of a high _____ price well above the seller's marginal cost that leads to a high _____ profit. The verb monopolise or monopolize refers to the process by which a company gains the ability to raise prices or exclude competitors. In economics, a _____ is a single seller. In law, a _____ is a business entity that has significant market power, that is, the power to charge overly high prices. Although monopolies may be big businesses, size is not a characteristic of a _____ . A small business may still have the power to raise prices in a small industry .

Exam Probability: **Low**

53. *Answer choices:*

(see index for correct answer)

- a. Third-party access
- b. Monopoly
- c. Patent portfolio
- d. Cost per procedure

Guidance: level 1

:: Telecommunication theory ::

In reliability theory and reliability engineering, the term _____ has the following meanings.

54. *Answer choices:*

(see index for correct answer)

- a. Received noise power
- b. Availability
- c. Bias distortion
- d. Balance return loss

Guidance: level 1

:: Automatic identification and data capture ::

_____ is human–computer interaction in which a computer is expected to be transported during normal usage, which allows for transmission of data, voice and video. _____ involves mobile communication, mobile hardware, and mobile software. Communication issues include ad hoc networks and infrastructure networks as well as communication properties, protocols, data formats and concrete technologies. Hardware includes mobile devices or device components. Mobile software deals with the characteristics and requirements of mobile applications.

55. *Answer choices:*

(see index for correct answer)

- a. Snake Eater
- b. Mobile computing
- c. Watchclock
- d. Radio-frequency identification

Guidance: level 1

:: ::

_____ is software designed to provide a platform for other software. Examples of _____ include operating systems like macOS, Ubuntu and Microsoft Windows, computational science software, game engines, industrial automation, and software as a service applications.

Exam Probability: **Medium**

56. *Answer choices:*

(see index for correct answer)

- a. cultural
- b. empathy
- c. Sarbanes-Oxley act of 2002
- d. System software

:: ::

_____ is an American video-sharing website headquartered in San Bruno, California. Three former PayPal employees—Chad Hurley, Steve Chen, and Jawed Karim—created the service in February 2005. Google bought the site in November 2006 for US$1.65 billion; _____ now operates as one of Google's subsidiaries.

Exam Probability: **High**

57. *Answer choices:*

(see index for correct answer)

- a. similarity-attraction theory
- b. functional perspective
- c. YouTube
- d. hierarchical perspective

:: Help desk ::

Data center management is the collection of tasks performed by those responsible for managing ongoing operation of a data center This includes Business service management and planning for the future.

Exam Probability: **Medium**

58. *Answer choices:*
(see index for correct answer)

- a. EHelp Corporation
- b. GLPI
- c. KnowledgeBase Manager Pro
- d. AetherPal

Guidance: level 1

:: Identity management ::

_____ is the ability of an individual or group to seclude themselves, or information about themselves, and thereby express themselves selectively. The boundaries and content of what is considered private differ among cultures and individuals, but share common themes. When something is private to a person, it usually means that something is inherently special or sensitive to them. The domain of _____ partially overlaps with security , which can include the concepts of appropriate use, as well as protection of information. _____ may also take the form of bodily integrity.

Exam Probability: **Low**

59. *Answer choices:*

(see index for correct answer)

- a. Identity verification service
- b. Privacy
- c. DigiD
- d. Directory information tree

Guidance: level 1

Marketing

Marketing is the study and management of exchange relationships. Marketing is
the business process of creating relationships with and satisfying customers.
With its focus on the customer, marketing is one of the premier components of
business management.

Marketing is defined by the American Marketing Association as "the activity,
set of institutions, and processes for creating, communicating, delivering, and
exchanging offerings that have value for customers, clients, partners, and
society at large."

:: ::

_____ consists of using generic or ad hoc methods in an orderly manner to find solutions to problems. Some of the problem-solving techniques developed and used in philosophy, artificial intelligence, computer science, engineering, mathematics, or medicine are related to mental problem-solving techniques studied in psychology.

Exam Probability: **Medium**

1. *Answer choices:*

(see index for correct answer)

- a. deep-level diversity
- b. information systems assessment
- c. personal values
- d. Problem Solving

Guidance: level 1

:: ::

_____ Motor Company is an American multinational automaker that has its main headquarter in Dearborn, Michigan, a suburb of Detroit. It was founded by Henry _____ and incorporated on June 16, 1903. The company sells automobiles and commercial vehicles under the _____ brand and most luxury cars under the Lincoln brand. _____ also owns Brazilian SUV manufacturer Troller, an 8% stake in Aston Martin of the United Kingdom and a 32% stake in Jiangling Motors. It also has joint-ventures in China , Taiwan , Thailand , Turkey , and Russia . The company is listed on the New York Stock Exchange and is controlled by the _____ family; they have minority ownership but the majority of the voting power.

Exam Probability: **Low**

2. *Answer choices:*

(see index for correct answer)

- a. functional perspective
- b. open system
- c. information systems assessment
- d. hierarchical

Guidance: level 1

:: Business ethics ::

_____ is a microeconomic pricing strategy where identical or largely similar goods or services are transacted at different prices by the same provider in different markets. _____ is distinguished from product differentiation by the more substantial difference in production cost for the differently priced products involved in the latter strategy. Price differentiation essentially relies on the variation in the customers' willingness to pay and in the elasticity of their demand.

Exam Probability: **Low**

3. *Answer choices:*

(see index for correct answer)

- a. Institute of Business Ethics
- b. The FCPA Blog
- c. Accounting scandals
- d. Minority business enterprise

Guidance: level 1

:: Marketing ::

_____ is a marketing practice of individuals or organizations . It allows them to sell products or services to other companies or organizations that resell them, use them in their products or services or use them to support their works.

Exam Probability: **Medium**

4. Answer choices:

(see index for correct answer)

- a. Business marketing
- b. Licensing International Expo
- c. Pitching engine
- d. Macromarketing

Guidance: level 1

:: ::

_____ is the process whereby a business sets the price at which it will sell its products and services, and may be part of the business's marketing plan. In setting prices, the business will take into account the price at which it could acquire the goods, the manufacturing cost, the market place, competition, market condition, brand, and quality of product.

Exam Probability: **Medium**

5. Answer choices:

(see index for correct answer)

- a. deep-level diversity
- b. Pricing
- c. cultural
- d. corporate values

:: Logistics ::

_____ is generally the detailed organization and implementation of a complex operation. In a general business sense, _____ is the management of the flow of things between the point of origin and the point of consumption in order to meet requirements of customers or corporations. The resources managed in _____ may include tangible goods such as materials, equipment, and supplies, as well as food and other consumable items. The _____ of physical items usually involves the integration of information flow, materials handling, production, packaging, inventory, transportation, warehousing, and often security.

Exam Probability: **Low**

6. *Answer choices:*

(see index for correct answer)

- a. Tracking number
- b. The Institute of Transport Management
- c. Logistics
- d. Short shipment

:: Consumer behaviour ::

_____ refers to the ability of a company or product to retain its customers over some specified period. High _____ means customers of the product or business tend to return to, continue to buy or in some other way not defect to another product or business, or to non-use entirely. Selling organizations generally attempt to reduce customer defections. _____ starts with the first contact an organization has with a customer and continues throughout the entire lifetime of a relationship and successful retention efforts take this entire lifecycle into account. A company's ability to attract and retain new customers is related not only to its product or services, but also to the way it services its existing customers, the value the customers actually generate as a result of utilizing the solutions, and the reputation it creates within and across the marketplace.

Exam Probability: **Low**

7. *Answer choices:*

(see index for correct answer)

- a. Daniel Starch
- b. Consumer capitalism
- c. Customer retention
- d. Sustainable consumer behaviour

Guidance: level 1

:: Product management ::

A _____ is a professional role which is responsible for the development of products for an organization, known as the practice of product management. _____ s own the business strategy behind a product , specify its functional requirements and generally manage the launch of features. They coordinate work done by many other functions and are ultimately responsible for the business success of the product.

Exam Probability: **Low**

8. *Answer choices:*

(see index for correct answer)

- a. Product manager
- b. Crossing the Chasm
- c. Rapid prototyping
- d. Promise Index

Guidance: level 1

:: ::

An _____ is a contingent motivator. Traditional _____ s are extrinsic motivators which reward actions to yield a desired outcome. The effectiveness of traditional _____ s has changed as the needs of Western society have evolved. While the traditional _____ model is effective when there is a defined procedure and goal for a task, Western society started to require a higher volume of critical thinkers, so the traditional model became less effective. Institutions are now following a trend in implementing strategies that rely on intrinsic motivations rather than the extrinsic motivations that the traditional _____ s foster.

Exam Probability: **Low**

9. *Answer choices:*

(see index for correct answer)

- a. Sarbanes-Oxley act of 2002
- b. Incentive
- c. similarity-attraction theory
- d. information systems assessment

Guidance: level 1

:: Promotion and marketing communications ::

_____ is one of the elements of the promotional mix. . _____ uses both media and non-media marketing communications for a pre-determined, limited time to increase consumer demand, stimulate market demand or improve product availability. Examples include contests, coupons, freebies, loss leaders, point of purchase displays, premiums, prizes, product samples, and rebates.

10. *Answer choices:*

(see index for correct answer)

- a. Infoganda
- b. Sales promotion
- c. Puffery
- d. Next Jump

Guidance: level 1

:: Belief ::

_____ is an umbrella term of influence. _____ can attempt to influence a person's beliefs, attitudes, intentions, motivations, or behaviors. In business, _____ is a process aimed at changing a person's attitude or behavior toward some event, idea, object, or other person, by using written, spoken words or visual tools to convey information, feelings, or reasoning, or a combination thereof. _____ is also an often used tool in the pursuit of personal gain, such as election campaigning, giving a sales pitch, or in trial advocacy. _____ can also be interpreted as using one's personal or positional resources to change people's behaviors or attitudes. Systematic _____ is the process through which attitudes or beliefs are leveraged by appeals to logic and reason. Heuristic _____ on the other hand is the process through which attitudes or beliefs are leveraged by appeals to habit or emotion.

11. *Answer choices:*

(see index for correct answer)

- a. Political myth
- b. False pleasure
- c. Persuasion
- d. Faith literate

Guidance: level 1

:: ::

_____ is the collection of techniques, skills, methods, and processes used in the production of goods or services or in the accomplishment of objectives, such as scientific investigation. _____ can be the knowledge of techniques, processes, and the like, or it can be embedded in machines to allow for operation without detailed knowledge of their workings. Systems applying _____ by taking an input, changing it according to the system`s use, and then producing an outcome are referred to as _____ systems or technological systems.

Exam Probability: **Medium**

12. *Answer choices:*

(see index for correct answer)

- a. open system
- b. Technology

- c. empathy
- d. information systems assessment

Guidance: level 1

:: ::

A _____ is a person who trades in commodities produced by other people. Historically, a _____ is anyone who is involved in business or trade. _____ s have operated for as long as industry, commerce, and trade have existed. During the 16th-century, in Europe, two different terms for _____ s emerged: One term, meerseniers, described local traders such as bakers, grocers, etc.; while a new term, koopman (Dutch: koopman, described _____ s who operated on a global stage, importing and exporting goods over vast distances, and offering added-value services such as credit and finance.

Exam Probability: **Medium**

13. *Answer choices:*

(see index for correct answer)

- a. information systems assessment
- b. Merchant
- c. personal values
- d. similarity-attraction theory

Guidance: level 1

:: Marketing ::

_____ is the marketing of products that are presumed to be environmentally safe. It incorporates a broad range of activities, including product modification, changes to the production process, sustainable packaging, as well as modifying advertising. Yet defining _____ is not a simple task where several meanings intersect and contradict each other; an example of this will be the existence of varying social, environmental and retail definitions attached to this term. Other similar terms used are environmental marketing and ecological marketing.

Exam Probability: **Medium**

14. *Answer choices:*

(see index for correct answer)

- a. Narrowcasting
- b. Business marketing
- c. Audience development
- d. Customer dynamics

Guidance: level 1

:: Economic globalization ::

_____ is an agreement in which one company hires another company to be responsible for a planned or existing activity that is or could be done internally,and sometimes involves transferring employees and assets from one firm to another.

Exam Probability: **Low**

15. *Answer choices:*

(see index for correct answer)

- a. reshoring
- b. global financial

Guidance: level 1

:: Marketing analytics ::

_____ is a long-term, forward-looking approach to planning with the fundamental goal of achieving a sustainable competitive advantage. Strategic planning involves an analysis of the company's strategic initial situation prior to the formulation, evaluation and selection of market-oriented competitive position that contributes to the company's goals and marketing objectives.

Exam Probability: **Medium**

16. *Answer choices:*

(see index for correct answer)

- a. Marketing effectiveness
- b. Marketing strategy
- c. Mission-driven marketing
- d. Advertising adstock

Guidance: level 1

:: Goods ::

In most contexts, the concept of _____ denotes the conduct that should be preferred when posed with a choice between possible actions. _____ is generally considered to be the opposite of evil, and is of interest in the study of morality, ethics, religion and philosophy. The specific meaning and etymology of the term and its associated translations among ancient and contemporary languages show substantial variation in its inflection and meaning depending on circumstances of place, history, religious, or philosophical context.

Exam Probability: **Low**

17. *Answer choices:*

(see index for correct answer)

- a. Experience good
- b. Neutral good
- c. Good

- d. Credence good

Guidance: level 1

:: E-commerce ::

_____ is the activity of buying or selling of products on online services or over the Internet. Electronic commerce draws on technologies such as mobile commerce, electronic funds transfer, supply chain management, Internet marketing, online transaction processing, electronic data interchange , inventory management systems, and automated data collection systems.

Exam Probability: **Medium**

18. *Answer choices:*

(see index for correct answer)

- a. EPAS
- b. Center for the Connected Consumer
- c. Eurocheque
- d. E-commerce

Guidance: level 1

:: Management ::

A _____ is a promise of value to be delivered, communicated, and acknowledged. It is also a belief from the customer about how value will be delivered, experienced and acquired.

Exam Probability: **Low**

19. *Answer choices:*

(see index for correct answer)

- a. Value proposition
- b. Libertarian management
- c. Logistics management
- d. Design management

Guidance: level 1

:: Marketing by medium ::

_____ or viral advertising is a business strategy that uses existing social networks to promote a product. Its name refers to how consumers spread information about a product with other people in their social networks, much in the same way that a virus spreads from one person to another. It can be delivered by word of mouth or enhanced by the network effects of the Internet and mobile networks.

Exam Probability: **High**

20. *Answer choices:*

(see index for correct answer)

- a. Brand infiltration
- b. New media marketing
- c. Viral marketing
- d. Social marketing intelligence

Guidance: level 1

:: Auctioneering ::

An _____ is a process of buying and selling goods or services by offering them up for bid, taking bids, and then selling the item to the highest bidder. The open ascending price _____ is arguably the most common form of _____ in use today. Participants bid openly against one another, with each subsequent bid required to be higher than the previous bid. An _____ eer may announce prices, bidders may call out their bids themselves , or bids may be submitted electronically with the highest current bid publicly displayed. In a Dutch _____ , the _____ eer begins with a high asking price for some quantity of like items; the price is lowered until a participant is willing to accept the _____ eer`s price for some quantity of the goods in the lot or until the seller`s reserve price is met. While _____ s are most associated in the public imagination with the sale of antiques, paintings, rare collectibles and expensive wines, _____ s are also used for commodities, livestock, radio spectrum and used cars. In economic theory, an _____ may refer to any mechanism or set of trading rules for exchange.

Exam Probability: **Low**

21. *Answer choices:*

(see index for correct answer)

- a. National Auctioneers Association
- b. How Much Wood Would a Woodchuck Chuck
- c. Auction
- d. Calor licitantis

Guidance: level 1

:: ::

_____ or accountancy is the measurement, processing, and communication of financial information about economic entities such as businesses and corporations. The modern field was established by the Italian mathematician Luca Pacioli in 1494. _____ , which has been called the "language of business", measures the results of an organization's economic activities and conveys this information to a variety of users, including investors, creditors, management, and regulators. Practitioners of _____ are known as accountants. The terms "_____" and "financial reporting" are often used as synonyms.

Exam Probability: **Medium**

22. *Answer choices:*

(see index for correct answer)

- a. levels of analysis
- b. interpersonal communication

- c. functional perspective
- d. Accounting

Guidance: level 1

:: ::

Bloomberg Businessweek is an American weekly business magazine published since 2009 by Bloomberg L.P. Businessweek, founded in 1929, aimed to provide information and interpretation about events in the business world. The magazine is headquartered in New York City. Megan Murphy served as editor from November 2016; she stepped down from the role in January 2018 and Joel Weber was appointed in her place.The magazine is published 47 times a year.

Exam Probability: **High**

23. *Answer choices:*

(see index for correct answer)

- a. co-culture
- b. Business Week
- c. hierarchical
- d. Sarbanes-Oxley act of 2002

Guidance: level 1

:: Market research ::

An _____ or lighthouse customer is an early customer of a given company, product, or technology. The term originates from Everett M. Rogers' Diffusion of Innovations .

Exam Probability: **Low**

24. *Answer choices:*

(see index for correct answer)

- a. Early adopter
- b. Portable People Meter
- c. High Mark Credit Information Services
- d. Fuld-Gilad-Herring Academy of Competitive Intelligence

Guidance: level 1

:: Mereology ::

_____ , in the abstract, is what belongs to or with something, whether as an attribute or as a component of said thing. In the context of this article, it is one or more components , whether physical or incorporeal, of a person's estate; or so belonging to, as in being owned by, a person or jointly a group of people or a legal entity like a corporation or even a society. Depending on the nature of the _____ , an owner of _____ has the right to consume, alter, share, redefine, rent, mortgage, pawn, sell, exchange, transfer, give away or destroy it, or to exclude others from doing these things, as well as to perhaps abandon it; whereas regardless of the nature of the _____ , the owner thereof has the right to properly use it , or at the very least exclusively keep it.

25. *Answer choices:*

(see index for correct answer)

- a. Mereology
- b. Property
- c. Meronomy
- d. Mereological essentialism

Guidance: level 1

:: Management ::

A _____ is a comprehensive document or blueprint that outlines the advertising and marketing efforts for the coming year. It describes business activities involved in accomplishing specific marketing objectives within a set time frame. A _____ also includes a description of the current marketing position of a business, a discussion of the target market and a description of the marketing mix that a business will use to achieve their marketing goals. A _____ has a formal structure, but can be used as a formal or informal document which makes it very flexible. It contains some historical data, future predictions, and methods or strategies to achieve the marketing objectives. _____ s start with the identification of customer needs through a market research and how the business can satisfy these needs while generating an acceptable return. This includes processes such as market situation analysis, action programs, budgets, sales forecasts, strategies and projected financial statements. A _____ can also be described as a technique that helps a business to decide on the best use of its resources to achieve corporate objectives. It can also contain a full analysis of the strengths and weaknesses of a company, its organization and its products.

26. *Answer choices:*

(see index for correct answer)

- a. Director
- b. The Toyota Way
- c. Supplier relationship management
- d. Process capability

Guidance: level 1

:: ::

Competition arises whenever at least two parties strive for a goal which cannot be shared: where one's gain is the other's loss .

Exam Probability: **Medium**

27. *Answer choices:*

(see index for correct answer)

- a. Competitor
- b. process perspective
- c. levels of analysis
- d. similarity-attraction theory

:: Retailing ::

_____ is the process of selling consumer goods or services to customers through multiple channels of distribution to earn a profit. _____ ers satisfy demand identified through a supply chain. The term " _____ er" is typically applied where a service provider fills the small orders of a large number of individuals, who are end-users, rather than large orders of a small number of wholesale, corporate or government clientele. Shopping generally refers to the act of buying products. Sometimes this is done to obtain final goods, including necessities such as food and clothing; sometimes it takes place as a recreational activity. Recreational shopping often involves window shopping and browsing; it does not always result in a purchase.

Exam Probability: **High**

28. *Answer choices:*

(see index for correct answer)

- a. Shop in a box
- b. Brick and mortar
- c. Retail
- d. Showroom

:: Generally Accepted Accounting Principles ::

In accounting, _____ is the income that a business have from its normal business activities, usually from the sale of goods and services to customers. _____ is also referred to as sales or turnover.Some companies receive _____ from interest, royalties, or other fees. _____ may refer to business income in general, or it may refer to the amount, in a monetary unit, earned during a period of time, as in "Last year, Company X had _____ of $42 million". Profits or net income generally imply total _____ minus total expenses in a given period. In accounting, in the balance statement it is a subsection of the Equity section and _____ increases equity, it is often referred to as the "top line" due to its position on the income statement at the very top. This is to be contrasted with the "bottom line" which denotes net income .

Exam Probability: **High**

29. *Answer choices:*

(see index for correct answer)

- a. Statement of recommended practice
- b. Revenue
- c. Fin 48
- d. Revenue recognition

Guidance: level 1

:: ::

_____ is change in the heritable characteristics of biological populations over successive generations. These characteristics are the expressions of genes that are passed on from parent to offspring during reproduction. Different characteristics tend to exist within any given population as a result of mutation, genetic recombination and other sources of genetic variation. _____ occurs when _____ ary processes such as natural selection and genetic drift act on this variation, resulting in certain characteristics becoming more common or rare within a population. It is this process of _____ that has given rise to biodiversity at every level of biological organisation, including the levels of species, individual organisms and molecules.

Exam Probability: **High**

30. *Answer choices:*

(see index for correct answer)

- a. Sarbanes-Oxley act of 2002
- b. co-culture
- c. empathy
- d. Evolution

Guidance: level 1

:: Meetings ::

A _____ is a body of one or more persons that is subordinate to a deliberative assembly. Usually, the assembly sends matters into a _____ as a way to explore them more fully than would be possible if the assembly itself were considering them. _____ s may have different functions and their type of work differ depending on the type of the organization and its needs.

Exam Probability: **High**

31. *Answer choices:*

(see index for correct answer)

- a. Program book
- b. Conference hall
- c. Committee
- d. Annual Georgia European Union Summit

Guidance: level 1

:: Sales ::

_____ is a business discipline which is focused on the practical application of sales techniques and the management of a firm's sales operations. It is an important business function as net sales through the sale of products and services and resulting profit drive most commercial business. These are also typically the goals and performance indicators of _____ .

Exam Probability: **Medium**

32. *Answer choices:*

(see index for correct answer)

- a. Upselling
- b. Account-based marketing
- c. Richard Christiansen
- d. Sales management

Guidance: level 1

:: ::

Consumer behaviour is the study of individuals, groups, or organizations and all the activities associated with the purchase, use and disposal of goods and services, including the consumer's emotional, mental and behavioural responses that precede or follow these activities. Consumer behaviour emerged in the 1940s and 50s as a distinct sub-discipline in the marketing area.

Exam Probability: **High**

33. *Answer choices:*

(see index for correct answer)

- a. information systems assessment
- b. Consumer behavior
- c. functional perspective
- d. co-culture

:: Public relations ::

_____ is the public visibility or awareness for any product, service or company. It may also refer to the movement of information from its source to the general public, often but not always via the media. The subjects of _____ include people , goods and services, organizations, and works of art or entertainment.

Exam Probability: **Medium**

34. *Answer choices:*

(see index for correct answer)

- a. Sparkpr
- b. Public diplomacy
- c. Media monitoring service
- d. Publicity

:: Marketing ::

_____ is a pricing strategy where the price of a product is initially set low to rapidly reach a wide fraction of the market and initiate word of mouth. The strategy works on the expectation that customers will switch to the new brand because of the lower price. _____ is most commonly associated with marketing objectives of enlarging market share and exploiting economies of scale or experience.

Exam Probability: **Low**

35. *Answer choices:*

(see index for correct answer)

- a. Penetration pricing
- b. Pitching engine
- c. Chaotics
- d. Negotiation

Guidance: level 1

:: ::

A _____ is an organized collection of data, generally stored and accessed electronically from a computer system. Where _____ s are more complex they are often developed using formal design and modeling techniques.

Exam Probability: **Low**

36. *Answer choices:*

(see index for correct answer)

- a. similarity-attraction theory
- b. Database
- c. levels of analysis
- d. corporate values

Guidance: level 1

:: Business terms ::

_____ occurs when a sales representative meets with a potential client for the purpose of transacting a sale. Many sales representatives rely on a sequential sales process that typically includes nine steps. Some sales representatives develop scripts for all or part of the sales process. The sales process can be used in face-to-face encounters and in telemarketing.

Exam Probability: **Low**

37. *Answer choices:*

(see index for correct answer)

- a. churn rate
- b. Personal selling
- c. Owner Controlled Insurance Program
- d. Mission statement

:: ::

_____ is a term frequently used in marketing. It is a measure of how products and services supplied by a company meet or surpass customer expectation. _____ is defined as "the number of customers, or percentage of total customers, whose reported experience with a firm, its products, or its services exceeds specified satisfaction goals."

Exam Probability: **High**

38. *Answer choices:*

(see index for correct answer)

- a. information systems assessment
- b. open system
- c. imperative
- d. personal values

:: Advertising techniques ::

In promotion and of advertising, a _____ or show consists of a person's written or spoken statement extolling the virtue of a product. The term " _____ " most commonly applies to the sales-pitches attributed to ordinary citizens, whereas the word "endorsement" usually applies to pitches by celebrities. _____ s can be part of communal marketing. Sometimes, the cartoon character can be a _____ in a commercial.

Exam Probability: **Medium**

39. *Answer choices:*
(see index for correct answer)

- a. Testimonial
- b. Hard sell
- c. Unipole sign
- d. Inconsistent comparison

Guidance: level 1

:: ::

_____ LLC is an American multinational technology company that specializes in Internet-related services and products, which include online advertising technologies, search engine, cloud computing, software, and hardware. It is considered one of the Big Four technology companies, alongside Amazon, Apple and Facebook.

Exam Probability: **High**

40. *Answer choices:*

(see index for correct answer)

- a. Google
- b. interpersonal communication
- c. personal values
- d. functional perspective

Guidance: level 1

:: Progressive Era in the United States ::

The Clayton Antitrust Act of 1914 , was a part of United States antitrust law with the goal of adding further substance to the U.S. antitrust law regime; the _____ sought to prevent anticompetitive practices in their incipiency. That regime started with the Sherman Antitrust Act of 1890, the first Federal law outlawing practices considered harmful to consumers . The _____ specified particular prohibited conduct, the three-level enforcement scheme, the exemptions, and the remedial measures.

Exam Probability: **Medium**

41. *Answer choices:*

(see index for correct answer)

- a. Mann Act
- b. Clayton Act
- c. Clayton Antitrust Act

:: Stock market ::

The _____ of a corporation is all of the shares into which ownership of the corporation is divided. In American English, the shares are commonly known as " _____ s". A single share of the _____ represents fractional ownership of the corporation in proportion to the total number of shares. This typically entitles the _____ holder to that fraction of the company's earnings, proceeds from liquidation of assets , or voting power, often dividing these up in proportion to the amount of money each _____ holder has invested. Not all _____ is necessarily equal, as certain classes of _____ may be issued for example without voting rights, with enhanced voting rights, or with a certain priority to receive profits or liquidation proceeds before or after other classes of shareholders.

Exam Probability: **Low**

42. *Answer choices:*

(see index for correct answer)

- a. Stock
- b. Stock market
- c. Program trading
- d. Yellow strip

:: Income ::

_____ is a ratio between the net profit and cost of investment resulting from an investment of some resources. A high ROI means the investment's gains favorably to its cost. As a performance measure, ROI is used to evaluate the efficiency of an investment or to compare the efficiencies of several different investments. In purely economic terms, it is one way of relating profits to capital invested. _____ is a performance measure used by businesses to identify the efficiency of an investment or number of different investments.

Exam Probability: **High**

43. *Answer choices:*

(see index for correct answer)

- a. Independent income
- b. Return on investment
- c. Aggregate expenditure
- d. bottom line

Guidance: level 1

:: ::

A _____ consists of one people who live in the same dwelling and share meals. It may also consist of a single family or another group of people. A dwelling is considered to contain multiple _____ s if meals or living spaces are not shared. The _____ is the basic unit of analysis in many social, microeconomic and government models, and is important to economics and inheritance.

Exam Probability: **Low**

44. *Answer choices:*

(see index for correct answer)

- a. cultural
- b. Sarbanes-Oxley act of 2002
- c. Household
- d. co-culture

Guidance: level 1

:: National accounts ::

_____ is a monetary measure of the market value of all the final goods and services produced in a period of time, often annually. GDP per capita does not, however, reflect differences in the cost of living and the inflation rates of the countries; therefore using a basis of GDP per capita at purchasing power parity is arguably more useful when comparing differences in living standards between nations.

45. *Answer choices:*

(see index for correct answer)

- a. Gross domestic product
- b. capital formation
- c. National Income

Guidance: level 1

:: Human resource management ::

_____ encompasses values and behaviors that contribute to the unique social and psychological environment of a business. The _____ influences the way people interact, the context within which knowledge is created, the resistance they will have towards certain changes, and ultimately the way they share knowledge. _____ represents the collective values, beliefs and principles of organizational members and is a product of factors such as history, product, market, technology, strategy, type of employees, management style, and national culture; culture includes the organization`s vision, values, norms, systems, symbols, language, assumptions, environment, location, beliefs and habits.

46. *Answer choices:*

(see index for correct answer)

- a. Organizational culture
- b. Lego Serious Play
- c. Bradford Factor
- d. Reward management

Guidance: level 1

:: Business planning ::

_____ is an organization's process of defining its strategy, or direction, and making decisions on allocating its resources to pursue this strategy. It may also extend to control mechanisms for guiding the implementation of the strategy. _____ became prominent in corporations during the 1960s and remains an important aspect of strategic management. It is executed by strategic planners or strategists, who involve many parties and research sources in their analysis of the organization and its relationship to the environment in which it competes.

Exam Probability: **Medium**

47. *Answer choices:*

(see index for correct answer)

- a. Exit planning
- b. Community Futures
- c. Customer Demand Planning
- d. Strategic planning

:: Network theory ::

A _____ is a social structure made up of a set of social actors , sets of dyadic ties, and other social interactions between actors. The _____ perspective provides a set of methods for analyzing the structure of whole social entities as well as a variety of theories explaining the patterns observed in these structures. The study of these structures uses _____ analysis to identify local and global patterns, locate influential entities, and examine network dynamics.

Exam Probability: **Low**

48. *Answer choices:*

(see index for correct answer)

- a. Centrality
- b. Social objects
- c. Weighted network
- d. Social network

:: Brokered programming ::

An _____ is a form of television commercial, which generally includes a toll-free telephone number or website. Most often used as a form of direct response television , long-form _____ s are typically 28:30 or 58:30 minutes in length. _____ s are also known as paid programming . This phenomenon started in the United States, where _____ s were typically shown overnight , outside peak prime time hours for commercial broadcasters. Some television stations chose to air _____ s as an alternative to the former practice of signing off. Some channels air _____ s 24 hours. Some stations also choose to air _____ s during the daytime hours mostly on weekends to fill in for unscheduled network or syndicated programming. By 2009, most _____ spending in the U.S. occurred during the early morning, daytime and evening hours, or in the afternoon. Stations in most countries around the world have instituted similar media structures. The _____ industry is worth over $200 billion.

Exam Probability: **High**

49. *Answer choices:*

(see index for correct answer)

- a. Brokered programming
- b. One Magnificent Morning
- c. Infomercial
- d. Toonzai

Guidance: level 1

:: ::

_____ s uses different marketing channels and tools in combination: _____ channels focus on any way a business communicates a message to its desired market, or the market in general. A _____ tool can be anything from: advertising, personal selling, direct marketing, sponsorship, communication, and promotion to public relations.

Exam Probability: **High**

50. *Answer choices:*

(see index for correct answer)

- a. similarity-attraction theory
- b. Character
- c. Marketing communication
- d. imperative

Guidance: level 1

:: Management ::

In economics and marketing, _____ is the process of distinguishing a product or service from others, to make it more attractive to a particular target market. This involves differentiating it from competitors' products as well as a firm's own products. The concept was proposed by Edward Chamberlin in his 1933 The Theory of Monopolistic Competition.

Exam Probability: **Low**

51. *Answer choices:*

- a. Product differentiation
- b. Target operating model
- c. Scrum
- d. Intopia

Guidance: level 1

:: ::

_____ is an abstract concept of management of complex systems according to a set of rules and trends. In systems theory, these types of rules exist in various fields of biology and society, but the term has slightly different meanings according to context. For example.

Exam Probability: **Medium**

52. *Answer choices:*

- a. Regulation
- b. surface-level diversity
- c. levels of analysis
- d. empathy

:: Management accounting ::

_____ s are costs that change as the quantity of the good or service that a business produces changes. _____ s are the sum of marginal costs over all units produced. They can also be considered normal costs. Fixed costs and _____ s make up the two components of total cost. Direct costs are costs that can easily be associated with a particular cost object. However, not all _____ s are direct costs. For example, variable manufacturing overhead costs are _____ s that are indirect costs, not direct costs. _____ s are sometimes called unit-level costs as they vary with the number of units produced.

Exam Probability: **Medium**

53. *Answer choices:*

(see index for correct answer)

- a. Variable cost
- b. Accounting management
- c. Direct material usage variance
- d. Total benefits of ownership

:: Information technology management ::

B2B is often contrasted with business-to-consumer . In B2B commerce, it is often the case that the parties to the relationship have comparable negotiating power, and even when they do not, each party typically involves professional staff and legal counsel in the negotiation of terms, whereas B2C is shaped to a far greater degree by economic implications of information asymmetry. However, within a B2B context, large companies may have many commercial, resource and information advantages over smaller businesses. The United Kingdom government, for example, created the post of Small Business Commissioner under the Enterprise Act 2016 to "enable small businesses to resolve disputes" and "consider complaints by small business suppliers about payment issues with larger businesses that they supply."

Exam Probability: **Medium**

54. *Answer choices:*

(see index for correct answer)

- a. Records life-cycle
- b. Corporate Governance of ICT
- c. Remote access policy
- d. Business-to-business

Guidance: level 1

:: Management occupations ::

_____ ship is the process of designing, launching and running a new business, which is often initially a small business. The people who create these businesses are called _____ s.

55. *Answer choices:*

(see index for correct answer)

- a. Ceco
- b. Chief design officer
- c. Entrepreneur
- d. Chief reputation officer

Guidance: level 1

:: Production economics ::

In microeconomics, _____ are the cost advantages that enterprises obtain due to their scale of operation , with cost per unit of output decreasing with increasing scale.

Exam Probability: **Medium**

56. *Answer choices:*

(see index for correct answer)

- a. Marginal cost of capital schedule
- b. Economies of scale
- c. Industrial production index
- d. Split-off point

:: Promotion and marketing communications ::

A _____ is the intended audience or readership of a publication, advertisement, or other message. In marketing and advertising, it is a particular group of consumers within the predetermined target market, identified as the targets or recipients for a particular advertisement or message. Businesses that have a wide target market will focus on a specific _____ for certain messages to send, such as The Body Shops Mother's Day advertisements, which were aimed at the children and spouses of women, rather than the whole market which would have included the women themselves.

Exam Probability: **Low**

57. *Answer choices:*

(see index for correct answer)

- a. Press release
- b. One Club
- c. Youth marketing
- d. direct-mail

:: Types of marketing ::

_____ is "marketing on a worldwide scale reconciling or taking commercial advantage of global operational differences, similarities and opportunities in order to meet global objectives".

Exam Probability: **High**

58. *Answer choices:*

(see index for correct answer)

- a. Influencer marketing
- b. Z-CARD
- c. Vertical integration
- d. Global marketing

Guidance: level 1

:: Market research ::

_____ is the action of defining, gathering, analyzing, and distributing intelligence about products, customers, competitors, and any aspect of the environment needed to support executives and managers in strategic decision making for an organization.

Exam Probability: **Medium**

59. *Answer choices:*

(see index for correct answer)

- a. Competitive intelligence
- b. 6-3-5 Brainwriting
- c. Nielsen VideoScan
- d. Eddie Chung

Guidance: level 1

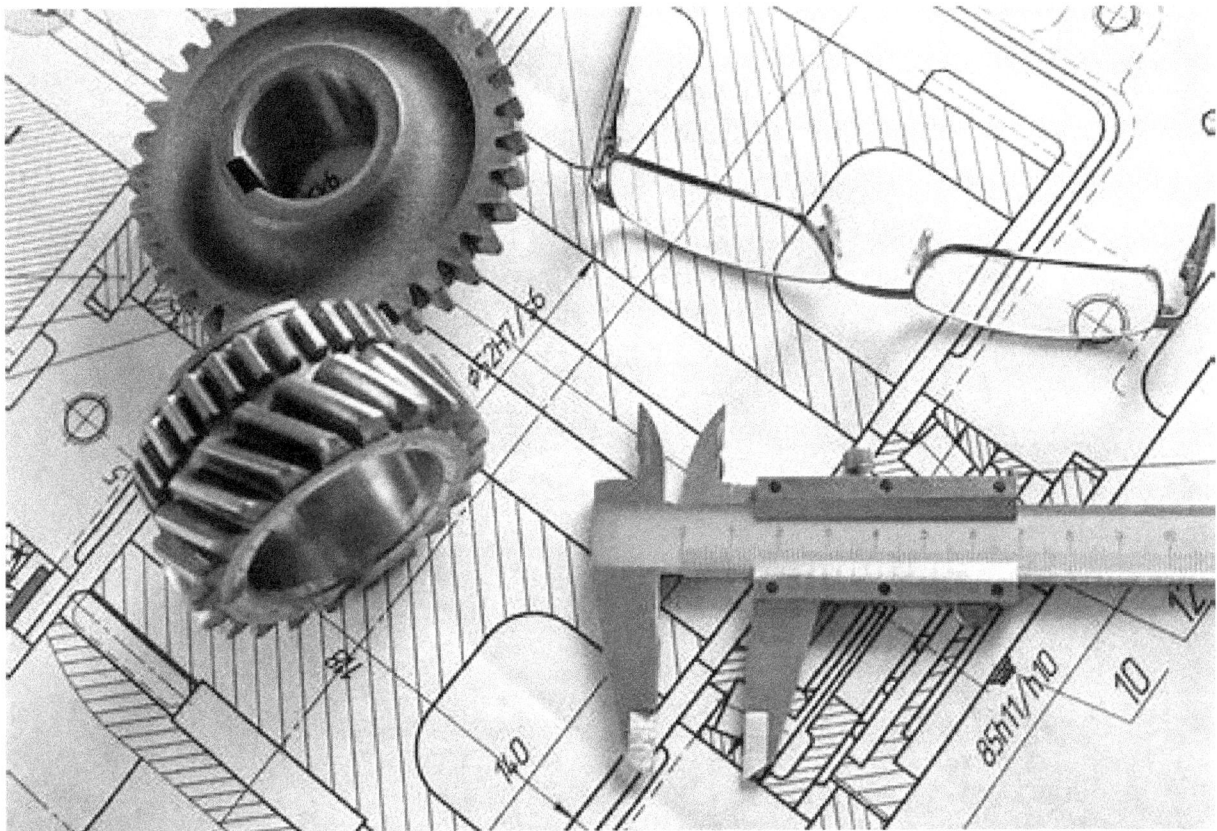

Manufacturing

Manufacturing is the production of merchandise for use or sale using labor and machines, tools, chemical and biological processing, or formulation. The term may refer to a range of human activity, from handicraft to high tech, but is most commonly applied to industrial design , in which raw materials are transformed into finished goods on a large scale. Such finished goods may be sold to other manufacturers for the production of other, more complex products, such as aircraft, household appliances, furniture, sports equipment or automobiles, or sold to wholesalers, who in turn sell them to retailers, who then sell them to end users and consumers.

:: Management ::

_____ is a process by which entities review the quality of all factors involved in production. ISO 9000 defines _____ as "A part of quality management focused on fulfilling quality requirements".

Exam Probability: **High**

1. *Answer choices:*
(see index for correct answer)

- a. Concept of operations
- b. Supply chain network
- c. Quality control
- d. Shamrock Organization

Guidance: level 1

:: Outsourcing ::

_____ is an institutional procurement process that continuously improves and re-evaluates the purchasing activities of a company. In the services industry, _____ refers to a service solution, sometimes called a strategic partnership, which is specifically customized to meet the client`s individual needs. In a production environment, it is often considered one component of supply chain management. Modern supply chain management professionals have placed emphasis on defining the distinct differences between _____ and procurement. Procurement operations support tactical day-to-day transactions such as issuing Purchase Orders to suppliers, whereas _____ represents to strategic planning, supplier development, contract negotiation, supply chain infrastructure, and outsourcing models.

2. *Answer choices:*

- a. Print and mail outsourcing
- b. MITIE Group
- c. Strategic sourcing
- d. Divestment

Guidance: level 1

:: Industrial engineering ::

_____ , in its contemporary conceptualisation, is a comparison of perceived expectations of a service with perceived performance , giving rise to the equation SQ=P-E. This conceptualistion of _____ has its origins in the expectancy-disconfirmation paradigm.

Exam Probability: **Medium**

3. *Answer choices:*

- a. Activity relationship chart
- b. Needs analysis
- c. Service quality

- d. Work Measurement

Guidance: level 1

:: Production and manufacturing ::

_____ is a systematic method to improve the "value" of goods or products and services by using an examination of function. Value, as defined, is the ratio of function to cost. Value can therefore be manipulated by either improving the function or reducing the cost. It is a primary tenet of _____ that basic functions be preserved and not be reduced as a consequence of pursuing value improvements.

Exam Probability: **High**

4. *Answer choices:*

(see index for correct answer)

- a. Scientific management
- b. Nesting
- c. Value engineering
- d. Digital materialization

Guidance: level 1

:: Metals ::

A _____ is a material that, when freshly prepared, polished, or fractured, shows a lustrous appearance, and conducts electricity and heat relatively well. _____ s are typically malleable or ductile . A _____ may be a chemical element such as iron, or an alloy such as stainless steel.

Exam Probability: **Medium**

5. *Answer choices:*

(see index for correct answer)

- a. Non-ferrous metal
- b. Metallic bonding
- c. Metals of antiquity
- d. Metal

Guidance: level 1

:: ::

A _____ consists of an orchestrated and repeatable pattern of business activity enabled by the systematic organization of resources into processes that transform materials, provide services, or process information. It can be depicted as a sequence of operations, the work of a person or group, the work of an organization of staff, or one or more simple or complex mechanisms.

Exam Probability: **High**

6. *Answer choices:*

(see index for correct answer)

- a. open system
- b. Workflow
- c. process perspective
- d. cultural

Guidance: level 1

:: Lean manufacturing ::

_____ is the Sino-Japanese word for "improvement". In business, _____ refers to activities that continuously improve all functions and involve all employees from the CEO to the assembly line workers. It also applies to processes, such as purchasing and logistics, that cross organizational boundaries into the supply chain. It has been applied in healthcare, psychotherapy, life-coaching, government, and banking.

Exam Probability: **Low**

7. *Answer choices:*

(see index for correct answer)

- a. Manufacturing supermarket
- b. Kaizen
- c. Lean services
- d. Continuous improvement

:: Project management ::

A _____ is a type of bar chart that illustrates a project schedule, named after its inventor, Henry Gantt , who designed such a chart around the years 1910–1915. Modern _____ s also show the dependency relationships between activities and current schedule status.

Exam Probability: **High**

8. *Answer choices:*

(see index for correct answer)

- a. Sustainable event management
- b. Changes clause
- c. Initiative
- d. Opportunity management

:: Promotion and marketing communications ::

The _____ of American Manufacturers, now ThomasNet, is an online platform for supplier discovery and product sourcing in the US and Canada. It was once known as the "big green books" and "Thomas Registry", and was a multi-volume directory of industrial product information covering 650,000 distributors, manufacturers and service companies within 67,000-plus industrial categories that is now published on ThomasNet.

Exam Probability: **High**

9. *Answer choices:*

(see index for correct answer)

- a. Thomas Register
- b. Pentagon rapid response operation
- c. Aisle411
- d. Pakistan Electronic Media Regulatory Authority

Guidance: level 1

:: ::

_____ is the process of making predictions of the future based on past and present data and most commonly by analysis of trends. A commonplace example might be estimation of some variable of interest at some specified future date. Prediction is a similar, but more general term. Both might refer to formal statistical methods employing time series, cross-sectional or longitudinal data, or alternatively to less formal judgmental methods. Usage can differ between areas of application: for example, in hydrology the terms "forecast" and "_____" are sometimes reserved for estimates of values at certain specific future times, while the term "prediction" is used for more general estimates, such as the number of times floods will occur over a long period.

Exam Probability: **Medium**

10. *Answer choices:*

(see index for correct answer)

- a. similarity-attraction theory
- b. personal values
- c. process perspective
- d. Forecasting

Guidance: level 1

:: ::

In production, research, retail, and accounting, a _____ is the value of money that has been used up to produce something or deliver a service, and hence is not available for use anymore. In business, the _____ may be one of acquisition, in which case the amount of money expended to acquire it is counted as _____ . In this case, money is the input that is gone in order to acquire the thing. This acquisition _____ may be the sum of the _____ of production as incurred by the original producer, and further _____ s of transaction as incurred by the acquirer over and above the price paid to the producer. Usually, the price also includes a mark-up for profit over the _____ of production.

Exam Probability: **High**

11. *Answer choices:*

(see index for correct answer)

- a. co-culture
- b. deep-level diversity
- c. Cost
- d. information systems assessment

Guidance: level 1

:: Business process ::

_____ is the value to an enterprise which is derived from the techniques, procedures, and programs that implement and enhance the delivery of goods and services. _____ is one of the three components of structural capital, itself a component of intellectual capital. _____ can be seen as the value of processes to any entity, whether for profit or not-for profit, but is most commonly used in reference to for-profit entities.

Exam Probability: **Low**

12. *Answer choices:*

(see index for correct answer)

- a. Signavio
- b. Software ecosystem
- c. Communication-enabled business process
- d. Feasibility study

Guidance: level 1

:: Production economics ::

_____ is the joint use of a resource or space. It is also the process of dividing and distributing. In its narrow sense, it refers to joint or alternating use of inherently finite goods, such as a common pasture or a shared residence. Still more loosely, "_____" can actually mean giving something as an outright gift: for example, to "share" one's food really means to give some of it as a gift. _____ is a basic component of human interaction, and is responsible for strengthening social ties and ensuring a person's well-being.

13. *Answer choices:*

(see index for correct answer)

- a. Isocost
- b. Sharing
- c. Productivity Alpha
- d. Specialization

Guidance: level 1

:: Casting (manufacturing) ::

A _____ is a regularity in the world, man-made design, or abstract ideas. As such, the elements of a _____ repeat in a predictable manner. A geometric _____ is a kind of _____ formed of geometric shapes and typically repeated like a wallpaper design.

Exam Probability: **Low**

14. *Answer choices:*

(see index for correct answer)

- a. Entrainment defect
- b. Investment casting
- c. Dross

- d. Tundish

Guidance: level 1

:: Information technology management ::

_____ concerns a cycle of organizational activity: the acquisition of information from one or more sources, the custodianship and the distribution of that information to those who need it, and its ultimate disposition through archiving or deletion.

Exam Probability: **Low**

15. *Answer choices:*
(see index for correct answer)

- a. IT service management
- b. Software factory
- c. ISO/IEC 20000
- d. Business-to-business

Guidance: level 1

:: ::

_____ is a kind of action that occur as two or more objects have an effect upon one another. The idea of a two-way effect is essential in the concept of _____ , as opposed to a one-way causal effect. A closely related term is interconnectivity, which deals with the _____ s of _____ s within systems: combinations of many simple _____ s can lead to surprising emergent phenomena. _____ has different tailored meanings in various sciences. Changes can also involve _____ .

Exam Probability: **Low**

16. *Answer choices:*

(see index for correct answer)

- a. information systems assessment
- b. surface-level diversity
- c. open system
- d. levels of analysis

Guidance: level 1

:: Business planning ::

_____ is an organization's process of defining its strategy, or direction, and making decisions on allocating its resources to pursue this strategy. It may also extend to control mechanisms for guiding the implementation of the strategy. _____ became prominent in corporations during the 1960s and remains an important aspect of strategic management. It is executed by strategic planners or strategists, who involve many parties and research sources in their analysis of the organization and its relationship to the environment in which it competes.

Exam Probability: **Medium**

17. *Answer choices:*

(see index for correct answer)

- a. Exit planning
- b. Open Options Corporation
- c. Gap analysis
- d. Strategic planning

Guidance: level 1

:: Consortia ::

A _____ is an association of two or more individuals, companies, organizations or governments with the objective of participating in a common activity or pooling their resources for achieving a common goal.

Exam Probability: **High**

18. *Answer choices:*

(see index for correct answer)

- a. Open Data Center Alliance
- b. International Internet Preservation Consortium
- c. Aero Propulsion Alliance
- d. Bonyad

Guidance: level 1

:: Quality management ::

In quality management system, a _____ is a document developed by management to express the directive of the top management with respect to quality. _____ management is a strategic item.

Exam Probability: **High**

19. *Answer choices:*

(see index for correct answer)

- a. Bureau Veritas
- b. Quality policy
- c. Product quality risk in supply chain
- d. TL 9000

Guidance: level 1

:: Project management ::

A _____ is the approximation of the cost of a program, project, or operation. The _____ is the product of the cost estimating process. The _____ has a single total value and may have identifiable component values. A problem with a cost overrun can be avoided with a credible, reliable, and accurate _____ . A cost estimator is the professional who prepares _____ s. There are different types of cost estimators, whose title may be preceded by a modifier, such as building estimator, or electrical estimator, or chief estimator. Other professionals such as quantity surveyors and cost engineers may also prepare _____ s or contribute to _____ s. In the US, according to the Bureau of Labor Statistics, there were 185,400 cost estimators in 2010. There are around 75,000 professional quantity surveyors working in the UK.

Exam Probability: **High**

20. *Answer choices:*

(see index for correct answer)

- a. Legal matter management
- b. Cost estimate
- c. Cash flow diagram
- d. RationalPlan

Guidance: level 1

:: Information systems ::

_____ is the process of creating, sharing, using and managing the knowledge and information of an organisation. It refers to a multidisciplinary approach to achieving organisational objectives by making the best use of knowledge.

Exam Probability: **Medium**

21. *Answer choices:*

(see index for correct answer)

- a. Value sensitive design
- b. Censhare
- c. Information engineering
- d. Knowledge management

Guidance: level 1

:: Process management ::

When used in the context of communication networks, such as Ethernet or packet radio, _____ or network _____ is the rate of successful message delivery over a communication channel. The data these messages belong to may be delivered over a physical or logical link, or it can pass through a certain network node. _____ is usually measured in bits per second , and sometimes in data packets per second or data packets per time slot.

Exam Probability: **High**

22. *Answer choices:*

(see index for correct answer)

- a. Throughput
- b. YAWL
- c. Work domain analysis
- d. Proactive contracting

Guidance: level 1

:: Unit operations ::

_____ is a discipline of thermal engineering that concerns the generation, use, conversion, and exchange of thermal energy between physical systems. _____ is classified into various mechanisms, such as thermal conduction, thermal convection, thermal radiation, and transfer of energy by phase changes. Engineers also consider the transfer of mass of differing chemical species, either cold or hot, to achieve _____ . While these mechanisms have distinct characteristics, they often occur simultaneously in the same system.

Exam Probability: **Medium**

23. *Answer choices:*

(see index for correct answer)

- a. Heat transfer
- b. Solvent impregnated resin

- c. Settling
- d. Unit operation

Guidance: level 1

:: Project management ::

In economics, _____ is the assignment of available resources to various uses. In the context of an entire economy, resources can be allocated by various means, such as markets or central planning.

Exam Probability: **Low**

24. *Answer choices:*

(see index for correct answer)

- a. Effort management
- b. Project blog
- c. Hart Mason Index
- d. Resource allocation

Guidance: level 1

:: Unit operations ::

_____ is the process of separating the components or substances from a liquid mixture by using selective boiling and condensation. _____ may result in essentially complete separation , or it may be a partial separation that increases the concentration of selected components in the mixture. In either case, the process exploits differences in the volatility of the mixture's components. In industrial chemistry, _____ is a unit operation of practically universal importance, but it is a physical separation process, not a chemical reaction.

Exam Probability: **High**

25. *Answer choices:*

(see index for correct answer)

- a. Clearing factor
- b. Theoretical plate
- c. Separation process
- d. Unit Operations of Chemical Engineering

Guidance: level 1

:: Management ::

_____ is a term used in business and Information Technology to describe the in-depth process of capturing customer's expectations, preferences and aversions. Specifically, the _____ is a market research technique that produces a detailed set of customer wants and needs, organized into a hierarchical structure, and then prioritized in terms of relative importance and satisfaction with current alternatives. _____ studies typically consist of both qualitative and quantitative research steps. They are generally conducted at the start of any new product, process, or service design initiative in order to better understand the customer's wants and needs, and as the key input for new product definition, Quality Function Deployment , and the setting of detailed design specifications.

Exam Probability: **Medium**

26. *Answer choices:*

(see index for correct answer)

- a. Cross ownership
- b. Voice of the customer
- c. Investment control
- d. Organizational space

Guidance: level 1

:: Data management ::

_____ is the ability of a physical product to remain functional, without requiring excessive maintenance or repair, when faced with the challenges of normal operation over its design lifetime. There are several measures of _____ in use, including years of life, hours of use, and number of operational cycles. In economics, goods with a long usable life are referred to as durable goods.

Exam Probability: **Medium**

27. *Answer choices:*

(see index for correct answer)

- a. Durability
- b. PureXML
- c. Client-side persistent data
- d. Photo recovery

Guidance: level 1

:: Metal heat treatments ::

_____ is a group of industrial and metalworking processes used to alter the physical, and sometimes chemical, properties of a material. The most common application is metallurgical. Heat treatments are also used in the manufacture of many other materials, such as glass. Heat treatment involves the use of heating or chilling, normally to extreme temperatures, to achieve a desired result such as hardening or softening of a material. Heat treatment techniques include annealing, case hardening, precipitation strengthening, tempering, carburizing, normalizing and quenching. It is noteworthy that while the term heat treatment applies only to processes where the heating and cooling are done for the specific purpose of altering properties intentionally, heating and cooling often occur incidentally during other manufacturing processes such as hot forming or welding.

Exam Probability: **High**

28. *Answer choices:*

(see index for correct answer)

- a. Differential heat treatment
- b. Quench polish quench
- c. Heat treating
- d. Carbonitriding

Guidance: level 1

:: Project management ::

A _____ is a professional in the field of project management. _____ s have the responsibility of the planning, procurement and execution of a project, in any undertaking that has a defined scope, defined start and a defined finish; regardless of industry. _____ s are first point of contact for any issues or discrepancies arising from within the heads of various departments in an organization before the problem escalates to higher authorities. Project management is the responsibility of a _____ . This individual seldom participates directly in the activities that produce the end result, but rather strives to maintain the progress, mutual interaction and tasks of various parties in such a way that reduces the risk of overall failure, maximizes benefits, and minimizes costs.

Exam Probability: **Medium**

29. *Answer choices:*

(see index for correct answer)

- a. Bottleneck
- b. Stages of project finance
- c. Project manager
- d. IPMA

Guidance: level 1

:: Metrics ::

_____ is a computer model developed by the University of Idaho, that uses Landsat satellite data to compute and map evapotranspiration . _____ calculates ET as a residual of the surface energy balance, where ET is estimated by keeping account of total net short wave and long wave radiation at the vegetation or soil surface, the amount of heat conducted into soil, and the amount of heat convected into the air above the surface. The difference in these three terms represents the amount of energy absorbed during the conversion of liquid water to vapor, which is ET. _____ expresses near-surface temperature gradients used in heat convection as indexed functions of radio _____ surface temperature, thereby eliminating the need for absolutely accurate surface temperature and the need for air-temperature measurements.

Exam Probability: **High**

30. *Answer choices:*

(see index for correct answer)

- a. Neighbourhood unit
- b. METRIC
- c. Software metric
- d. Accommodation index

Guidance: level 1

:: Management accounting ::

_____ are costs that are not directly accountable to a cost object .
_____ may be either fixed or variable. _____ include administration, personnel and security costs. These are those costs which are not directly related to production. Some _____ may be overhead. But some overhead costs can be directly attributed to a project and are direct costs.

Exam Probability: **Medium**

31. *Answer choices:*

(see index for correct answer)

- a. Target costing
- b. Indirect costs
- c. Pre-determined overhead rate
- d. Operating profit margin

Guidance: level 1

:: Quality awards ::

The _____ recognizes U.S. organizations in the business, health care, education, and nonprofit sectors for performance excellence. The Baldrige Award is the only formal recognition of the performance excellence of both public and private U.S. organizations given by the President of the United States. It is administered by the Baldrige Performance Excellence Program, which is based at and managed by the National Institute of Standards and Technology , an agency of the U.S. Department of Commerce.

32. *Answer choices:*

(see index for correct answer)

- a. European Quality Award
- b. Rajiv Gandhi National Quality Award
- c. EFQM Excellence Award
- d. Deming Prize

Guidance: level 1

:: Management accounting ::

" _____ s are the structural determinants of the cost of an activity, reflecting any linkages or interrelationships that affect it". Therefore we could assume that the _____ s determine the cost behavior within the activities, reflecting the links that these have with other activities and relationships that affect them.

Exam Probability: **Low**

33. *Answer choices:*

(see index for correct answer)

- a. Cash and cash equivalents
- b. Cost driver

- c. Variance
- d. Average per-bit delivery cost

Guidance: level 1

:: Management ::

Business _____ is a discipline in operations management in which people use various methods to discover, model, analyze, measure, improve, optimize, and automate business processes. BPM focuses on improving corporate performance by managing business processes. Any combination of methods used to manage a company's business processes is BPM. Processes can be structured and repeatable or unstructured and variable. Though not required, enabling technologies are often used with BPM.

Exam Probability: **Low**

34. *Answer choices:*
(see index for correct answer)

- a. Risk management
- b. Security management
- c. Target culture
- d. Critical path method

Guidance: level 1

:: Project management ::

_____ is a process of setting goals, planning and/or controlling the organizing and leading the execution of any type of activity, such as.

Exam Probability: **Low**

35. *Answer choices:*
(see index for correct answer)

- a. Association for Project Management
- b. Site survey
- c. Rolling Wave planning
- d. Project Management Professional

Guidance: level 1

:: Information technology management ::

_____ is the discipline of engineering concerned with the principles and practice of product and service quality assurance and control. In the software development, it is the management, development, operation and maintenance of IT systems and enterprise architectures with a high quality standard.

Exam Probability: **Low**

36. *Answer choices:*

(see index for correct answer)

- a. Skills Framework for the Information Age
- b. IT asset management
- c. Information Lifecycle Management
- d. Storage virtualization

Guidance: level 1

:: Manufacturing ::

A _____ is an object used to extend the ability of an individual to modify features of the surrounding environment. Although many animals use simple _____ s, only human beings, whose use of stone _____ s dates back hundreds of millennia, use _____ s to make other _____ s. The set of _____ s needed to perform different tasks that are part of the same activity is called gear or equipment.

Exam Probability: **Low**

37. *Answer choices:*

(see index for correct answer)

- a. Gunsmith
- b. Molecular assembler
- c. Ppc cycle
- d. Component engineering

:: Quality control tools ::

A _____ is a type of diagram that represents an algorithm, workflow or process. _____ can also be defined as a diagramatic representation of an algorithm .

Exam Probability: **Medium**

38. *Answer choices:*

(see index for correct answer)

- a. Cause-and-effect diagram
- b. EWMA chart
- c. Flowchart
- d. Robustness validation

:: Industrial equipment ::

_____s are heat exchangers typically used to provide heat to the bottom of industrial distillation columns. They boil the liquid from the bottom of a distillation column to generate vapors which are returned to the column to drive the distillation separation. The heat supplied to the column by the _____ at the bottom of the column is removed by the condenser at the top of the column.

Exam Probability: **Low**

39. *Answer choices:*

(see index for correct answer)

- a. Separator
- b. Choke manifold
- c. Reboiler
- d. Material handling

Guidance: level 1

:: E-commerce ::

_____ is the activity of buying or selling of products on online services or over the Internet. Electronic commerce draws on technologies such as mobile commerce, electronic funds transfer, supply chain management, Internet marketing, online transaction processing, electronic data interchange , inventory management systems, and automated data collection systems.

Exam Probability: **Low**

40. *Answer choices:*

(see index for correct answer)

- a. Online Shopping in Bangladesh
- b. Buyhatke
- c. E-commerce
- d. Electronic trading

Guidance: level 1

:: Data management ::

_____ is an object-oriented program and library developed by CERN. It was originally designed for particle physics data analysis and contains several features specific to this field, but it is also used in other applications such as astronomy and data mining. The latest release is 6.16.00, as of 2018-11-14.

Exam Probability: **Low**

41. *Answer choices:*

(see index for correct answer)

- a. EU Open Data Portal
- b. Data independence
- c. Data migration
- d. ROOT

:: Management ::

_____ is the process of thinking about the activities required to achieve a desired goal. It is the first and foremost activity to achieve desired results. It involves the creation and maintenance of a plan, such as psychological aspects that require conceptual skills. There are even a couple of tests to measure someone's capability of _____ well. As such, _____ is a fundamental property of intelligent behavior. An important further meaning, often just called " _____ " is the legal context of permitted building developments.

Exam Probability: **Medium**

42. *Answer choices:*

(see index for correct answer)

- a. Planning
- b. Vendor relationship management
- c. Force-field analysis
- d. Environmental stewardship

Guidance: level 1

:: Production and manufacturing ::

_____ is a comprehensive and rigorous industrial process by which a previously sold, leased, used, worn or non-functional product or part is returned to a 'like-new' or 'better-than-new' condition, from both a quality and performance perspective, through a controlled, reproducible and sustainable process.

Exam Probability: **High**

43. *Answer choices:*

(see index for correct answer)

- a. Remanufacturing
- b. Plant layout study
- c. Resource Breakdown
- d. Transfer line

Guidance: level 1

:: ::

_____ refers to a business or organization attempting to acquire goods or services to accomplish its goals. Although there are several organizations that attempt to set standards in the _____ process, processes can vary greatly between organizations. Typically the word " _____ " is not used interchangeably with the word "procurement", since procurement typically includes expediting, supplier quality, and transportation and logistics in addition to _____ .

44. *Answer choices:*

(see index for correct answer)

- a. Sarbanes-Oxley act of 2002
- b. empathy
- c. information systems assessment
- d. personal values

Guidance: level 1

:: Quality management ::

_____ ensures that an organization, product or service is consistent. It has four main components: quality planning, quality assurance, quality control and quality improvement. _____ is focused not only on product and service quality, but also on the means to achieve it. _____ , therefore, uses quality assurance and control of processes as well as products to achieve more consistent quality.What a customer wants and is willing to pay for it determines quality. It is written or unwritten commitment to a known or unknown consumer in the market . Thus, quality can be defined as fitness for intended use or, in other words, how well the product performs its intended function

45. *Answer choices:*

(see index for correct answer)

- a. Good Clinical Laboratory Practice
- b. Indian Register Quality Systems
- c. Quality management
- d. Quality Management Maturity Grid

Guidance: level 1

:: Marketing ::

_____ or stock control can be broadly defined as "the activity of checking a shop's stock." However, a more focused definition takes into account the more science-based, methodical practice of not only verifying a business` inventory but also focusing on the many related facets of inventory management "within an organisation to meet the demand placed upon that business economically." Other facets of _____ include supply chain management, production control, financial flexibility, and customer satisfaction. At the root of _____, however, is the _____ problem, which involves determining when to order, how much to order, and the logistics of those decisions.

Exam Probability: **High**

46. *Answer choices:*
(see index for correct answer)

- a. History of marketing
- b. Inventory control
- c. customer-perceived value
- d. Impulse buying

:: Commercial item transport and distribution ::

_____ in logistics and supply chain management is an organization's use of third-party businesses to outsource elements of its distribution, warehousing, and fulfillment services.

Exam Probability: **Low**

47. *Answer choices:*

(see index for correct answer)

- a. Inland navigation
- b. Third-party logistics
- c. Cabotage
- d. Interchange

:: Information technology management ::

The term _____ is used to refer to periods when a system is unavailable. _____ or outage duration refers to a period of time that a system fails to provide or perform its primary function. Reliability, availability, recovery, and unavailability are related concepts. The unavailability is the proportion of a time-span that a system is unavailable or offline. This is usually a result of the system failing to function because of an unplanned event, or because of routine maintenance .

Exam Probability: **High**

48. *Answer choices:*

(see index for correct answer)

- a. Information technology consulting
- b. User account policy
- c. IT portfolio management
- d. Downtime

Guidance: level 1

:: Costs ::

In process improvement efforts, _____ or cost of quality is a means to quantify the total cost of quality-related efforts and deficiencies. It was first described by Armand V. Feigenbaum in a 1956 Harvard Business Review article.

Exam Probability: **Medium**

49. *Answer choices:*

(see index for correct answer)

- a. Cost of products sold
- b. Joint cost
- c. Cost curve
- d. Quality costs

Guidance: level 1

:: Infographics ::

The _____ is a form used to collect data in real time at the location where the data is generated. The data it captures can be quantitative or qualitative. When the information is quantitative, the _____ is sometimes called a tally sheet.

Exam Probability: **Low**

50. *Answer choices:*

(see index for correct answer)

- a. Surya Majapahit
- b. Information sign
- c. Hazard symbol
- d. Check sheet

:: ::

Catalysis is the process of increasing the rate of a chemical reaction by adding a substance known as a _____ , which is not consumed in the catalyzed reaction and can continue to act repeatedly. Because of this, only very small amounts of _____ are required to alter the reaction rate in principle.

Exam Probability: **Medium**

51. *Answer choices:*

(see index for correct answer)

- a. deep-level diversity
- b. Catalyst
- c. open system
- d. hierarchical

:: ::

A _____ is a covering that is applied to the surface of an object, usually referred to as the substrate. The purpose of applying the _____ may be decorative, functional, or both. The _____ itself may be an all-over _____ , completely covering the substrate, or it may only cover parts of the substrate. An example of all of these types of _____ is a product label on many drinks bottles- one side has an all-over functional _____ and the other side has one or more decorative _____ s in an appropriate pattern to form the words and images.

Exam Probability: **Medium**

52. *Answer choices:*

(see index for correct answer)

- a. similarity-attraction theory
- b. cultural
- c. co-culture
- d. process perspective

Guidance: level 1

:: Production economics ::

In economics and related disciplines, a _____ is a cost in making any economic trade when participating in a market.

Exam Probability: **Low**

53. *Answer choices:*

(see index for correct answer)

- a. Average fixed cost
- b. Specialization
- c. Marginal rate of technical substitution
- d. Product pipeline

Guidance: level 1

:: Industrial engineering ::

The _____ is the design of any task that aims to describe or explain the variation of information under conditions that are hypothesized to reflect the variation. The term is generally associated with experiments in which the design introduces conditions that directly affect the variation, but may also refer to the design of quasi-experiments, in which natural conditions that influence the variation are selected for observation.

Exam Probability: **Low**

54. *Answer choices:*

(see index for correct answer)

- a. Design of experiments
- b. Service quality
- c. Material flow
- d. Lang factor

:: Supply chain management terms ::

In business and finance, _____ is a system of organizations, people, activities, information, and resources involved inmoving a product or service from supplier to customer. _____ activities involve the transformation of natural resources, raw materials, and components into a finished product that is delivered to the end customer. In sophisticated _____ systems, used products may re-enter the _____ at any point where residual value is recyclable. _____ s link value chains.

Exam Probability: **Medium**

55. *Answer choices:*

(see index for correct answer)

- a. Supply chain
- b. Supply-chain management
- c. Consumable
- d. Cool Chain Quality Indicator

:: ::

An _____ is a company that produces parts and equipment that may be marketed by another manufacturer. For example, Foxconn, a Taiwanese electronics contract manufacturing company, which produces a variety of parts and equipment for companies such as Apple Inc., Dell, Google, Huawei, Nintendo, etc., is the largest OEM company in the world by both scale and revenue.

Exam Probability: **Low**

56. *Answer choices:*
(see index for correct answer)

- a. functional perspective
- b. hierarchical
- c. open system
- d. levels of analysis

Guidance: level 1

:: Metalworking ::

A _____ is a round object with various uses. It is used in _____ games, where the play of the game follows the state of the _____ as it is hit, kicked or thrown by players. _____ s can also be used for simpler activities, such as catch or juggling. _____ s made from hard-wearing materials are used in engineering applications to provide very low friction bearings, known as _____ bearings. Black-powder weapons use stone and metal _____ s as projectiles.

57. *Answer choices:*

- a. Slotted angle
- b. Metal injection molding
- c. Indo-MIM
- d. Powder metallurgy

Guidance: level 1

:: Commercial item transport and distribution ::

In commerce, supply-chain management , the management of the flow of goods and services, involves the movement and storage of raw materials, of work-in-process inventory, and of finished goods from point of origin to point of consumption. Interconnected or interlinked networks, channels and node businesses combine in the provision of products and services required by end customers in a supply chain. Supply-chain management has been defined as the "design, planning, execution, control, and monitoring of supply-chain activities with the objective of creating net value, building a competitive infrastructure, leveraging worldwide logistics, synchronizing supply with demand and measuring performance globally."SCM practice draws heavily from the areas of industrial engineering, systems engineering, operations management, logistics, procurement, information technology, and marketing and strives for an integrated approach. Marketing channels play an important role in supply-chain management. Current research in supply-chain management is concerned with topics related to sustainability and risk management, among others. Some suggest that the "people dimension" of SCM, ethical issues, internal integration, transparency/visibility, and human capital/talent management are topics that have, so far, been underrepresented on the research agenda.

Exam Probability: **Medium**

58. *Answer choices:*

(see index for correct answer)

- a. Unit load
- b. Slip sheet
- c. E2open
- d. Supply chain management

Guidance: level 1

:: Procurement ::

A _____ is a standard business process whose purpose is to invite suppliers into a bidding process to bid on specific products or services. RfQ generally means the same thing as Call for bids and Invitation for bid .

Exam Probability: **Medium**

59. *Answer choices:*

(see index for correct answer)

- a. Inverted Sourcing
- b. Request for quotation
- c. FAPPO
- d. Procure-to-pay

Guidance: level 1

Commerce

Commerce relates to "the exchange of goods and services, especially on a large scale." It includes legal, economic, political, social, cultural and technological systems that operate in any country or internationally.

:: ::

An _____ is a contingent motivator. Traditional _____ s are extrinsic motivators which reward actions to yield a desired outcome. The effectiveness of traditional _____ s has changed as the needs of Western society have evolved. While the traditional _____ model is effective when there is a defined procedure and goal for a task, Western society started to require a higher volume of critical thinkers, so the traditional model became less effective. Institutions are now following a trend in implementing strategies that rely on intrinsic motivations rather than the extrinsic motivations that the traditional _____ s foster.

Exam Probability: **High**

1. *Answer choices:*

(see index for correct answer)

- a. Incentive
- b. levels of analysis
- c. surface-level diversity
- d. Sarbanes-Oxley act of 2002

Guidance: level 1

:: E-commerce ::

E-commerce is the activity of buying or selling of products on online services or over the Internet. _____ draws on technologies such as mobile commerce, electronic funds transfer, supply chain management, Internet marketing, online transaction processing, electronic data interchange , inventory management systems, and automated data collection systems.

2. *Answer choices:*

- a. Public eProcurement
- b. Cart32
- c. GS1 Sweden
- d. Address Verification System

Guidance: level 1

:: Goods ::

In most contexts, the concept of _____ denotes the conduct that should be preferred when posed with a choice between possible actions. _____ is generally considered to be the opposite of evil, and is of interest in the study of morality, ethics, religion and philosophy. The specific meaning and etymology of the term and its associated translations among ancient and contemporary languages show substantial variation in its inflection and meaning depending on circumstances of place, history, religious, or philosophical context.

Exam Probability: **Medium**

3. *Answer choices:*

- a. Experience good
- b. Complementary good
- c. Neutral good
- d. Good

Guidance: level 1

:: Real estate ::

_____ s serve several societal needs – primarily as shelter from weather, security, living space, privacy, to store belongings, and to comfortably live and work. A _____ as a shelter represents a physical division of the human habitat and the outside .

Exam Probability: **Low**

4. *Answer choices:*

(see index for correct answer)

- a. Owner-occupier
- b. Discount brokerage
- c. Building
- d. Healthcare real estate

Guidance: level 1

:: Production economics ::

In economics, _____ is the change in the total cost that arises when the quantity produced is incremented by one unit; that is, it is the cost of producing one more unit of a good. Intuitively, _____ at each level of production includes the cost of any additional inputs required to produce the next unit. At each level of production and time period being considered, _____ s include all costs that vary with the level of production, whereas other costs that do not vary with production are fixed and thus have no _____ . For example, the _____ of producing an automobile will generally include the costs of labor and parts needed for the additional automobile but not the fixed costs of the factory that have already been incurred. In practice, marginal analysis is segregated into short and long-run cases, so that, over the long run, all costs become marginal. Where there are economies of scale, prices set at _____ will fail to cover total costs, thus requiring a subsidy. _____ pricing is not a matter of merely lowering the general level of prices with the aid of a subsidy; with or without subsidy it calls for a drastic restructuring of pricing practices, with opportunities for very substantial improvements in efficiency at critical points.

Exam Probability: **High**

5. *Answer choices:*

(see index for correct answer)

- a. Transaction cost
- b. Returns to scale
- c. Division of work
- d. Marginal cost

Guidance: level 1

:: Commercial item transport and distribution ::

A _____ in common law countries is a person or company that transports goods or people for any person or company and that is responsible for any possible loss of the goods during transport. A _____ offers its services to the general public under license or authority provided by a regulatory body. The regulatory body has usually been granted "ministerial authority" by the legislation that created it. The regulatory body may create, interpret, and enforce its regulations upon the _____ with independence and finality, as long as it acts within the bounds of the enabling legislation.

Exam Probability: **Medium**

6. *Answer choices:*
(see index for correct answer)

- a. Ship transport
- b. Courier software
- c. Common carrier
- d. Port centric logistics

Guidance: level 1

:: Consortia ::

A _____ is an association of two or more individuals, companies, organizations or governments with the objective of participating in a common activity or pooling their resources for achieving a common goal.

Exam Probability: **Medium**

7. *Answer choices:*

(see index for correct answer)

- a. TranSys
- b. RVU Alliance
- c. Meritas
- d. Consortium

Guidance: level 1

:: Direct marketing ::

_____ is a form of advertising where organizations communicate directly to customers through a variety of media including cell phone text messaging, email, websites, online adverts, database marketing, fliers, catalog distribution, promotional letters, targeted television, newspapers, magazine advertisements, and outdoor advertising. Among practitioners, it is also known as direct response marketing.

Exam Probability: **High**

8. *Answer choices:*

(see index for correct answer)

- a. Stream Energy
- b. The Cobra Group
- c. Publishers Clearing House
- d. Ed Valenti

Guidance: level 1

:: Marketing ::

_____ or stock is the goods and materials that a business holds for the ultimate goal of resale .

Exam Probability: **Low**

9. *Answer choices:*

(see index for correct answer)

- a. Inventory
- b. Predatory pricing
- c. Bass diffusion model
- d. Loyalty program

Guidance: level 1

:: Regulators ::

A _____ is a public authority or government agency responsible for exercising autonomous authority over some area of human activity in a regulatory or supervisory capacity. An independent _____ is a _____ that is independent from other branches or arms of the government.

Exam Probability: **High**

10. *Answer choices:*

(see index for correct answer)

- a. Independent regulatory agencies in Turkey
- b. Energy and Utilities Board
- c. Alberta Energy Regulator
- d. Crofters Commission

Guidance: level 1

:: ::

In international relations, _____ is – from the perspective of governments – a voluntary transfer of resources from one country to another.

Exam Probability: **Medium**

11. *Answer choices:*

(see index for correct answer)

- a. process perspective
- b. Aid
- c. corporate values
- d. Sarbanes-Oxley act of 2002

Guidance: level 1

:: ::

In law, an _____ is the process in which cases are reviewed, where parties request a formal change to an official decision. _____ s function both as a process for error correction as well as a process of clarifying and interpreting law. Although appellate courts have existed for thousands of years, common law countries did not incorporate an affirmative right to _____ into their jurisprudence until the 19th century.

Exam Probability: **Medium**

12. *Answer choices:*

(see index for correct answer)

- a. Character
- b. levels of analysis
- c. hierarchical
- d. Appeal

:: ::

In mathematics, computer science and operations research, mathematical optimization or mathematical programming is the selection of a best element from some set of available alternatives.

Exam Probability: **Low**

13. *Answer choices:*

(see index for correct answer)

- a. Character
- b. cultural
- c. co-culture
- d. Optimum

:: Supply chain management ::

_____ is a variable pricing strategy, based on understanding, anticipating and influencing consumer behavior in order to maximize revenue or profits from a fixed, time-limited resource . As a specific, inventory-focused branch of revenue management, _____ involves strategic control of inventory to sell the right product to the right customer at the right time for the right price. This process can result in price discrimination, in which customers consuming identical goods or services are charged different prices. _____ is a large revenue generator for several major industries; Robert Crandall, former Chairman and CEO of American Airlines, gave _____ its name and has called it "the single most important technical development in transportation management since we entered deregulation."

Exam Probability: **Low**

14. *Answer choices:*

- a. Reverse auction
- b. Netchain analysis
- c. Demand sensing
- d. Yield management

Guidance: level 1

:: Information retrieval ::

_____ is a technique used by recommender systems. _____ has two senses, a narrow one and a more general one.

15. *Answer choices:*

(see index for correct answer)

- a. MAREC
- b. ChemRefer
- c. DtSearch
- d. Collaborative filtering

Guidance: level 1

:: ::

Walter Elias Disney was an American entrepreneur, animator, voice actor and film producer. A pioneer of the American animation industry, he introduced several developments in the production of cartoons. As a film producer, Disney holds the record for most Academy Awards earned by an individual, having won 22 Oscars from 59 nominations. He was presented with two Golden Globe Special Achievement Awards and an Emmy Award, among other honors. Several of his films are included in the National Film Registry by the Library of Congress.

Exam Probability: **High**

16. *Answer choices:*

(see index for correct answer)

- a. Walt Disney

- b. process perspective
- c. information systems assessment
- d. imperative

Guidance: level 1

:: Management ::

The term _____ refers to measures designed to increase the degree of autonomy and self-determination in people and in communities in order to enable them to represent their interests in a responsible and self-determined way, acting on their own authority. It is the process of becoming stronger and more confident, especially in controlling one's life and claiming one's rights. _____ as action refers both to the process of self- _____ and to professional support of people, which enables them to overcome their sense of powerlessness and lack of influence, and to recognize and use their resources. To do work with power.

Exam Probability: **Low**

17. *Answer choices:*

(see index for correct answer)

- a. Project cost management
- b. Line manager
- c. Empowerment
- d. Place management

Guidance: level 1

:: Banking ::

A _____ is a financial institution that accepts deposits from the public and creates credit. Lending activities can be performed either directly or indirectly through capital markets. Due to their importance in the financial stability of a country, _____ s are highly regulated in most countries. Most nations have institutionalized a system known as fractional reserve _____ ing under which _____ s hold liquid assets equal to only a portion of their current liabilities. In addition to other regulations intended to ensure liquidity, _____ s are generally subject to minimum capital requirements based on an international set of capital standards, known as the Basel Accords.

Exam Probability: **High**

18. *Answer choices:*

(see index for correct answer)

- a. Annual percentage rate
- b. Joint account
- c. Monetary base
- d. Narrow banking

Guidance: level 1

:: ::

_____ is getting a diploma or academic degree or the ceremony that is sometimes associated with it, in which students become graduates. The date of _____ is often called _____ day. The _____ ceremony itself is also called commencement, convocation or invocation.

Exam Probability: **Medium**

19. *Answer choices:*

(see index for correct answer)

- a. hierarchical
- b. hierarchical perspective
- c. Graduation
- d. interpersonal communication

Guidance: level 1

:: Debt ::

_____ , in finance and economics, is payment from a borrower or deposit-taking financial institution to a lender or depositor of an amount above repayment of the principal sum , at a particular rate. It is distinct from a fee which the borrower may pay the lender or some third party. It is also distinct from dividend which is paid by a company to its shareholders from its profit or reserve, but not at a particular rate decided beforehand, rather on a pro rata basis as a share in the reward gained by risk taking entrepreneurs when the revenue earned exceeds the total costs.

20. *Answer choices:*

(see index for correct answer)

- a. Debt-lag
- b. Interest
- c. Borrowing base
- d. Asset protection

Guidance: level 1

:: ::

A _____ is any person who contracts to acquire an asset in return for some form of consideration.

21. *Answer choices:*

(see index for correct answer)

- a. Character
- b. information systems assessment
- c. functional perspective
- d. interpersonal communication

:: Auctioneering ::

A _____ is one of several similar kinds of auctions. Most commonly, it means an auction in which the auctioneer begins with a high asking price, and lowers it until some participant accepts the price, or it reaches a predetermined reserve price. This has also been called a clock auction or open-outcry descending-price auction. This type of auction is good for auctioning goods quickly, since a sale never requires more than one bid. Strategically, it's similar to a first-price sealed-bid auction.

Exam Probability: **Medium**

22. *Answer choices:*

(see index for correct answer)

- a. Estate sale
- b. National Auctioneers Association
- c. Dutch auction
- d. Vehicle impoundment

:: Stock market ::

The _____ of a corporation is all of the shares into which ownership of the corporation is divided. In American English, the shares are commonly known as " _____ s". A single share of the _____ represents fractional ownership of the corporation in proportion to the total number of shares. This typically entitles the _____ holder to that fraction of the company's earnings, proceeds from liquidation of assets , or voting power, often dividing these up in proportion to the amount of money each _____ holder has invested. Not all _____ is necessarily equal, as certain classes of _____ may be issued for example without voting rights, with enhanced voting rights, or with a certain priority to receive profits or liquidation proceeds before or after other classes of shareholders.

Exam Probability: **Low**

23. *Answer choices:*

(see index for correct answer)

- a. Stub
- b. Rogue trader
- c. Stock
- d. Big boy letter

Guidance: level 1

:: ::

A trade fair is an exhibition organized so that companies in a specific industry can showcase and demonstrate their latest products and services, meet with industry partners and customers, study activities of rivals, and examine recent market trends and opportunities. In contrast to consumer fairs, only some trade fairs are open to the public, while others can only be attended by company representatives and members of the press, therefore _____ s are classified as either "public" or "trade only". A few fairs are hybrids of the two; one example is the Frankfurt Book Fair, which is trade only for its first three days and open to the general public on its final two days. They are held on a continuing basis in virtually all markets and normally attract companies from around the globe. For example, in the U.S., there are currently over 10,000 _____ s held every year, and several online directories have been established to help organizers, attendees, and marketers identify appropriate events.

Exam Probability: **High**

24. *Answer choices:*

(see index for correct answer)

- a. Trade show
- b. process perspective
- c. functional perspective
- d. Character

Guidance: level 1

:: Business law ::

A _____ is an arrangement where parties, known as partners, agree to cooperate to advance their mutual interests. The partners in a _____ may be individuals, businesses, interest-based organizations, schools, governments or combinations. Organizations may partner to increase the likelihood of each achieving their mission and to amplify their reach. A _____ may result in issuing and holding equity or may be only governed by a contract.

Exam Probability: **High**

25. *Answer choices:*

(see index for correct answer)

- a. Statutory authority
- b. Tacit relocation
- c. Independent contractor
- d. Partnership

Guidance: level 1

:: Business terms ::

_____ ning is an organization's process of defining its strategy, or direction, and making decisions on allocating its resources to pursue this strategy. It may also extend to control mechanisms for guiding the implementation of the strategy. _____ ning became prominent in corporations during the 1960s and remains an important aspect of strategic management. It is executed by _____ ners or strategists, who involve many parties and research sources in their analysis of the organization and its relationship to the environment in which it competes.

26. *Answer choices:*

(see index for correct answer)

- a. Owner Controlled Insurance Program
- b. organizational capital
- c. Strategic plan
- d. noncommercial

Guidance: level 1

:: Management accounting ::

In economics, _____ s, indirect costs or overheads are business expenses that are not dependent on the level of goods or services produced by the business. They tend to be time-related, such as interest or rents being paid per month, and are often referred to as overhead costs. This is in contrast to variable costs, which are volume-related and unknown at the beginning of the accounting year. For a simple example, such as a bakery, the monthly rent for the baking facilities, and the monthly payments for the security system and basic phone line are _____ s, as they do not change according to how much bread the bakery produces and sells. On the other hand, the wage costs of the bakery are variable, as the bakery will have to hire more workers if the production of bread increases. Economists reckon _____ as a entry barrier for new entrepreneurs.

27. *Answer choices:*

(see index for correct answer)

- a. Overhead
- b. Indirect costs
- c. Fixed cost
- d. Certified Management Accountant

Guidance: level 1

:: ::

A _____ is a sworn body of people convened to render an impartial verdict officially submitted to them by a court, or to set a penalty or judgment. Modern juries tend to be found in courts to ascertain the guilt or lack thereof in a crime. In Anglophone jurisdictions, the verdict may be guilty or not guilty . The old institution of grand juries still exists in some places, particularly the United States, to investigate whether enough evidence of a crime exists to bring someone to trial.

Exam Probability: **High**

28. *Answer choices:*

(see index for correct answer)

- a. Jury
- b. interpersonal communication
- c. hierarchical perspective

- d. functional perspective

:: ::

_____ is a type of government support for the citizens of that society. _____ may be provided to people of any income level, as with social security , but it is usually intended to ensure that the poor can meet their basic human needs such as food and shelter. _____ attempts to provide poor people with a minimal level of well-being, usually either a free- or a subsidized-supply of certain goods and social services, such as healthcare, education, and vocational training.

Exam Probability: **Medium**

29. *Answer choices:*

(see index for correct answer)

- a. information systems assessment
- b. corporate values
- c. levels of analysis
- d. Welfare

Guidance: level 1

:: Dot-com bubble ::

_____ is an internet portal launched in 1995 that provides a variety of content including news and weather, a metasearch engine, a web-based email, instant messaging, stock quotes, and a customizable user homepage. It is currently operated by IAC Applications of IAC, and _____ Networks. In the U.S., the main _____ site has long been a personal start page called My _____ . _____ also operates an e-mail service, although it is no longer open for new customers.

Exam Probability: **Medium**

30. *Answer choices:*

(see index for correct answer)

- a. Epidemic Marketing
- b. Lycos
- c. Excite
- d. @Home Network

Guidance: level 1

:: Cash flow ::

_____ s are narrowly interconnected with the concepts of value, interest rate and liquidity. A _____ that shall happen on a future day tN can be transformed into a _____ of the same value in t0.

Exam Probability: **High**

31. *Answer choices:*

- a. Cash flow forecasting
- b. Cash flow
- c. Cash flow loan
- d. Discounted payback period

Guidance: level 1

:: Retailing ::

A _____ or trolley , also known by a variety of other names, is a cart supplied by a shop, especially supermarkets, for use by customers inside the shop for transport of merchandise to the checkout counter during shopping. In many cases customers can then also use the cart to transport their purchased goods to their vehicles, but some carts are designed to prevent them from leaving the shop.

Exam Probability: **Low**

32. *Answer choices:*

- a. Shopping cart
- b. Used bookstore
- c. Shopping hours
- d. Hardware store

:: Behavior modification ::

In psychotherapy and mental health, _____ has a positive sense of empowering individuals, or a negative sense of encouraging dysfunctional behavior.

Exam Probability: **High**

33. *Answer choices:*

(see index for correct answer)

- a. Enabling
- b. Thought stopping

:: Land value taxation ::

_____ , sometimes referred to as dry _____ , is the solid surface of Earth that is not permanently covered by water. The vast majority of human activity throughout history has occurred in _____ areas that support agriculture, habitat, and various natural resources. Some life forms have developed from predecessor species that lived in bodies of water.

34. *Answer choices:*

(see index for correct answer)

- a. Prosper Australia
- b. Lands Valuation Appeal Court
- c. Land
- d. Georgism

Guidance: level 1

:: Auctioneering ::

An _____ is a process of buying and selling goods or services by offering them up for bid, taking bids, and then selling the item to the highest bidder. The open ascending price _____ is arguably the most common form of _____ in use today. Participants bid openly against one another, with each subsequent bid required to be higher than the previous bid. An _____ eer may announce prices, bidders may call out their bids themselves, or bids may be submitted electronically with the highest current bid publicly displayed. In a Dutch _____ , the _____ eer begins with a high asking price for some quantity of like items; the price is lowered until a participant is willing to accept the _____ eer`s price for some quantity of the goods in the lot or until the seller`s reserve price is met. While _____ s are most associated in the public imagination with the sale of antiques, paintings, rare collectibles and expensive wines, _____ s are also used for commodities, livestock, radio spectrum and used cars. In economic theory, an _____ may refer to any mechanism or set of trading rules for exchange.

35. *Answer choices:*

(see index for correct answer)

- a. Bid shading
- b. Public auction
- c. Auction
- d. Online trading community

Guidance: level 1

:: Income ::

_____ is the application of disciplined analytics that predict consumer behaviour at the micro-market levels and optimize product availability and price to maximize revenue growth. The primary aim of _____ is selling the right product to the right customer at the right time for the right price and with the right pack. The essence of this discipline is in understanding customers` perception of product value and accurately aligning product prices, placement and availability with each customer segment.

Exam Probability: **Medium**

36. *Answer choices:*

(see index for correct answer)

- a. Imputed income

- b. Revenue management
- c. Aggregate expenditure
- d. National average salary

Guidance: level 1

:: Marketing by medium ::

_____ , also called online marketing or Internet advertising or web advertising, is a form of marketing and advertising which uses the Internet to deliver promotional marketing messages to consumers. Many consumers find _____ disruptive and have increasingly turned to ad blocking for a variety of reasons. When software is used to do the purchasing, it is known as programmatic advertising.

Exam Probability: **High**

37. *Answer choices:*

(see index for correct answer)

- a. Growth hacking
- b. Online advertising
- c. Social marketing intelligence
- d. New media marketing

Guidance: level 1

:: ::

_____ characterises the behaviour of a system or model whose components interact in multiple ways and follow local rules, meaning there is no reasonable higher instruction to define the various possible interactions.

Exam Probability: **High**

38. *Answer choices:*

(see index for correct answer)

- a. Complexity
- b. imperative
- c. personal values
- d. information systems assessment

Guidance: level 1

:: ::

_____ is the provision of service to customers before, during and after a purchase. The perception of success of such interactions is dependent on employees "who can adjust themselves to the personality of the guest". _____ concerns the priority an organization assigns to _____ relative to components such as product innovation and pricing. In this sense, an organization that values good _____ may spend more money in training employees than the average organization or may proactively interview customers for feedback.

39. *Answer choices:*

(see index for correct answer)

- a. functional perspective
- b. Customer service
- c. similarity-attraction theory
- d. Character

Guidance: level 1

:: Packaging ::

In work place, _____ or job _____ means good ranking with the hypothesized conception of requirements of a role. There are two types of job _____ s: contextual and task. Task _____ is related to cognitive ability while contextual _____ is dependent upon personality. Task _____ are behavioral roles that are recognized in job descriptions and by remuneration systems, they are directly related to organizational _____ , whereas, contextual _____ are value based and additional behavioral roles that are not recognized in job descriptions and covered by compensation; they are extra roles that are indirectly related to organizational _____ .
Citizenship _____ like contextual _____ means a set of individual activity/contribution that supports the organizational culture.

Exam Probability: **Low**

40. *Answer choices:*

(see index for correct answer)

- a. Vacuum packing
- b. Matchbox
- c. Performance
- d. ISPM 15

Guidance: level 1

:: ::

_____ is both a research area and a practical skill encompassing the ability of an individual or organization to "lead" or guide other individuals, teams, or entire organizations. Specialist literature debates various viewpoints, contrasting Eastern and Western approaches to _____ , and also United States versus European approaches. U.S. academic environments define _____ as "a process of social influence in which a person can enlist the aid and support of others in the accomplishment of a common task".

Exam Probability: **High**

41. *Answer choices:*

(see index for correct answer)

- a. Leadership
- b. process perspective
- c. cultural
- d. personal values

:: Human resource management ::

_____ are the people who make up the workforce of an organization, business sector, or economy. "Human capital" is sometimes used synonymously with " _____ ", although human capital typically refers to a narrower effect . Likewise, other terms sometimes used include manpower, talent, labor, personnel, or simply people.

Exam Probability: **Low**

42. *Answer choices:*

(see index for correct answer)

- a. Succession planning
- b. Organizational culture
- c. Job knowledge
- d. E-HRM

:: Business ethics ::

_____ is a type of harassment technique that relates to a sexual nature and the unwelcome or inappropriate promise of rewards in exchange for sexual favors. _____ includes a range of actions from mild transgressions to sexual abuse or assault. Harassment can occur in many different social settings such as the workplace, the home, school, churches, etc. Harassers or victims may be of any gender.

Exam Probability: **Low**

43. *Answer choices:*

(see index for correct answer)

- a. Sustainability Accounting Standards Board
- b. Anatomy of Greed
- c. Accounting scandals
- d. Sexual harassment

Guidance: level 1

:: ::

In marketing jargon, product lining is offering several related products for sale individually. Unlike product bundling, where several products are combined into one group, which is then offered for sale as a units, product lining involves offering the products for sale separately. A line can comprise related products of various sizes, types, colors, qualities, or prices. Line depth refers to the number of subcategories a category has. Line consistency refers to how closely related the products that make up the line are. Line vulnerability refers to the percentage of sales or profits that are derived from only a few products in the line.

Exam Probability: **Low**

44. *Answer choices:*

(see index for correct answer)

- a. levels of analysis
- b. Product mix
- c. corporate values
- d. empathy

Guidance: level 1

:: Workplace ::

_____ is asystematic determination of a subject's merit, worth and significance, using criteria governed by a set of standards. It can assist an organization, program, design, project or any other intervention or initiative to assess any aim, realisable concept/proposal, or any alternative, to help in decision-making; or to ascertain the degree of achievement or value in regard to the aim and objectives and results of any such action that has been completed. The primary purpose of _____ , in addition to gaining insight into prior or existing initiatives, is to enable reflection and assist in the identification of future change.

Exam Probability: **Medium**

45. *Answer choices:*

(see index for correct answer)

- a. Work motivation
- b. Workplace friendship
- c. Evaluation
- d. Micromanagement

Guidance: level 1

:: Price fixing convictions ::

_____ AG is a German multinational conglomerate company headquartered in Berlin and Munich and the largest industrial manufacturing company in Europe with branch offices abroad.

Exam Probability: **Low**

46. *Answer choices:*

(see index for correct answer)

- a. Siemens
- b. Northwest Airlines
- c. SK Foods
- d. Asahi Glass Co.

Guidance: level 1

:: E-commerce ::

_____ , cybersecurity or information technology security is the
protection of computer systems from theft or damage to their hardware, software
or electronic data, as well as from disruption or misdirection of the services
they provide.

Exam Probability: **Medium**

47. *Answer choices:*

(see index for correct answer)

- a. Electronic Commerce Directive
- b. Mobile ticketing
- c. EPages

- d. Donna Hoffman

:: ::

According to the philosopher Piyush Mathur , "Tangibility is the property that a phenomenon exhibits if it has and/or transports mass and/or energy and/or momentum".

Exam Probability: **Low**

48. *Answer choices:*

- a. imperative
- b. Tangible
- c. hierarchical perspective
- d. Character

:: Dot-com bubble ::

Yahoo! _____ was a web hosting service. It was founded in November 1994 by David Bohnett and John Rezner, and was called Beverly Hills Internet for a very short time before being named _____ .

49. *Answer choices:*

(see index for correct answer)

- a. GeoCities
- b. Cyberian Outpost
- c. E-Dreams
- d. Dot-com bubble

Guidance: level 1

:: Auctioneering ::

Unlike sealed-bid auctions , an _____ is "open" or fully transparent, as the identity of all bidders is disclosed to each other during the auction. More generally, an auction mechanism is considered "English" if it involves an iterative process of adjusting the price in a direction that is unfavorable to the bidders . In contrast, a Dutch auction would adjust the price in a direction that favored the bidders .

50. *Answer choices:*

(see index for correct answer)

- a. Call for bids
- b. Chinese auction
- c. Bidding fee auction
- d. English auction

Guidance: level 1

:: Management accounting ::

_____ s are costs that change as the quantity of the good or service that a business produces changes. _____ s are the sum of marginal costs over all units produced. They can also be considered normal costs. Fixed costs and _____ s make up the two components of total cost. Direct costs are costs that can easily be associated with a particular cost object. However, not all _____ s are direct costs. For example, variable manufacturing overhead costs are _____ s that are indirect costs, not direct costs. _____ s are sometimes called unit-level costs as they vary with the number of units produced.

Exam Probability: **Low**

51. *Answer choices:*

(see index for correct answer)

- a. Average per-bit delivery cost
- b. Invested capital

- c. Variable cost
- d. Direct material price variance

Guidance: level 1

:: Economics terminology ::

_____ is the total receipts a seller can obtain from selling goods or services to buyers. It can be written as P × Q, which is the price of the goods multiplied by the quantity of the sold goods.

Exam Probability: **High**

52. *Answer choices:*

(see index for correct answer)

- a. Total revenue
- b. Currency trading
- c. marginal revenue
- d. Bond issue

Guidance: level 1

:: Marketing ::

The _____ is a foundation model for businesses. The _____ has been defined as the "set of marketing tools that the firm uses to pursue its marketing objectives in the target market". Thus the _____ refers to four broad levels of marketing decision, namely: product, price, place, and promotion. Marketing practice has been occurring for millennia, but marketing theory emerged in the early twentieth century. The contemporary _____ , or the 4 Ps, which has become the dominant framework for marketing management decisions, was first published in 1960. In services marketing, an extended _____ is used, typically comprising 7 Ps, made up of the original 4 Ps extended by process, people, and physical evidence. Occasionally service marketers will refer to 8 Ps, comprising these 7 Ps plus performance.

Exam Probability: **Low**

53. *Answer choices:*

(see index for correct answer)

- a. Content marketing
- b. Golden sample
- c. Marketing mix
- d. Exploratory research

Guidance: level 1

:: Credit cards ::

The _____ Company, also known as Amex, is an American multinational financial services corporation headquartered in Three World Financial Center in New York City. The company was founded in 1850 and is one of the 30 components of the Dow Jones Industrial Average. The company is best known for its charge card, credit card, and traveler's cheque businesses.

Exam Probability: **High**

54. *Answer choices:*

(see index for correct answer)

- a. Centurion Card
- b. EnRoute
- c. American Express
- d. Credit card debt

Guidance: level 1

:: Insolvency ::

_____ is the process in accounting by which a company is brought to an end in the United Kingdom, Republic of Ireland and United States. The assets and property of the company are redistributed. _____ is also sometimes referred to as winding-up or dissolution, although dissolution technically refers to the last stage of _____ . The process of _____ also arises when customs, an authority or agency in a country responsible for collecting and safeguarding customs duties, determines the final computation or ascertainment of the duties or drawback accruing on an entry.

Exam Probability: **Low**

55. *Answer choices:*

(see index for correct answer)

- a. Conservatorship
- b. Official Committee of Equity Security Holders
- c. Liquidation
- d. Liquidator

Guidance: level 1

:: ::

_____ s is the linguistic and philosophical study of meaning, in language, programming languages, formal logics, and semiotics. It is concerned with the relationship between signifiers—like words, phrases, signs, and symbols—and what they stand for in reality, their denotation.

Exam Probability: **High**

56. *Answer choices:*

(see index for correct answer)

- a. imperative
- b. process perspective
- c. Semantic

- d. functional perspective

Guidance: level 1

:: ::

Regulatory economics is the economics of regulation. It is the application of law by government or independent administrative agencies for various purposes, including remedying market failure, protecting the environment, centrally-planning an economy, enriching well-connected firms, or benefiting politicians.

Exam Probability: **High**

57. *Answer choices:*

(see index for correct answer)

- a. levels of analysis
- b. Economic regulation
- c. functional perspective
- d. process perspective

Guidance: level 1

:: Business models ::

A _____, _____ company or daughter company is a company that is owned or controlled by another company, which is called the parent company, parent, or holding company. The _____ can be a company, corporation, or limited liability company. In some cases it is a government or state-owned enterprise. In some cases, particularly in the music and book publishing industries, subsidiaries are referred to as imprints.

58. *Answer choices:*

(see index for correct answer)

- a. Subsidiary
- b. The Community Company
- c. Professional open source
- d. Technology push

Guidance: level 1

:: Management accounting ::

_____ , or dollar contribution per unit, is the selling price per unit minus the variable cost per unit. "Contribution" represents the portion of sales revenue that is not consumed by variable costs and so contributes to the coverage of fixed costs. This concept is one of the key building blocks of break-even analysis.

59. *Answer choices:*

(see index for correct answer)

- a. Fixed cost
- b. Target income sales
- c. Dual overhead rate
- d. Contribution margin

Guidance: level 1

Business ethics

Business ethics (also known as corporate ethics) is a form of applied ethics or professional ethics, that examines ethical principles and moral or ethical problems that can arise in a business environment. It applies to all aspects of business conduct and is relevant to the conduct of individuals and entire organizations. These ethics originate from individuals, organizational statements or from the legal system. These norms, values, ethical, and unethical practices are what is used to guide business. They help those businesses maintain a better connection with their stakeholders.

:: ::

The _____ is an institution of the European Union, responsible for proposing legislation, implementing decisions, upholding the EU treaties and managing the day-to-day business of the EU. Commissioners swear an oath at the European Court of Justice in Luxembourg City, pledging to respect the treaties and to be completely independent in carrying out their duties during their mandate. Unlike in the Council of the European Union, where members are directly and indirectly elected, and the European Parliament, where members are directly elected, the Commissioners are proposed by the Council of the European Union, on the basis of suggestions made by the national governments, and then appointed by the European Council after the approval of the European Parliament.

Exam Probability: **High**

1. *Answer choices:*

(see index for correct answer)

- a. European Commission
- b. information systems assessment
- c. personal values
- d. surface-level diversity

Guidance: level 1

:: ::

The _____ to Fight AIDS, Tuberculosis and Malaria is an international financing organization that aims to "attract, leverage and invest additional resources to end the epidemics of HIV/AIDS, tuberculosis and malaria to support attainment of the Sustainable Development Goals established by the United Nations." A public-private partnership, the organization maintains its secretariat in Geneva, Switzerland. The organization began operations in January 2002. Microsoft founder Bill Gates was one of the first private foundations among many bilateral donors to provide seed money for the partnership.

Exam Probability: **Medium**

2. *Answer choices:*

(see index for correct answer)

- a. empathy
- b. interpersonal communication
- c. Global Fund
- d. information systems assessment

Guidance: level 1

:: Auditing ::

_____ , as defined by accounting and auditing, is a process for assuring of an organization's objectives in operational effectiveness and efficiency, reliable financial reporting, and compliance with laws, regulations and policies. A broad concept, _____ involves everything that controls risks to an organization.

3. *Answer choices:*

(see index for correct answer)

- a. Internal control
- b. audit log
- c. Audit plan
- d. ISACA

Guidance: level 1

:: Business ethics ::

_____ is a type of international private business self-regulation. While once it was possible to describe CSR as an internal organisational policy or a corporate ethic strategy, that time has passed as various international laws have been developed and various organisations have used their authority to push it beyond individual or even industry-wide initiatives. While it has been considered a form of corporate self-regulation for some time, over the last decade or so it has moved considerably from voluntary decisions at the level of individual organisations, to mandatory schemes at regional, national and even transnational levels.

4. *Answer choices:*

(see index for correct answer)

- a. Corporate social responsibility
- b. Corporate sustainable profitability
- c. Wheelmen
- d. Sullivan principles

Guidance: level 1

:: Business ethics ::

_____ is a type of harassment technique that relates to a sexual nature and the unwelcome or inappropriate promise of rewards in exchange for sexual favors. _____ includes a range of actions from mild transgressions to sexual abuse or assault. Harassment can occur in many different social settings such as the workplace, the home, school, churches, etc. Harassers or victims may be of any gender.

Exam Probability: **Low**

5. *Answer choices:*
(see index for correct answer)

- a. Society of Corporate Compliance and Ethics
- b. Eating your own dog food
- c. Institute for Business and Professional Ethics
- d. Sexual harassment

Guidance: level 1

:: Workplace ::

In business management, _____ is a management style whereby a manager closely observes and/or controls the work of his/her subordinates or employees.

Exam Probability: **High**

6. *Answer choices:*

(see index for correct answer)

- a. Workplace relationships
- b. Work motivation
- c. Micromanagement
- d. Toxic workplace

Guidance: level 1

:: Management ::

A _____ describes the rationale of how an organization creates, delivers, and captures value, in economic, social, cultural or other contexts. The process of _____ construction and modification is also called _____ innovation and forms a part of business strategy.

Exam Probability: **Medium**

7. *Answer choices:*

(see index for correct answer)

- a. Coworking
- b. Industrial forensics
- c. Double linking
- d. Business model

Guidance: level 1

:: Corporations law ::

A normal _____ consists of various departments that contribute to the company's overall mission and goals. Common departments include Marketing, [Finance, [[Operations managementOperations, Human Resource, and IT. These five divisions represent the major departments within a publicly traded company, though there are often smaller departments within autonomous firms. There is typically a CEO, and Board of Directors composed of the directors of each department. There are also company presidents, vice presidents, and CFOs. There is a great diversity in corporate forms as enterprises may range from single company to multi-corporate conglomerate. The four main _____ s are Functional, Divisional, Geographic, and the Matrix. Realistically, most corporations tend to have a "hybrid" structure, which is a combination of different models with one dominant strategy.

Exam Probability: **Medium**

8. *Answer choices:*

(see index for correct answer)

- a. South African company law
- b. Asset lock
- c. Prest v Petrodel Resources Ltd
- d. Corporate structure

Guidance: level 1

:: Culture ::

_____ is a society which is characterized by individualism, which is the prioritization or emphasis, of the individual over the entire group. _____ s are oriented around the self, being independent instead of identifying with a group mentality. They see each other as only loosely linked, and value personal goals over group interests. _____ s tend to have a more diverse population and are characterized with emphasis on personal achievements, and a rational assessment of both the beneficial and detrimental aspects of relationships with others. _____ s have such unique aspects of communication as being a low power-distance culture and having a low-context communication style. The United States, Australia, Great Britain, Canada, the Netherlands, and New Zealand have been identified as highly _____ s.

Exam Probability: **Low**

9. *Answer choices:*

(see index for correct answer)

- a. Low-context
- b. High-context
- c. cultural framework

- d. Intracultural

Guidance: level 1

:: White-collar criminals ::

_____ refers to financially motivated, nonviolent crime committed by businesses and government professionals. It was first defined by the sociologist Edwin Sutherland in 1939 as "a crime committed by a person of respectability and high social status in the course of their occupation". Typical _____ s could include wage theft, fraud, bribery, Ponzi schemes, insider trading, labor racketeering, embezzlement, cybercrime, copyright infringement, money laundering, identity theft, and forgery. Lawyers can specialize in _____ .

Exam Probability: **High**

10. *Answer choices:*

(see index for correct answer)

- a. White-collar crime
- b. Du Jun

Guidance: level 1

:: Minimum wage ::

A _____ is the lowest remuneration that employers can legally pay their workers—the price floor below which workers may not sell their labor. Most countries had introduced _____ legislation by the end of the 20th century.

Exam Probability: **Medium**

11. *Answer choices:*

(see index for correct answer)

- a. Working poor
- b. Minimum wage
- c. Guaranteed minimum income
- d. Minimum wage in Taiwan

Guidance: level 1

:: ::

The _____ is an 1848 political pamphlet by the German philosophers Karl Marx and Friedrich Engels. Commissioned by the Communist League and originally published in London just as the Revolutions of 1848 began to erupt, the Manifesto was later recognised as one of the world's most influential political documents. It presents an analytical approach to the class struggle and the conflicts of capitalism and the capitalist mode of production, rather than a prediction of communism's potential future forms.

Exam Probability: **High**

12. *Answer choices:*

(see index for correct answer)

- a. Communist Manifesto
- b. Sarbanes-Oxley act of 2002
- c. similarity-attraction theory
- d. Character

Guidance: level 1

:: ::

_____ is the introduction of contaminants into the natural environment that cause adverse change. _____ can take the form of chemical substances or energy, such as noise, heat or light. Pollutants, the components of _____ , can be either foreign substances/energies or naturally occurring contaminants. _____ is often classed as point source or nonpoint source _____ .In 2015, _____ killed 9 million people in the world.

Exam Probability: **Low**

13. *Answer choices:*

(see index for correct answer)

- a. Character
- b. empathy
- c. Pollution
- d. hierarchical

:: Hazard analysis ::

  Broadly speaking, a _____ is the combined effort of 1. identifying and analyzing potential events that may negatively impact individuals, assets, and/or the environment ; and 2. making judgments "on the tolerability of the risk on the basis of a risk analysis" while considering influencing factors . Put in simpler terms, a _____ analyzes what can go wrong, how likely it is to happen, what the potential consequences are, and how tolerable the identified risk is. As part of this process, the resulting determination of risk may be expressed in a quantitative or qualitative fashion. The _____ is an inherent part of an overall risk management strategy, which attempts to, after a _____ , "introduce control measures to eliminate or reduce" any potential risk-related consequences.

Exam Probability: **High**

14. *Answer choices:*

(see index for correct answer)

- a. Hazard identification
- b. Risk assessment
- c. Hazardous Materials Identification System

:: Water law ::

The _____ is the primary federal law in the United States governing water pollution. Its objective is to restore and maintain the chemical, physical, and biological integrity of the nation's waters; recognizing the responsibilities of the states in addressing pollution and providing assistance to states to do so, including funding for publicly owned treatment works for the improvement of wastewater treatment; and maintaining the integrity of wetlands. It is one of the United States' first and most influential modern environmental laws. As with many other major U.S. federal environmental statutes, it is administered by the U.S. Environmental Protection Agency , in coordination with state governments. Its implementing regulations are codified at 40 C.F.R. Subchapters D, N, and O .

Exam Probability: **Low**

15. *Answer choices:*

(see index for correct answer)

- a. Water quality law
- b. Berlin Rules on Water Resources
- c. The Helsinki Rules on the Uses of the Waters of International Rivers
- d. Return flow

Guidance: level 1

:: ::

An _____ is the release of a liquid petroleum hydrocarbon into the environment, especially the marine ecosystem, due to human activity, and is a form of pollution. The term is usually given to marine _____ s, where oil is released into the ocean or coastal waters, but spills may also occur on land. _____ s may be due to releases of crude oil from tankers, offshore platforms, drilling rigs and wells, as well as spills of refined petroleum products and their by-products, heavier fuels used by large ships such as bunker fuel, or the spill of any oily refuse or waste oil.

Exam Probability: **High**

16. *Answer choices:*

(see index for correct answer)

- a. levels of analysis
- b. Oil spill
- c. corporate values
- d. co-culture

Guidance: level 1

:: Competition regulators ::

The _____ is an independent agency of the United States government, established in 1914 by the _____ Act. Its principal mission is the promotion of consumer protection and the elimination and prevention of anticompetitive business practices, such as coercive monopoly. It is headquartered in the _____ Building in Washington, D.C.

Exam Probability: **High**

17. *Answer choices:*

(see index for correct answer)

- a. Commerce Commission
- b. Competition Appeal Tribunal
- c. Jersey Competition Regulatory Authority
- d. Federal Trade Commission

Guidance: level 1

:: Writs ::

In common law, a writ of _____ is a writ whereby a private individual who assists a prosecution can receive all or part of any penalty imposed. Its name is an abbreviation of the Latin phrase _____ pro domino rege quam pro se ipso in hac parte sequitur, meaning "[he] who sues in this matter for the king as well as for himself."

Exam Probability: **High**

18. *Answer choices:*

(see index for correct answer)

- a. Writ
- b. Writ of execution

- c. Qui tam

:: Social responsibility ::

The United Nations Global Compact is a non-binding United Nations pact to encourage businesses worldwide to adopt sustainable and socially responsible policies, and to report on their implementation. The _____ is a principle-based framework for businesses, stating ten principles in the areas of human rights, labor, the environment and anti-corruption. Under the Global Compact, companies are brought together with UN agencies, labor groups and civil society. Cities can join the Global Compact through the Cities Programme.

Exam Probability: **Medium**

19. *Answer choices:*
(see index for correct answer)

- a. UN Global Compact
- b. Enterprise 2020
- c. Mallen Baker
- d. Socially responsible business

:: Auditing ::

_____ is a general term that can reflect various types of evaluations intended to identify environmental compliance and management system implementation gaps, along with related corrective actions. In this way they perform an analogous function to financial audits. There are generally two different types of _____ s: compliance audits and management systems audits. Compliance audits tend to be the primary type in the US or within US-based multinationals.

Exam Probability: **Medium**

20. *Answer choices:*

(see index for correct answer)

- a. Audit Bureau of Circulations
- b. SOFT audit
- c. Control environment
- d. Audit management

Guidance: level 1

:: United States federal trade legislation ::

The _____ of 1914 established the Federal Trade Commission. The Act, signed into law by Woodrow Wilson in 1914, outlaws unfair methods of competition and outlaws unfair acts or practices that affect commerce.

Exam Probability: **High**

21. *Answer choices:*

(see index for correct answer)

- • a. Iran Nonproliferation Act of 2000
- • b. Tariff of 1792
- • c. Non-Intercourse Act
- • d. Federal Trade Commission Act

Guidance: level 1

:: Cultural appropriation ::

_____ is a social and economic order that encourages the acquisition of goods and services in ever-increasing amounts. With the industrial revolution, but particularly in the 20th century, mass production led to an economic crisis: there was overproduction—the supply of goods would grow beyond consumer demand, and so manufacturers turned to planned obsolescence and advertising to manipulate consumer spending. In 1899, a book on _____ published by Thorstein Veblen, called The Theory of the Leisure Class, examined the widespread values and economic institutions emerging along with the widespread "leisure time" in the beginning of the 20th century. In it Veblen "views the activities and spending habits of this leisure class in terms of conspicuous and vicarious consumption and waste. Both are related to the display of status and not to functionality or usefulness."

Exam Probability: **Low**

22. *Answer choices:*

(see index for correct answer)

- a. Cleveland Indians
- b. The Rebel Sell
- c. Consumerism
- d. Plastic Paddy

Guidance: level 1

:: ::

The _____ , founded in 1912, is a private, nonprofit organization whose self-described mission is to focus on advancing marketplace trust, consisting of 106 independently incorporated local BBB organizations in the United States and Canada, coordinated under the Council of _____ s in Arlington, Virginia.

Exam Probability: **High**

23. *Answer choices:*

(see index for correct answer)

- a. surface-level diversity
- b. deep-level diversity
- c. imperative
- d. Better Business Bureau

Guidance: level 1

:: ::

_____ is an eight-block-long street running roughly northwest to southeast from Broadway to South Street, at the East River, in the Financial District of Lower Manhattan in New York City. Over time, the term has become a metonym for the financial markets of the United States as a whole, the American financial services industry , or New York–based financial interests.

Exam Probability: **Medium**

24. *Answer choices:*

(see index for correct answer)

- a. Sarbanes-Oxley act of 2002
- b. deep-level diversity
- c. Wall Street
- d. co-culture

Guidance: level 1

:: ::

In ecology, a _____ is the type of natural environment in which a particular species of organism lives. It is characterized by both physical and biological features. A species` _____ is those places where it can find food, shelter, protection and mates for reproduction.

25. *Answer choices:*

(see index for correct answer)

- a. imperative
- b. Habitat
- c. levels of analysis
- d. functional perspective

Guidance: level 1

:: ::

_____ is a non-governmental environmental organization with offices in over 39 countries and an international coordinating body in Amsterdam, the Netherlands. _____ was founded in 1971 by Irving Stowe, and Dorothy Stowe, Canadian and US ex-pat environmental activists. _____ states its goal is to "ensure the ability of the Earth to nurture life in all its diversity" and focuses its campaigning on worldwide issues such as climate change, deforestation, overfishing, commercial whaling, genetic engineering, and anti-nuclear issues. It uses direct action, lobbying, research, and ecotage to achieve its goals. The global organization does not accept funding from governments, corporations, or political parties, relying on three million individual supporters and foundation grants. _____ has a general consultative status with the United Nations Economic and Social Council and is a founding member of the INGO Accountability Charter, an international non-governmental organization that intends to foster accountability and transparency of non-governmental organizations.

26. *Answer choices:*

(see index for correct answer)

- a. hierarchical perspective
- b. Greenpeace
- c. functional perspective
- d. Character

Guidance: level 1

:: Organizational structure ::

An _____ defines how activities such as task allocation, coordination, and supervision are directed toward the achievement of organizational aims.

Exam Probability: **High**

27. *Answer choices:*

(see index for correct answer)

- a. Organizational structure
- b. Blessed Unrest
- c. The Starfish and the Spider
- d. Organization of the New York City Police Department

:: Minimum wage ::

The _____ are working people whose incomes fall below a given poverty line due to lack of work hours and/or low wages.Largely because they are earning such low wages, the _____ face numerous obstacles that make it difficult for many of them to find and keep a job, save up money, and maintain a sense of self-worth.

Exam Probability: **Medium**

28. *Answer choices:*

(see index for correct answer)

- a. Guaranteed minimum income
- b. Working poor
- c. Minimum Wage Fairness Act
- d. National Anti-Sweating League

:: Agricultural labor ::

The _____ of America, or more commonly just _____ , is a labor union for farmworkers in the United States. It originated from the merger of two workers' rights organizations, the Agricultural Workers Organizing Committee led by organizer Larry Itliong, and the National Farm Workers Association led by César Chávez and Dolores Huerta. They became allied and transformed from workers' rights organizations into a union as a result of a series of strikes in 1965, when the mostly Filipino farmworkers of the AWOC in Delano, California initiated a grape strike, and the NFWA went on strike in support. As a result of the commonality in goals and methods, the NFWA and the AWOC formed the _____ Organizing Committee on August 22, 1966. This organization was accepted into the AFL-CIO in 1972 and changed its name to the _____ Union.

Exam Probability: **High**

29. *Answer choices:*

(see index for correct answer)

- a. Collective farming
- b. Kolkhoz
- c. California Agricultural Labor Relations Act
- d. United Farm Workers

Guidance: level 1

:: Professional ethics ::

In the mental health field, a _____ is a situation where multiple roles exist between a therapist, or other mental health practitioner, and a client. _____ s are also referred to as multiple relationships, and these two terms are used interchangeably in the research literature. The American Psychological Association Ethical Principles of Psychologists and Code of Conduct is a resource that outlines ethical standards and principles to which practitioners are expected to adhere. Standard 3.05 of the APA ethics code outlines the definition of multiple relationships. Dual or multiple relationships occur when.

Exam Probability: **Low**

30. *Answer choices:*

(see index for correct answer)

- a. Dual relationship
- b. ethical code
- c. Continuous professional development

Guidance: level 1

:: Renewable energy ::

_____ is the conversion of energy from sunlight into electricity, either directly using photovoltaics , indirectly using concentrated _____ , or a combination. Concentrated _____ systems use lenses or mirrors and tracking systems to focus a large area of sunlight into a small beam. Photovoltaic cells convert light into an electric current using the photovoltaic effect.

31. *Answer choices:*

(see index for correct answer)

- a. Solar power
- b. National Solar Conference and World Renewable Energy Forum 2012
- c. Solar thermal energy
- d. Microbial fuel cell

Guidance: level 1

:: Commercial crimes ::

_____ is an agreement between participants on the same side in a market to buy or sell a product, service, or commodity only at a fixed price, or maintain the market conditions such that the price is maintained at a given level by controlling supply and demand.

Exam Probability: **Low**

32. *Answer choices:*

(see index for correct answer)

- a. Price fixing
- b. National White Collar Crime Center
- c. Fraudulent conveyance

- d. Cheque fraud

Guidance: level 1

:: Socialism ::

_____ is a label used to define the first currents of modern socialist thought as exemplified by the work of Henri de Saint-Simon, Charles Fourier, Étienne Cabet and Robert Owen.

Exam Probability: **Low**

33. *Answer choices:*
(see index for correct answer)

- a. Socialist Resistance
- b. Accumulation by dispossession
- c. Utopian socialism
- d. Neosocialism

Guidance: level 1

:: ::

The Federal National Mortgage Association , commonly known as _____ , is a United States government-sponsored enterprise and, since 1968, a publicly traded company. Founded in 1938 during the Great Depression as part of the New Deal, the corporation's purpose is to expand the secondary mortgage market by securitizing mortgage loans in the form of mortgage-backed securities , allowing lenders to reinvest their assets into more lending and in effect increasing the number of lenders in the mortgage market by reducing the reliance on locally based savings and loan associations . Its brother organization is the Federal Home Loan Mortgage Corporation , better known as Freddie Mac. As of 2018, _____ is ranked #21 on the Fortune 500 rankings of the largest United States corporations by total revenue.

Exam Probability: **Low**

34. *Answer choices:*

(see index for correct answer)

- a. empathy
- b. process perspective
- c. interpersonal communication
- d. hierarchical

Guidance: level 1

:: ::

_____ is the means to see, hear, or become aware of something or someone through our fundamental senses. The term _____ derives from the Latin word perceptio, and is the organization, identification, and interpretation of sensory information in order to represent and understand the presented information, or the environment.

Exam Probability: **Medium**

35. *Answer choices:*

(see index for correct answer)

- a. cultural
- b. process perspective
- c. hierarchical
- d. levels of analysis

Guidance: level 1

:: ::

The Ethics & Compliance Initiative was formed in 2015 and consists of three nonprofit organizations: the Ethics Research Center, the Ethics & Compliance Association, and the Ethics & Compliance Certification Institute. Based in Arlington, Virginia, United States, ECI is devoted to the advancement of high ethical standards and practices in public and private institutions, and provides research about ethical standards, workplace integrity, and compliance practices and processes.

36. *Answer choices:*

(see index for correct answer)

- a. information systems assessment
- b. levels of analysis
- c. co-culture
- d. Ethics Resource Center

Guidance: level 1

:: Corporate crime ::

_____ LLP, based in Chicago, was an American holding company. Formerly one of the "Big Five" accounting firms , the firm had provided auditing, tax, and consulting services to large corporations. By 2001, it had become one of the world's largest multinational companies.

Exam Probability: **Low**

37. *Answer choices:*

(see index for correct answer)

- a. Walter Forbes
- b. Tip and Trade
- c. FirstEnergy

- d. Arthur Andersen

Guidance: level 1

:: ::

The _____ , the Calvinist work ethic or the Puritan work ethic is a work ethic concept in theology, sociology, economics and history that emphasizes that hard work, discipline and frugality are a result of a person's subscription to the values espoused by the Protestant faith, particularly Calvinism. The phrase was initially coined in 1904–1905 by Max Weber in his book The Protestant Ethic and the Spirit of Capitalism.

Exam Probability: **Low**

38. *Answer choices:*

(see index for correct answer)

- a. personal values
- b. empathy
- c. surface-level diversity
- d. Protestant work ethic

Guidance: level 1

:: Patent law ::

A _____ is generally any statement intended to specify or delimit the scope of rights and obligations that may be exercised and enforced by parties in a legally recognized relationship. In contrast to other terms for legally operative language, the term _____ usually implies situations that involve some level of uncertainty, waiver, or risk.

Exam Probability: **Medium**

39. *Answer choices:*

(see index for correct answer)

- a. Coverture
- b. Design around
- c. Disclaimer
- d. Patent war

Guidance: level 1

:: ::

Revenge is a form of justice enacted in the absence or defiance of the norms of formal law and jurisprudence. Often, revenge is defined as being a harmful action against a person or group in response to a grievance, be it real or perceived . It is used to punish a wrong by going outside the law. Francis Bacon described revenge as a kind of "wild justice" that "does... offend the law [and] putteth the law out of office." Primitive justice or retributive justice is often differentiated from more formal and refined forms of justice such as distributive justice and divine judgment.

40. *Answer choices:*

(see index for correct answer)

- a. levels of analysis
- b. Retaliation
- c. open system
- d. imperative

Guidance: level 1

:: Nepotism ::

_____ is the granting of favour to relatives in various fields, including business, politics, entertainment, sports, religion and other activities. The term originated with the assignment of nephews to important positions by Catholic popes and bishops. Trading parliamentary employment for favors is a modern-day example of _____ . Criticism of _____ , however, can be found in ancient Indian texts such as the Kural literature.

Exam Probability: **Medium**

41. *Answer choices:*

(see index for correct answer)

- a. Wasta
- b. Nepotism

- c. Cronyism
- d. Ethnic nepotism

Guidance: level 1

:: Monopoly (economics) ::

The _____ of 1890 was a United States antitrust law that regulates competition among enterprises, which was passed by Congress under the presidency of Benjamin Harrison.

Exam Probability: **High**

42. *Answer choices:*

(see index for correct answer)

- a. Special 301 Report
- b. Dominance
- c. Sherman Antitrust Act
- d. Electricity liberalization

Guidance: level 1

:: Leadership ::

_____ is leadership that is directed by respect for ethical beliefs and values and for the dignity and rights of others. It is thus related to concepts such as trust, honesty, consideration, charisma, and fairness.

Exam Probability: **Medium**

43. *Answer choices:*

(see index for correct answer)

- a. Ethical leadership
- b. Sex differences in leadership
- c. Transformational leadership
- d. Outstanding leadership theory

Guidance: level 1

:: Euthenics ::

_____ is an ethical framework and suggests that an entity, be it an organization or individual, has an obligation to act for the benefit of society at large. _____ is a duty every individual has to perform so as to maintain a balance between the economy and the ecosystems. A trade-off may exist between economic development, in the material sense, and the welfare of the society and environment, though this has been challenged by many reports over the past decade. _____ means sustaining the equilibrium between the two. It pertains not only to business organizations but also to everyone whose any action impacts the environment. This responsibility can be passive, by avoiding engaging in socially harmful acts, or active, by performing activities that directly advance social goals. _____ must be intergenerational since the actions of one generation have consequences on those following.

Exam Probability: **Medium**

44. *Answer choices:*

(see index for correct answer)

- a. Social responsibility
- b. Family and consumer science
- c. Euthenics
- d. Minnie Cumnock Blodgett

Guidance: level 1

:: Anti-Revisionism ::

_____ , officially the German Democratic Republic , was a country that existed from 1949 to 1990, when the eastern portion of Germany was part of the Eastern Bloc during the Cold War. It described itself as a socialist "workers` and peasants` state", and the territory was administered and occupied by Soviet forces at the end of World War II — the Soviet Occupation Zone of the Potsdam Agreement, bounded on the east by the Oder–Neisse line. The Soviet zone surrounded West Berlin but did not include it; as a result, West Berlin remained outside the jurisdiction of the GDR.

Exam Probability: **Low**

45. *Answer choices:*

(see index for correct answer)

- a. East Germany
- b. Hoxhaism
- c. Anti-Party Group
- d. Anti-Revisionism

Guidance: level 1

:: ::

Sustainability is the process of people maintaining change in a balanced environment, in which the exploitation of resources, the direction of investments, the orientation of technological development and institutional change are all in harmony and enhance both current and future potential to meet human needs and aspirations. For many in the field, sustainability is defined through the following interconnected domains or pillars: environment, economic and social, which according to Fritjof Capra is based on the principles of Systems Thinking. Sub-domains of _____ development have been considered also: cultural, technological and political. While _____ development may be the organizing principle for sustainability for some, for others, the two terms are paradoxical . _____ development is the development that meets the needs of the present without compromising the ability of future generations to meet their own needs. Brundtland Report for the World Commission on Environment and Development introduced the term of _____ development.

Exam Probability: **Medium**

46. *Answer choices:*

(see index for correct answer)

- a. levels of analysis
- b. Sustainable
- c. hierarchical perspective
- d. co-culture

Guidance: level 1

:: Private equity ::

In finance, a high-yield bond is a bond that is rated below investment grade. These bonds have a higher risk of default or other adverse credit events, but typically pay higher yields than better quality bonds in order to make them attractive to investors.

Exam Probability: **Medium**

47. *Answer choices:*

(see index for correct answer)

- a. Magix
- b. J curve
- c. Equity co-investment
- d. Growth capital

Guidance: level 1

:: Real estate ::

_____ s serve several societal needs – primarily as shelter from weather, security, living space, privacy, to store belongings, and to comfortably live and work. A _____ as a shelter represents a physical division of the human habitat and the outside .

Exam Probability: **Medium**

48. *Answer choices:*

- a. Peaceable possession
- b. AMP Technologies
- c. Real Estate Transaction Standard
- d. Rent control

Guidance: level 1

:: Toxicology ::

_____ or lead-based paint is paint containing lead. As pigment, lead chromate , Lead oxide, , and lead carbonate are the most common forms. Lead is added to paint to accelerate drying, increase durability, maintain a fresh appearance, and resist moisture that causes corrosion. It is one of the main health and environmental hazards associated with paint. In some countries, lead continues to be added to paint intended for domestic use, whereas countries such as the U.S. and the UK have regulations prohibiting this, although _____ may still be found in older properties painted prior to the introduction of such regulations. Although lead has been banned from household paints in the United States since 1978, paint used in road markings may still contain it. Alternatives such as water-based, lead-free traffic paint are readily available, and many states and federal agencies have changed their purchasing contracts to buy these instead.

Exam Probability: **Low**

49. *Answer choices:*

- a. Reye syndrome
- b. Lead paint
- c. Toxicodynamics
- d. Bioanalysis

Guidance: level 1

:: Human resource management ::

_____ is the ethics of an organization, and it is how an organization responds to an internal or external stimulus. _____ is interdependent with the organizational culture. Although it is akin to both organizational behavior and industrial and organizational psychology as well as business ethics on the micro and macro levels, _____ is neither OB or I/O psychology, nor is it solely business ethics . _____ express the values of an organization to its employees and/or other entities irrespective of governmental and/or regulatory laws.

Exam Probability: **Low**

50. *Answer choices:*

(see index for correct answer)

- a. Individual development plan
- b. Organizational ethics
- c. Potential analysis
- d. human resource

:: Leadership ::

_____ is a theory of leadership where a leader works with teams to identify needed change, creating a vision to guide the change through inspiration, and executing the change in tandem with committed members of a group; it is an integral part of the Full Range Leadership Model. _____ serves to enhance the motivation, morale, and job performance of followers through a variety of mechanisms; these include connecting the follower`s sense of identity and self to a project and to the collective identity of the organization; being a role model for followers in order to inspire them and to raise their interest in the project; challenging followers to take greater ownership for their work, and understanding the strengths and weaknesses of followers, allowing the leader to align followers with tasks that enhance their performance.

Exam Probability: **Medium**

51. *Answer choices:*

(see index for correct answer)

- a. servant leader
- b. Transformational leadership
- c. BTS Group
- d. Servant leadership

:: ::

The _____ of 1977 is a United States federal law known primarily for two of its main provisions: one that addresses accounting transparency requirements under the Securities Exchange Act of 1934 and another concerning bribery of foreign officials. The Act was amended in 1988 and in 1998, and has been subject to continued congressional concerns, namely whether its enforcement discourages U.S. companies from investing abroad.

Exam Probability: **High**

52. *Answer choices:*

(see index for correct answer)

- a. levels of analysis
- b. co-culture
- c. Foreign Corrupt Practices Act
- d. cultural

Guidance: level 1

:: ::

_____ is "property consisting of land and the buildings on it, along with its natural resources such as crops, minerals or water; immovable property of this nature; an interest vested in this an item of real property, buildings or housing in general. Also: the business of _____ ; the profession of buying, selling, or renting land, buildings, or housing." It is a legal term used in jurisdictions whose legal system is derived from English common law, such as India, England, Wales, Northern Ireland, United States, Canada, Pakistan, Australia, and New Zealand.

Exam Probability: **Medium**

53. *Answer choices:*

(see index for correct answer)

- a. personal values
- b. co-culture
- c. process perspective
- d. deep-level diversity

Guidance: level 1

:: Fraud ::

In law, _____ is intentional deception to secure unfair or unlawful gain, or to deprive a victim of a legal right. _____ can violate civil law , a criminal law , or it may cause no loss of money, property or legal right but still be an element of another civil or criminal wrong. The purpose of _____ may be monetary gain or other benefits, for example by obtaining a passport, travel document, or driver's license, or mortgage _____ , where the perpetrator may attempt to qualify for a mortgage by way of false statements.

Exam Probability: **High**

54. *Answer choices:*

(see index for correct answer)

- a. Parcel mule scam
- b. Clothing scam companies
- c. Adoption fraud
- d. Fraud

Guidance: level 1

:: Ethical banking ::

A _____ or community development finance institution - abbreviated in both cases to CDFI - is a financial institution that provides credit and financial services to underserved markets and populations, primarily in the USA but also in the UK. A CDFI may be a community development bank, a community development credit union , a community development loan fund , a community development venture capital fund , a microenterprise development loan fund, or a community development corporation.

Exam Probability: **Low**

55. *Answer choices:*

(see index for correct answer)

- a. Institute for Social Banking
- b. JAK Members Bank
- c. Reliance Bank
- d. GLS Bank

Guidance: level 1

:: Environmental economics ::

_____ is an institutional arrangement designed to help producers in developing countries achieve better trading conditions. Members of the _____ movement advocate the payment of higher prices to exporters, as well as improved social and environmental standards. The movement focuses in particular on commodities, or products which are typically exported from developing countries to developed countries, but also consumed in domestic markets most notably handicrafts, coffee, cocoa, wine, sugar, fresh fruit, chocolate, flowers and gold. The movement seeks to promote greater equity in international trading partnerships through dialogue, transparency, and respect. It promotes sustainable development by offering better trading conditions to, and securing the rights of, marginalized producers and workers in developing countries. _____ is grounded in three core beliefs; first, producers have the power to express unity with consumers. Secondly, the world trade practices that currently exist promote the unequal distribution of wealth between nations. Lastly, buying products from producers in developing countries at a fair price is a more efficient way of promoting sustainable development than traditional charity and aid.

Exam Probability: **High**

56. *Answer choices:*

(see index for correct answer)

- a. Environmental and Resource Economics
- b. Peak gas
- c. Tragedy of the commons
- d. Environmental impact assessment

Guidance: level 1

:: ::

The _____ is an agency of the United States Department of Labor. Congress established the agency under the Occupational Safety and Health Act , which President Richard M. Nixon signed into law on December 29, 1970. OSHA`s mission is to "assure safe and healthy working conditions for working men and women by setting and enforcing standards and by providing training, outreach, education and assistance". The agency is also charged with enforcing a variety of whistleblower statutes and regulations. OSHA is currently headed by Acting Assistant Secretary of Labor Loren Sweatt. OSHA`s workplace safety inspections have been shown to reduce injury rates and injury costs without adverse effects to employment, sales, credit ratings, or firm survival.

Exam Probability: **High**

57. *Answer choices:*

(see index for correct answer)

- a. corporate values
- b. process perspective
- c. information systems assessment
- d. open system

Guidance: level 1

:: Management ::

_____ is the identification, evaluation, and prioritization of risks followed by coordinated and economical application of resources to minimize, monitor, and control the probability or impact of unfortunate events or to maximize the realization of opportunities.

58. *Answer choices:*

(see index for correct answer)

- a. Event to knowledge
- b. Risk management
- c. Customer Benefit Package
- d. Virtual customer environment

Guidance: level 1

:: Utilitarianism ::

_____ is a family of consequentialist ethical theories that promotes actions that maximize happiness and well-being for the majority of a population. Although different varieties of _____ admit different characterizations, the basic idea behind all of them is to in some sense maximize utility, which is often defined in terms of well-being or related concepts. For instance, Jeremy Bentham, the founder of _____ , described utility as

Exam Probability: **Low**

59. *Answer choices:*

(see index for correct answer)

- a. Consequentialism

- b. Utilitarianism
- c. Felicific calculus
- d. Informed judge

Guidance: level 1

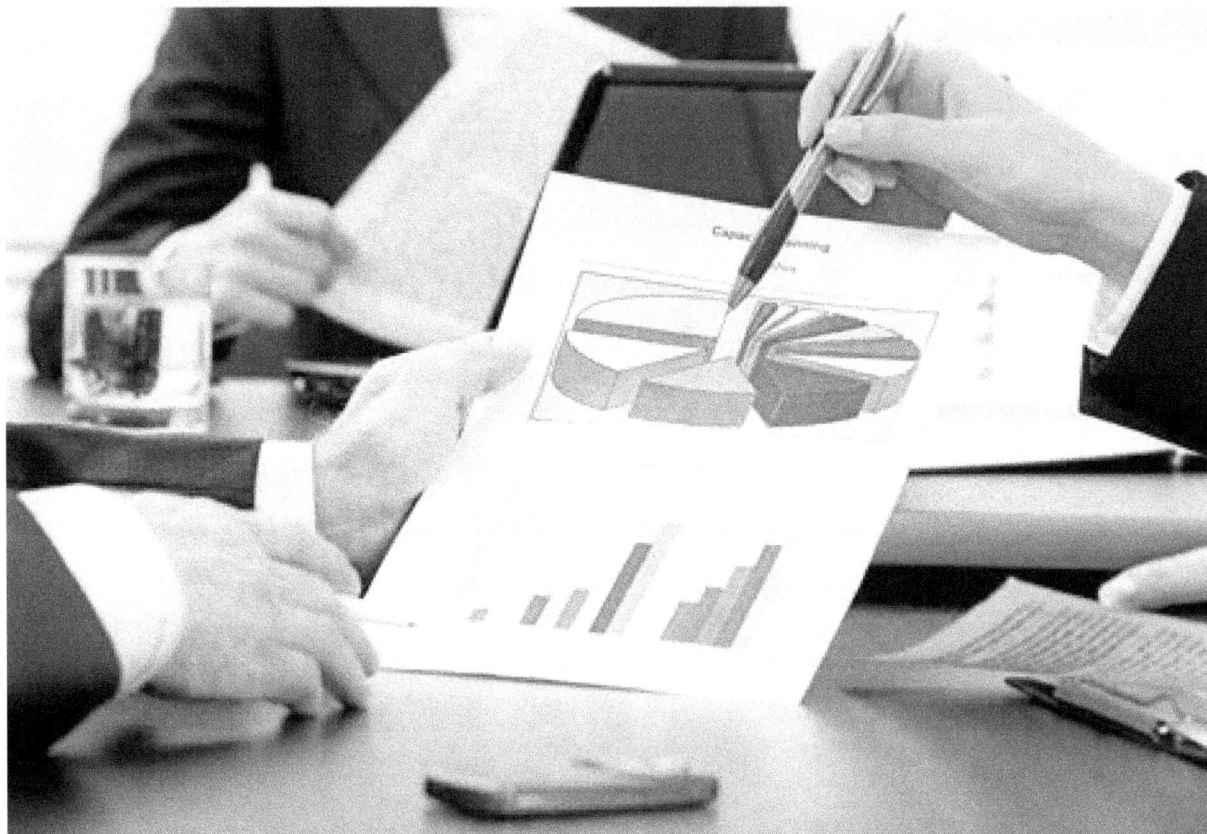

Accounting

Accounting or accountancy is the measurement, processing, and communication of financial information about economic entities such as businesses and corporations. The modern field was established by the Italian mathematician Luca Pacioli in 1494. Accounting, which has been called the "language of business", measures the results of an organization's economic activities and conveys this information to a variety of users, including investors, creditors, management, and regulators.

:: Budgets ::

_____ is a method of budgeting in which all expenses must be justified and approved for each new period. Developed by Peter Pyhrr in the 1970s, _____ starts from a "zero base" at the beginning of every budget period, analyzing needs and costs of every function within an organization and allocating funds accordingly, regardless of how much money has previously been budgeted to any given line item.

Exam Probability: **Low**

1. *Answer choices:*

- a. Programme budgeting
- b. Zero-based budgeting
- c. Public budgeting
- d. Railway Budget

Guidance: level 1

:: Stock market ::

A _____, securities exchange or bourse, is a facility where stock brokers and traders can buy and sell securities, such as shares of stock and bonds and other financial instruments. _____ s may also provide for facilities the issue and redemption of such securities and instruments and capital events including the payment of income and dividends. Securities traded on a _____ include stock issued by listed companies, unit trusts, derivatives, pooled investment products and bonds. _____ s often function as "continuous auction" markets with buyers and sellers consummating transactions via open outcry at a central location such as the floor of the exchange or by using an electronic trading platform.

Exam Probability: **Low**

2. *Answer choices:*

(see index for correct answer)

- a. Central limit order book
- b. Stock Exchange
- c. Qualified institutional placement
- d. Greenshoe

Guidance: level 1

:: Taxation and efficiency ::

_____ is the legal usage of the tax regime in a single territory to one's own advantage to reduce the amount of tax that is payable by means that are within the law. Tax sheltering is very similar, although unlike _____ tax sheltering is not necessarily legal. Tax havens are jurisdictions which facilitate reduced taxes.

Exam Probability: **Medium**

3. *Answer choices:*

(see index for correct answer)

- a. Tax avoidance
- b. Tax advantage
- c. Fiscal illusion
- d. Capital flight

Guidance: level 1

:: Accounting journals and ledgers ::

_____ is a daybook or journal which is used to record transactions relating to adjustment entries, opening stock, accounting errors etc. The source documents of this prime entry book are journal voucher, copy of management reports and invoices.

Exam Probability: **High**

4. *Answer choices:*

(see index for correct answer)

- a. Cash receipts journal
- b. Sales journal
- c. Check register
- d. General journal

Guidance: level 1

:: Management accounting ::

_____ s are costs that change as the quantity of the good or service that a business produces changes. _____ s are the sum of marginal costs over all units produced. They can also be considered normal costs. Fixed costs and _____ s make up the two components of total cost. Direct costs are costs that can easily be associated with a particular cost object. However, not all _____ s are direct costs. For example, variable manufacturing overhead costs are _____ s that are indirect costs, not direct costs. _____ s are sometimes called unit-level costs as they vary with the number of units produced.

Exam Probability: **Low**

5. *Answer choices:*

(see index for correct answer)

- a. Cost driver
- b. Job costing

- c. Variable cost
- d. Double counting

Guidance: level 1

:: Generally Accepted Accounting Principles ::

The term _____ is most often used to describe a practice or document that is provided as a courtesy or satisfies minimum requirements, conforms to a norm or doctrine, tends to be performed perfunctorily or is considered a formality.

Exam Probability: **Low**

6. *Answer choices:*

(see index for correct answer)

- a. Fin 48
- b. Cash method of accounting
- c. Matching principle
- d. Operating income before depreciation and amortization

Guidance: level 1

:: Inventory ::

In business and accounting/accountancy, _____ or continuous inventory describes systems of inventory where information on inventory quantity and availability is updated on a continuous basis as a function of doing business. Generally this is accomplished by connecting the inventory system with order entry and in retail the point of sale system. In this case, book inventory would be exactly the same as, or almost the same, as the real inventory.

Exam Probability: **High**

7. *Answer choices:*

(see index for correct answer)

- a. Average cost method
- b. Specific identification
- c. Perpetual inventory
- d. Stock mix

Guidance: level 1

:: International taxation ::

_____ is the levying of tax by two or more jurisdictions on the same declared income , asset , or financial transaction . Double liability is mitigated in a number of ways, for example.

Exam Probability: **High**

8. *Answer choices:*

(see index for correct answer)

- a. Spahn tax
- b. Advance pricing agreement
- c. Currency transaction tax
- d. Double taxation

Guidance: level 1

:: Inventory ::

_____ is a system of inventory in which updates are made on a periodic basis. This differs from perpetual inventory systems, where updates are made as seen fit.

Exam Probability: **Low**

9. *Answer choices:*

(see index for correct answer)

- a. Stock demands
- b. LIFO
- c. Cost of goods available for sale
- d. Stock control

Guidance: level 1

:: Accounting ::

_____ are key sources of information and evidence used to prepare, verify and/or audit the financial statements. They also include documentation to prove asset ownership for creation of liabilities and proof of monetary and non monetary transactions.

Exam Probability: **High**

10. *Answer choices:*

(see index for correct answer)

- a. Accounting research
- b. Profit model
- c. Teeming and lading
- d. Accounting records

Guidance: level 1

:: Management ::

The _____ is a strategy performance management tool – a semi-standard structured report, that can be used by managers to keep track of the execution of activities by the staff within their control and to monitor the consequences arising from these actions.

11. *Answer choices:*

(see index for correct answer)

- a. Financial planning
- b. Unified interoperability
- c. Energy management software
- d. Innovation management

Guidance: level 1

:: Financial ratios ::

In finance, the _____ , also known as the acid-test ratio   is a type of liquidity ratio which measures the ability of a company to use its near cash or quick assets to extinguish or retire its current liabilities immediately. Quick assets include those current assets that presumably can be quickly converted to cash at close to their book values. It is the ratio between quickly available or liquid assets and current liabilities.

Exam Probability: **Medium**

12. *Answer choices:*

(see index for correct answer)

- a. Operating leverage
- b. Sharpe ratio

- c. Quick ratio
- d. Omega ratio

Guidance: level 1

:: Financial ratios ::

_____ is a measure of how revenue growth translates into growth in operating income. It is a measure of leverage, and of how risky, or volatile, a company's operating income is.

Exam Probability: **Low**

13. *Answer choices:*

(see index for correct answer)

- a. Asset turnover
- b. Yield gap
- c. Operating leverage
- d. stock turnover

Guidance: level 1

:: Management accounting ::

_____ accounting is a traditional cost accounting method introduced in the 1920s, as an alternative for the traditional cost accounting method based on historical costs.

Exam Probability: **Low**

14. *Answer choices:*

(see index for correct answer)

- a. Direct material price variance
- b. Standard cost
- c. Direct material total variance
- d. Management accounting

Guidance: level 1

:: ::

A tax is a compulsory financial charge or some other type of levy imposed upon a taxpayer by a governmental organization in order to fund various public expenditures. A failure to pay, along with evasion of or resistance to _____ , is punishable by law. Taxes consist of direct or indirect taxes and may be paid in money or as its labour equivalent.

Exam Probability: **Low**

15. *Answer choices:*

(see index for correct answer)

- a. Sarbanes-Oxley act of 2002
- b. hierarchical
- c. Taxation
- d. process perspective

Guidance: level 1

:: Management accounting ::

_____ , or dollar contribution per unit, is the selling price per unit minus the variable cost per unit. "Contribution" represents the portion of sales revenue that is not consumed by variable costs and so contributes to the coverage of fixed costs. This concept is one of the key building blocks of break-even analysis.

Exam Probability: **Low**

16. *Answer choices:*

(see index for correct answer)

- a. Contribution margin
- b. Activity-based management
- c. Direct material total variance
- d. Direct material price variance

:: Basic financial concepts ::

_____ is a sustained increase in the general price level of goods and services in an economy over a period of time. When the general price level rises, each unit of currency buys fewer goods and services; consequently, _____ reflects a reduction in the purchasing power per unit of money a loss of real value in the medium of exchange and unit of account within the economy. The measure of _____ is the _____ rate, the annualized percentage change in a general price index, usually the consumer price index, over time. The opposite of _____ is deflation.

Exam Probability: **High**

17. *Answer choices:*

(see index for correct answer)

- a. Financial transaction
- b. Tax shield
- c. Present value of costs
- d. Eurodollar

:: ::

An _____ , for United States federal income tax, is a closely held corporation that makes a valid election to be taxed under Subchapter S of Chapter 1 of the Internal Revenue Code. In general, _____ s do not pay any income taxes. Instead, the corporation's income or losses are divided among and passed through to its shareholders. The shareholders must then report the income or loss on their own individual income tax returns.

Exam Probability: **Medium**

18. *Answer choices:*

(see index for correct answer)

- a. information systems assessment
- b. hierarchical perspective
- c. S corporation
- d. levels of analysis

Guidance: level 1

:: ::

_____ or accountancy is the measurement, processing, and communication of financial information about economic entities such as businesses and corporations. The modern field was established by the Italian mathematician Luca Pacioli in 1494. _____ , which has been called the "language of business", measures the results of an organization's economic activities and conveys this information to a variety of users, including investors, creditors, management, and regulators. Practitioners of _____ are known as accountants. The terms "_____" and "financial reporting" are often used as synonyms.

Exam Probability: **Low**

19. *Answer choices:*

(see index for correct answer)

- a. Accounting
- b. process perspective
- c. similarity-attraction theory
- d. imperative

Guidance: level 1

:: Financial ratios ::

The _____ or dividend-price ratio of a share is the dividend per share, divided by the price per share. It is also a company's total annual dividend payments divided by its market capitalization, assuming the number of shares is constant. It is often expressed as a percentage.

20. *Answer choices:*

(see index for correct answer)

- a. Market-to-book
- b. Operating ratio
- c. Short interest ratio
- d. Dividend yield

Guidance: level 1

:: Accounting in the United States ::

The _____ was formed by the American Institute of Certified Public Accountants in 1972, and developed the Objective of Financial Statements. The committee's goal was to create financial statements that helped external users make decisions about the economics of companies. In 1978, the Financial Accounting Standards Board , whose purpose is to develop generally accepted accounting principles, adopted the key objectives established by the _____

.

Exam Probability: **Medium**

21. *Answer choices:*

(see index for correct answer)

- a. Trueblood Committee

- b. Cotton Plantation Record and Account Book
- c. Norwalk Agreement
- d. Other postemployment benefits

Guidance: level 1

:: Accounting software ::

_____ is any item or verifiable record that is generally accepted as payment for goods and services and repayment of debts, such as taxes, in a particular country or socio-economic context. The main functions of _____ are distinguished as: a medium of exchange, a unit of account, a store of value and sometimes, a standard of deferred payment. Any item or verifiable record that fulfils these functions can be considered as _____ .

Exam Probability: **Low**

22. *Answer choices:*

(see index for correct answer)

- a. Money
- b. Accounting software
- c. Billback
- d. Costpoint

Guidance: level 1

:: Business economics ::

_____ is one of the constituents of a leasing calculus or operation. It describes the future value of a good in terms of absolute value in monetary terms and it is sometimes abbreviated into a percentage of the initial price when the item was new.

Exam Probability: **Low**

23. *Answer choices:*

(see index for correct answer)

- a. Kaizen costing
- b. Willingness to pay
- c. Creditor Reference
- d. Gross operating surplus

Guidance: level 1

:: Budgets ::

An _____ is the annual budget of an activity stated in terms of Budget Classification Code, functional/subfunctional categories and cost accounts. It contains estimates of the total value of resources required for the performance of the operation including reimbursable work or services for others. It also includes estimates of workload in terms of total work units identified by cost accounts.

24. *Answer choices:*

(see index for correct answer)

- a. Budgeted cost of work scheduled
- b. Film budgeting
- c. Operating budget
- d. Personal budget

Guidance: level 1

:: ::

The U.S. _____ is an independent agency of the United States federal government. The SEC holds primary responsibility for enforcing the federal securities laws, proposing securities rules, and regulating the securities industry, the nation's stock and options exchanges, and other activities and organizations, including the electronic securities markets in the United States.

Exam Probability: **High**

25. *Answer choices:*

(see index for correct answer)

- a. Securities and Exchange Commission
- b. cultural

- c. hierarchical
- d. deep-level diversity

Guidance: level 1

:: Commerce ::

Continuation of an entity as a _____ is presumed as the basis for financial reporting unless and until the entity's liquidation becomes imminent. Preparation of financial statements under this presumption is commonly referred to as the _____ basis of accounting. If and when an entity's liquidation becomes imminent, financial statements are prepared under the liquidation basis of accounting .

Exam Probability: **High**

26. *Answer choices:*

(see index for correct answer)

- a. Recommerce
- b. GT Nexus
- c. Commodity market
- d. Economic entity

Guidance: level 1

:: ::

A _____ is the period used by governments for accounting and budget purposes, which varies between countries. It is also used for financial reporting by business and other organizations. Laws in many jurisdictions require company financial reports to be prepared and published on an annual basis, but generally do not require the reporting period to align with the calendar year . Taxation laws generally require accounting records to be maintained and taxes calculated on an annual basis, which usually corresponds to the _____ used for government purposes. The calculation of tax on an annual basis is especially relevant for direct taxation, such as income tax. Many annual government fees—such as Council rates, licence fees, etc.—are also levied on a _____ basis, while others are charged on an anniversary basis.

Exam Probability: **High**

27. *Answer choices:*

(see index for correct answer)

- a. co-culture
- b. Character
- c. hierarchical perspective
- d. Fiscal year

Guidance: level 1

:: ::

In the field of analysis of algorithms in computer science, the _____ is a method of amortized analysis based on accounting. The _____ often gives a more intuitive account of the amortized cost of an operation than either aggregate analysis or the potential method. Note, however, that this does not guarantee such analysis will be immediately obvious; often, choosing the correct parameters for the _____ requires as much knowledge of the problem and the complexity bounds one is attempting to prove as the other two methods.

Exam Probability: **Medium**

28. *Answer choices:*

(see index for correct answer)

- a. Accounting method
- b. personal values
- c. process perspective
- d. hierarchical perspective

Guidance: level 1

:: Management accounting ::

_____ are costs that are not directly accountable to a cost object . _____ may be either fixed or variable. _____ include administration, personnel and security costs. These are those costs which are not directly related to production. Some _____ may be overhead. But some overhead costs can be directly attributed to a project and are direct costs.

29. *Answer choices:*

(see index for correct answer)

- a. Cost accounting
- b. Indirect costs
- c. Entity-level controls
- d. Overhead

Guidance: level 1

:: Money ::

In economics, _____ is money in the physical form of currency, such as banknotes and coins. In bookkeeping and finance, _____ is current assets comprising currency or currency equivalents that can be accessed immediately or near-immediately . _____ is seen either as a reserve for payments, in case of a structural or incidental negative _____ flow or as a way to avoid a downturn on financial markets.

Exam Probability: **Medium**

30. *Answer choices:*

(see index for correct answer)

- a. Cash
- b. World Money Fair

- c. Lump sum
- d. Token money

Guidance: level 1

:: Generally Accepted Accounting Principles ::

A _____ , in accrual accounting, is any account where the asset or liability is not realized until a future date , e.g. annuities, charges, taxes, income, etc. The deferred item may be carried, dependent on type of _____ , as either an asset or liability. See also accrual.

Exam Probability: **Low**

31. *Answer choices:*

(see index for correct answer)

- a. Standard Business Reporting
- b. Deferral
- c. Petty cash
- d. Depreciation

Guidance: level 1

:: Accounting systems ::

In accounting, a business or an organization and its owners are treated as two separately identifiable parties. This is called the _____ . The business stands apart from other organizations as a separate economic unit. It is necessary to record the business`s transactions separately, to distinguish them from the owners` personal transactions. This helps to give a correct determination of the true financial condition of the business. This concept can be extended to accounting separately for the various divisions of a business in order to ascertain the financial results for each division. Under the business _____ , a business holds separate entity and distinct from its owners. "The entity view holds the business `enterprise to be an institution in its own right separate and distinct from the parties who furnish the funds"

Exam Probability: **Medium**

32. *Answer choices:*

(see index for correct answer)

- a. Entity concept
- b. Inflation accounting
- c. Momentum accounting and triple-entry bookkeeping
- d. Cookie jar accounting

Guidance: level 1

:: Financial accounting ::

_____ refers to any one of several methods by which a company, for 'financial accounting' or tax purposes, depreciates a fixed asset in such a way that the amount of depreciation taken each year is higher during the earlier years of an asset's life. For financial accounting purposes, _____ is expected to be much more productive during its early years, so that depreciation expense will more accurately represent how much of an asset's usefulness is being used up each year. For tax purposes, _____ provides a way of deferring corporate income taxes by reducing taxable income in current years, in exchange for increased taxable income in future years. This is a valuable tax incentive that encourages businesses to purchase new assets.

Exam Probability: **Low**

33. *Answer choices:*

(see index for correct answer)

- a. Authorised capital
- b. Accelerated depreciation
- c. Exit rate
- d. Associate company

Guidance: level 1

:: Financial accounting ::

In accounting, _____ is the value of an asset according to its balance sheet account balance. For assets, the value is based on the original cost of the asset less any depreciation, amortization or impairment costs made against the asset. Traditionally, a company's _____ is its total assets minus intangible assets and liabilities. However, in practice, depending on the source of the calculation, _____ may variably include goodwill, intangible assets, or both. The value inherent in its workforce, part of the intellectual capital of a company, is always ignored. When intangible assets and goodwill are explicitly excluded, the metric is often specified to be "tangible _____".

Exam Probability: **Low**

34. *Answer choices:*

(see index for correct answer)

- a. Book value
- b. Money measurement
- c. Finance charge
- d. Exit rate

Guidance: level 1

:: Accounting in the United States ::

The _____ is the source of generally accepted accounting principles used by state and local governments in the United States. As with most of the entities involved in creating GAAP in the United States, it is a private, non-governmental organization.

35. *Answer choices:*

(see index for correct answer)

- a. Financial Accounting Foundation
- b. Cotton Plantation Record and Account Book
- c. Norwalk Agreement
- d. Governmental Accounting Standards Board

Guidance: level 1

:: Taxation ::

A _____ is a person or organization subject to pay a tax. _____ s have an Identification Number, a reference number issued by a government to its citizens.

Exam Probability: **Medium**

36. *Answer choices:*

(see index for correct answer)

- a. Taxpayer
- b. Value capture
- c. Tax lien
- d. Paulette

:: Project management ::

_____ is the widespread practice of collecting information and attempting to spot a pattern. In some fields of study, the term " _____ " has more formally defined meanings.

Exam Probability: **Medium**

37. *Answer choices:*

(see index for correct answer)

- a. Advanced Integrated Practice
- b. Life-cycle cost analysis
- c. Project management 2.0
- d. Trend analysis

:: Personal taxes ::

A _____ is the completion of documentation that calculates an entity's income earned with the amount of tax payable to the government, government organisations or to potential taxpayers.

38. *Answer choices:*

(see index for correct answer)

- a. Scottish variable rate
- b. 26 USC 102
- c. Vehicle registration tax
- d. Taxation in Canada

Guidance: level 1

:: Marketing ::

_____ or stock is the goods and materials that a business holds for the ultimate goal of resale .

Exam Probability: **Low**

39. *Answer choices:*

(see index for correct answer)

- a. Permission marketing
- b. Inventory
- c. Medical science liaison
- d. Global Center for Health Innovation

:: United States Generally Accepted Accounting Principles ::

A _____ is a set of U.S. government financial statements comprising the financial report of a state, municipal or other governmental entity that complies with the accounting requirements promulgated by the Governmental Accounting Standards Board . GASB provides standards for the content of a CAFR in its annually updated publication Codification of Governmental Accounting and Financial Reporting Standards. The U.S. Federal Government adheres to standards determined by the Federal Accounting Standards Advisory Board .

Exam Probability: **Medium**

40. *Answer choices:*

(see index for correct answer)

- a. Impaired asset
- b. Working Group on Financial Markets
- c. Comprehensive annual financial report
- d. GASB 45

:: Generally Accepted Accounting Principles ::

The first published description of the process is found in Luca Pacioli`s 1494 work Summa de arithmetica, in the section titled Particularis de Computis et Scripturis. Although he did not use the term, he essentially prescribed a technique similar to a post-closing _____ .

Exam Probability: **Medium**

41. *Answer choices:*

(see index for correct answer)

- a. Liability
- b. Closing entries
- c. Petty cash
- d. Revenue recognition

Guidance: level 1

:: Financial ratios ::

_____ is the difference between revenue and cost of goods sold divided by revenue. _____ is expressed as a percentage. Generally, it is calculated as the selling price of an item, less the cost of goods sold .
_____ is often used interchangeably with Gross Profit, but the terms are different. When speaking about a monetary amount, it is technically correct to use the term Gross Profit; when referring to a percentage or ratio, it is correct to use _____ . In other words, _____ is a percentage value, while Gross Profit is a monetary value.

Exam Probability: **Medium**

42. *Answer choices:*

(see index for correct answer)

- a. Return on event
- b. K-factor
- c. Gross margin
- d. CASA ratio

Guidance: level 1

:: Manufacturing ::

_____ costs are all manufacturing costs that are related to the cost object but cannot be traced to that cost object in an economically feasible way.

Exam Probability: **Low**

43. *Answer choices:*

(see index for correct answer)

- a. Rite-Hite
- b. Agile manufacturing
- c. Manufacturing overhead
- d. Reconfigurable Manufacturing System

:: Management accounting ::

_____ is the process of reviewing and analyzing a company's financial statements to make better economic decisions to earn income in future. These statements include the income statement, balance sheet, statement of cash flows, notes to accounts and a statement of changes in equity . _____ is a method or process involving specific techniques for evaluating risks, performance, financial health, and future prospects of an organization.

Exam Probability: **Low**

44. *Answer choices:*

(see index for correct answer)

- a. Holding cost
- b. Target income sales
- c. Financial statement analysis
- d. Constraints accounting

:: Information systems ::

_____ are formal, sociotechnical, organizational systems designed to collect, process, store, and distribute information. In a sociotechnical perspective, _____ are composed by four components: task, people, structure , and technology.

Exam Probability: **Low**

45. *Answer choices:*

(see index for correct answer)

- a. Reason maintenance
- b. Heritage Operations Processing System
- c. Website Meta Language
- d. Information systems

Guidance: level 1

:: ::

In accounting, the _____ is a measure of the number of times inventory is sold or used in a time period such as a year. It is calculated to see if a business has an excessive inventory in comparison to its sales level. The equation for _____ equals the cost of goods sold divided by the average inventory. _____ is also known as inventory turns, merchandise turnover, stockturn, stock turns, turns, and stock turnover.

Exam Probability: **Medium**

46. *Answer choices:*

(see index for correct answer)

- a. Inventory turnover
- b. surface-level diversity
- c. process perspective
- d. cultural

Guidance: level 1

:: Generally Accepted Accounting Principles ::

_____ is, in accrual accounting, money received for goods or services which have not yet been delivered. According to the revenue recognition principle, it is recorded as a liability until delivery is made, at which time it is converted into revenue.

Exam Probability: **Low**

47. *Answer choices:*

(see index for correct answer)

- a. Revenue recognition
- b. Statement of recommended practice
- c. Generally accepted accounting principles
- d. Deferred income

:: Management accounting ::

_____ is an accountancy practice, the aim of which is to provide an offset to the mark-to-market movement of the derivative in the profit and loss account. There are two types of hedge recognized. For a fair value hedge the offset is achieved either by marking-to-market an asset or a liability which offsets the P&L movement of the derivative. For a cash flow hedge some of the derivative volatility into a separate component of the entity's equity called the cash flow hedge reserve. Where a hedge relationship is effective , most of the mark-to-market derivative volatility will be offset in the profit and loss account. _____ entails much compliance - involving documenting the hedge relationship and both prospectively and retrospectively proving that the hedge relationship is effective.

Exam Probability: **Low**

48. *Answer choices:*

(see index for correct answer)

- a. Cash and cash equivalents
- b. Process costing
- c. Cost driver
- d. Hedge accounting

:: E-commerce ::

A _____ is a plastic payment card that can be used instead of cash when making purchases. It is similar to a credit card, but unlike a credit card, the money is immediately transferred directly from the cardholder's bank account when performing a transaction.

Exam Probability: **High**

49. *Answer choices:*

(see index for correct answer)

- a. Public exchange
- b. Triton
- c. Government-to-business
- d. Andy Dunn

Guidance: level 1

:: Management ::

_____ is the identification, evaluation, and prioritization of risks followed by coordinated and economical application of resources to minimize, monitor, and control the probability or impact of unfortunate events or to maximize the realization of opportunities.

Exam Probability: **Medium**

50. *Answer choices:*

(see index for correct answer)

- a. Risk management
- b. Security management
- c. Dynamic enterprise modeling
- d. Flat organization

Guidance: level 1

:: Management ::

Business _____ is a discipline in operations management in which people use various methods to discover, model, analyze, measure, improve, optimize, and automate business processes. BPM focuses on improving corporate performance by managing business processes. Any combination of methods used to manage a company's business processes is BPM. Processes can be structured and repeatable or unstructured and variable. Though not required, enabling technologies are often used with BPM.

Exam Probability: **Low**

51. *Answer choices:*

(see index for correct answer)

- a. Operations management
- b. Process Management
- c. Distributed management

- d. Libertarian management

Guidance: level 1

:: Management accounting ::

In finance, the _____ or net present worth applies to a series of cash flows occurring at different times. The present value of a cash flow depends on the interval of time between now and the cash flow. It also depends on the discount rate. NPV accounts for the time value of money. It provides a method for evaluating and comparing capital projects or financial products with cash flows spread over time, as in loans, investments, payouts from insurance contracts plus many other applications.

Exam Probability: **Low**

52. *Answer choices:*

(see index for correct answer)

- a. Standard cost
- b. Net present value
- c. Extended cost
- d. Fixed cost

Guidance: level 1

:: Management accounting ::

_____ is an accounting methodology that traces and accumulates direct costs, and allocates indirect costs of a manufacturing process. Costs are assigned to products, usually in a large batch, which might include an entire month's production. Eventually, costs have to be allocated to individual units of product. It assigns average costs to each unit, and is the opposite extreme of Job costing which attempts to measure individual costs of production of each unit. _____ is usually a significant chapter. It is a method of assigning costs to units of production in companies producing large quantities of homogeneous products..

Exam Probability: **Medium**

53. *Answer choices:*

(see index for correct answer)

- a. Indirect costs
- b. Process costing
- c. Activity-based management
- d. Entity-level controls

Guidance: level 1

:: Generally Accepted Accounting Principles ::

_____ is the accounting classification of an account. It is part of double-entry book-keeping technique.

Exam Probability: **High**

54. *Answer choices:*

(see index for correct answer)

- a. Reserve
- b. Revenue
- c. Historical cost
- d. Normal balance

Guidance: level 1

:: Banking terms ::

An _____ occurs when money is withdrawn from a bank account and the available balance goes below zero. In this situation the account is said to be "overdrawn". If there is a prior agreement with the account provider for an _____ , and the amount overdrawn is within the authorized _____ limit, then interest is normally charged at the agreed rate. If the negative balance exceeds the agreed terms, then additional fees may be charged and higher interest rates may apply.

Exam Probability: **Medium**

55. *Answer choices:*

(see index for correct answer)

- a. Originating Depository Financial Institution
- b. Payable-through
- c. Overdraft

- d. Bank reserves

Guidance: level 1

:: ::

The _____ of 1934 is a law governing the secondary trading of securities in the United States of America. A landmark of wide-ranging legislation, the Act of `34 and related statutes form the basis of regulation of the financial markets and their participants in the United States. The 1934 Act also established the Securities and Exchange Commission , the agency primarily responsible for enforcement of United States federal securities law.

Exam Probability: **Low**

56. *Answer choices:*
(see index for correct answer)

- a. process perspective
- b. functional perspective
- c. corporate values
- d. Securities Exchange Act

Guidance: level 1

:: Valuation (finance) ::

The _____ is one of three major groups of methodologies, called valuation approaches, used by appraisers. It is particularly common in commercial real estate appraisal and in business appraisal. The fundamental math is similar to the methods used for financial valuation, securities analysis, or bond pricing. However, there are some significant and important modifications when used in real estate or business valuation.

Exam Probability: **Medium**

57. *Answer choices:*

(see index for correct answer)

- a. Graham number
- b. Value date
- c. The Appraisal Foundation
- d. Pre-money valuation

Guidance: level 1

:: Management accounting ::

_____ is a professional business study of Accounts and management in which we learn importance of accounts in our management system.

Exam Probability: **Medium**

58. *Answer choices:*

- a. Relevant cost
- b. Accounting management
- c. Cost accounting
- d. Resource consumption accounting

Guidance: level 1

:: Debt ::

A _____ is a party that has a claim on the services of a second party. It is a person or institution to whom money is owed. The first party, in general, has provided some property or service to the second party under the assumption that the second party will return an equivalent property and service. The second party is frequently called a debtor or borrower. The first party is called the _____ , which is the lender of property, service, or money.

Exam Probability: **Medium**

59. *Answer choices:*

- a. Least developed country
- b. Phantom debt
- c. Debt-lag
- d. Consumer debt

Guidance: level 1

INDEX: Correct Answers

Foundations of Business

1. c: Review

2. b: Industry

3. c: Feedback

4. a: Strategic alliance

5. b: Federal Trade Commission

6. : Subsidiary

7. : Quality control

8. c: Economic Development

9. b: Best practice

10. b: Commerce

11. a: Market segmentation

12. a: Shareholders

13. a: Productivity

14. d: Currency

15. b: Business model

16. c: Marketing mix

17. d: Tariff

18. : Benchmarking

19. b: Sharing

20. b: Foreign direct investment

21. : Market research

22. b: Industrial Revolution

23. d: Need

24. : Pattern

25. a: Comparative advantage

26. d: Credit card

27. a: Consumer Protection

28. d: Size

29. d: Number

30. a: Strategy

31. c: Brainstorming

32. d: Business process

33. : Trade agreement

34. b: Asset

35. : Risk management

36. d: Interest

37. : Planning

38. d: Cash

39. : Fraud

40. d: Corporate governance

41. c: Human resources

42. b: Resource management

43. b: Bankruptcy

44. b: ASEAN

45. d: Description

46. a: Small business

47. c: Stock market

48. d: Mission statement

49. c: Exercise

50. : Buyer

51. b: Capital market

52. b: Insurance

53. a: Cooperative

54. a: Income statement

55. c: Initiative

56. c: Credit

57. b: Building

58. c: Incentive

59. a: Sustainability

Management

1. c: Review

2. c: Efficiency

3. : Quality circle

4. a: Vertical integration

5. : Office

6. : Bargaining

7. d: Social capital

8. : Chief executive officer

9. b: Expatriate

10. c: Offshoring

11. d: Training and development

12. c: Consultant

13. b: Resource management

14. d: Workforce

15. a: Management process

16. a: Variable cost

17. d: Glass ceiling

18. : Integrity

19. b: Environmental protection

20. a: Customs

21. c: Utility

22. a: Job enlargement

23. a: Income

24. c: Asset

25. c: Recruitment

26. b: Statistic

27. : Quality assurance

28. d: International trade

29. b: Inventory

30. : Task force

31. b: Virtual team

32. c: Insurance

33. d: Expert power

34. d: Bias

35. : 360-degree feedback

36. d: Governance

37. a: Customer

38. b: Time management

39. d: Overtime

40. d: Export

41. b: Cash flow

42. : Dimension

43. b: Empowerment

44. b: Sales

45. b: Incentive

46. : Pension

47. d: Risk management

48. a: Argument

49. d: Ratio

50. c: Vendor

51. : Interdependence

52. a: Human resource management

53. : Reinforcement

54. a: Transformational leadership

55. : Supervisor

56. : Product life cycle

57. d: Stereotype

58. d: Authority

59. a: Analysis

Business law

1. : Argument

2. c: Assignee

3. d: Security

4. a: Regulation

5. : Advertisement

6. b: Credit

7. d: S corporation

8. a: Constitutional law

9. a: Verdict

10. a: Trade

11. : Brand

12. : Rehabilitation Act

13. c: Merchant

14. b: Summary judgment

15. c: Subsidiary

16. d: Accounting

17. : Forgery

18. : Ford

19. : Offeree

20. : Warehouse

21. : Technology

22. a: Petition

23. a: Federal government

24. a: Welfare

25. b: Guarantee

26. c: Clayton Act

27. b: White-collar crime

28. b: Patent

29. d: Comparative negligence

30. b: Securities Act

31. : Contract

32. c: Unconscionability

33. d: Prohibition

34. c: Option contract

35. b: Negotiation

36. a: Perfection

37. d: Liquidated damages

38. b: Competitor

39. c: Holder in due course

40. a: Anticipatory repudiation

41. b: Beneficiary

42. : Licensee

43. d: Proximate cause

44. : Product liability

45. b: Relevant market

46. c: Utilitarianism

47. b: Criminal procedure

48. b: Intellectual property

49. d: Wage

50. d: Security interest

51. d: Interest

52. : Computer fraud

53. : Advertising

54. a: Plaintiff

55. d: Identity theft

56. a: Insolvency

57. b: Lanham Act

58. d: Arbitration

59. : Financial privacy

Finance

1. : Bank

2. c: INDEX

3. a: Capital asset pricing model

4. : Capital budgeting

5. : Rate of return

6. d: Forward contract

7. a: Financial instrument

8. a: Bank statement

9. c: Comprehensive income

10. a: Enron

11. b: Break-even

12. c: Present value

13. a: Sole proprietorship

14. b: Historical cost

15. c: Yield curve

16. c: Ending inventory

17. d: Deferral

18. : Merger

19. c: Capital structure

20. b: Government bond

21. a: Perpetual inventory

22. : Firm

23. d: Activity-based costing

24. : Financial market

25. c: Matching principle

26. a: Residual value

27. b: Liquidation

28. b: Risk assessment

29. d: Standard deviation

30. a: Net worth

31. b: Financial crisis

32. : Initial public offering

33. b: Management accounting

34. b: Volume

35. c: Stock

36. : Accounts receivable

37. : Cash equivalent

38. : Incentive

39. d: Internal control

40. d: Treasury stock

41. a: Accountant

42. a: Credit

43. a: Financial management

44. d: Annuity

45. : Vacation

46. d: Sales

47. a: Quick ratio

48. d: Marketing

49. d: Discounting

50. : Operating Income

51. d: Long-term liabilities

52. a: Market risk

53. d: Social security

54. b: Variable cost

55. b: Fiscal year

56. d: Cost of goods sold

57. b: Asset turnover

58. d: Opportunity cost

59. d: Convertible bond

Human resource management

1. d: Employment

2. d: Bargaining unit

3. c: Coaching

4. b: Xerox Corporation

5. d: Workforce planning

6. c: Featherbedding

7. b: Reasonable person

8. c: Expatriate

9. a: Concurrent validity

10. : Employee benefit

11. : Mergers and acquisitions

12. b: Global sourcing

13. c: Substance abuse

14. : On-the-job training

15. : Arbitration

16. a: Phantom stock

17. : Transformational leadership

18. a: Human resources

19. : Person Analysis

20. d: Mediation

21. : Prevailing wage

22. c: Grievance

23. : Job performance

24. b: Intuition

25. b: Theory Z

26. c: Meeting

27. b: Management

28. c: Affirmative action

29. a: Job analysis

30. d: Data collection

31. d: Family violence

32. d: Training and development

33. b: Minnesota Multiphasic Personality Inventory

34. c: Job enrichment

35. d: Survey research

36. : Closed shop

37. a: Sexual harassment

38. c: McDonnell Douglas Corp. v. Green

39. a: Employee retention

40. b: Externship

41. : Organizational learning

42. d: Structured interview

43. c: Total Reward

44. b: Unemployment insurance

45. c: Workforce management

46. : Absenteeism

47. d: Parental leave

48. d: Executive officer

49. c: Work ethic

50. b: Graveyard shift

51. b: Analysis

52. a: Needs assessment

53. c: Performance management

54. c: Fair Labor Standards Act

55. : Ingratiation

56. d: Socialization

57. b: Whistleblower

58. d: Alcoholism

59. a: Cafeteria plan

Information systems

1. d: Bit rate

2. a: Output device

3. a: Phishing

4. a: Positioning system

5. b: Facebook

6. d: Data model

7. c: Authentication protocol

8. : Analytics

9. a: Dashboard

10. a: Blogger

11. b: Mouse

12. d: Drill down

13. a: Service-oriented architecture

14. : Relational database

15. : Automation

16. c: Transaction processing

17. : Data redundancy

18. : Manifesto

19. c: Random access

20. b: QR code

21. a: PageRank

22. a: Zynga

23. a: Copyright

24. a: Consumer-to-consumer

25. c: Reputation management

26. : Total cost of ownership

27. d: Domain name

28. d: Fraud

29. c: Extensible Markup Language

30. c: Service level

31. : M-Pesa

32. a: Sustainable

33. d: Intrusion detection system

34. a: Commercial off-the-shelf

35. b: Google Docs

36. : Data

37. c: Authentication

38. c: Database management system

39. : Electronic data interchange

40. : Interaction

41. : Fault tolerance

42. a: Enterprise search

43. a: Query language

44. c: Google Maps

45. a: Computer-integrated manufacturing

46. : Data cleansing

47. c: Information flow

48. : Data visualization

49. c: Outsourcing

50. a: Competitive intelligence

51. c: Documentation

52. a: Long tail

53. b: Monopoly

54. b: Availability

55. b: Mobile computing

56. d: System software

57. c: YouTube

58. : Help desk

59. b: Privacy

Marketing

1. d: Problem Solving

2. : Ford

3. : Price discrimination

4. a: Business marketing

5. b: Pricing

6. c: Logistics

7. c: Customer retention

8. a: Product manager

9. b: Incentive

10. b: Sales promotion

11. c: Persuasion

12. b: Technology

13. b: Merchant

14. : Green marketing

15. c: Outsourcing

16. b: Marketing strategy

17. c: Good

18. d: E-commerce

19. a: Value proposition

20. c: Viral marketing

21. c: Auction

22. d: Accounting

23. b: Business Week

24. a: Early adopter

25. b: Property

26. : Marketing plan

27. a: Competitor

28. c: Retail

29. b: Revenue

30. d: Evolution

31. c: Committee

32. d: Sales management

33. b: Consumer behavior

34. d: Publicity

35. a: Penetration pricing

36. b: Database

37. b: Personal selling

38. : Customer satisfaction

39. a: Testimonial

40. a: Google

41. b: Clayton Act

42. a: Stock

43. b: Return on investment

44. c: Household

45. a: Gross domestic product

46. a: Organizational culture

47. d: Strategic planning

48. d: Social network

49. c: Infomercial

50. c: Marketing communication

51. a: Product differentiation

52. a: Regulation

53. a: Variable cost

54. d: Business-to-business

55. c: Entrepreneur

56. b: Economies of scale

57. : Target audience

58. d: Global marketing

59. a: Competitive intelligence

Manufacturing

1. c: Quality control

2. c: Strategic sourcing

3. c: Service quality

4. c: Value engineering

5. d: Metal

6. b: Workflow

7. b: Kaizen

8. : Gantt chart

9. a: Thomas Register

10. d: Forecasting

11. c: Cost

12. : Process capital

13. b: Sharing

14. : Pattern

15. : Information management

16. : Interaction

17. d: Strategic planning

18. : Consortium

19. b: Quality policy

20. b: Cost estimate

21. d: Knowledge management

22. a: Throughput

23. a: Heat transfer

24. d: Resource allocation

25. : Distillation

26. b: Voice of the customer

27. a: Durability

28. c: Heat treating

29. c: Project manager

30. b: METRIC

31. b: Indirect costs

32. : Malcolm Baldrige National Quality Award

33. b: Cost driver

34. : Process management

35. : Management process

36. : Quality Engineering

37. : Tool

38. c: Flowchart

39. c: Reboiler

40. c: E-commerce

41. d: ROOT

42. a: Planning

43. a: Remanufacturing

44. : Purchasing

45. c: Quality management

46. b: Inventory control

47. b: Third-party logistics

48. d: Downtime

49. d: Quality costs

50. d: Check sheet

51. b: Catalyst

52. : Coating

53. : Transaction cost

54. a: Design of experiments

55. a: Supply chain

56. : Original equipment manufacturer

57. : Ball

58. d: Supply chain management

59. b: Request for quotation

Commerce

1. a: Incentive

2. : Electronic commerce

3. d: Good

4. c: Building

5. d: Marginal cost

6. c: Common carrier

7. d: Consortium

8. : Direct marketing

9. a: Inventory

10. : Regulatory agency

11. b: Aid

12. d: Appeal

13. d: Optimum

14. d: Yield management

15. d: Collaborative filtering

16. a: Walt Disney

17. c: Empowerment

18. : Bank

19. c: Graduation

20. b: Interest

21. : Buyer

22. c: Dutch auction

23. c: Stock

24. a: Trade show

25. d: Partnership

26. c: Strategic plan

27. c: Fixed cost

28. a: Jury

29. d: Welfare

30. c: Excite

31. b: Cash flow

32. a: Shopping cart

33. a: Enabling

34. c: Land

35. c: Auction

36. b: Revenue management

37. b: Online advertising

38. a: Complexity

39. b: Customer service

40. c: Performance

41. a: Leadership

42. : Human resources

43. d: Sexual harassment

44. b: Product mix

45. c: Evaluation

46. a: Siemens

47. : Computer security

48. b: Tangible

49. a: GeoCities

50. d: English auction

51. c: Variable cost

52. a: Total revenue

53. c: Marketing mix

54. c: American Express

55. c: Liquidation

56. c: Semantic

57. b: Economic regulation

58. a: Subsidiary

59. d: Contribution margin

Business ethics

1. a: European Commission

2. c: Global Fund

3. a: Internal control

4. a: Corporate social responsibility

5. d: Sexual harassment

6. c: Micromanagement

7. d: Business model

8. d: Corporate structure

9. : Individualistic culture

10. a: White-collar crime

11. b: Minimum wage

12. a: Communist Manifesto

13. c: Pollution

14. b: Risk assessment

15. : Clean Water Act

16. b: Oil spill

17. d: Federal Trade Commission

18. c: Qui tam

19. a: UN Global Compact

20. : Environmental audit

21. d: Federal Trade Commission Act

22. c: Consumerism

23. d: Better Business Bureau

24. c: Wall Street

25. b: Habitat

26. b: Greenpeace

27. a: Organizational structure

28. b: Working poor

29. d: United Farm Workers

30. a: Dual relationship

31. a: Solar power

32. a: Price fixing

33. c: Utopian socialism

34. : Fannie Mae

35. : Perception

36. d: Ethics Resource Center

37. d: Arthur Andersen

38. d: Protestant work ethic

39. c: Disclaimer

40. b: Retaliation

41. b: Nepotism

42. c: Sherman Antitrust Act

43. a: Ethical leadership

44. a: Social responsibility

45. a: East Germany

46. b: Sustainable

47. : Junk bond

48. : Building

49. b: Lead paint

50. b: Organizational ethics

51. b: Transformational leadership

52. c: Foreign Corrupt Practices Act

53. : Real estate

54. d: Fraud

55. : Community development financial institution

56. : Fair trade

57. : Occupational Safety and Health Administration

58. b: Risk management

59. b: Utilitarianism

Accounting

1. b: Zero-based budgeting

2. b: Stock Exchange

3. a: Tax avoidance

4. d: General journal

5. c: Variable cost

6. : Pro forma

7. c: Perpetual inventory

8. d: Double taxation

9. : Periodic inventory

10. d: Accounting records

11. : Balanced scorecard

12. c: Quick ratio

13. c: Operating leverage

14. b: Standard cost

15. c: Taxation

16. a: Contribution margin

17. : Inflation

18. c: S corporation

19. a: Accounting

20. d: Dividend yield

21. a: Trueblood Committee

22. a: Money

23. : Residual value

24. c: Operating budget

25. a: Securities and Exchange Commission

26. : Going concern

27. d: Fiscal year

28. a: Accounting method

29. b: Indirect costs

30. a: Cash

31. b: Deferral

32. a: Entity concept

33. b: Accelerated depreciation

34. a: Book value

35. d: Governmental Accounting Standards Board

36. a: Taxpayer

37. d: Trend analysis

38. : Tax return

39. b: Inventory

40. c: Comprehensive annual financial report

41. : Trial balance

42. c: Gross margin

43. c: Manufacturing overhead

44. c: Financial statement analysis

45. d: Information systems

46. a: Inventory turnover

47. d: Deferred income

48. d: Hedge accounting

49. : Debit card

50. a: Risk management

51. b: Process Management

52. b: Net present value

53. b: Process costing

54. d: Normal balance

55. c: Overdraft

56. d: Securities Exchange Act

57. : Income approach

58. b: Accounting management

59. : Creditor

9 781538 860113